T0115440

TALK TO ME

TALK to ME

How to ASK BETTER QUESTIONS, GET BETTER ANSWERS, and INTERVIEW ANYONE LIKE a PRO

DEAN NELSON

HARPER PERENNIAL

NEW YORK • LONDON • TORONTO • SYDNEY • NEW DELHI • AUCKLAND

HARPER ● PERENNIAL

HarperCollins books may be purchased for educational, business, or sales promotional use. For information, please email the Special Markets Department at SPsales@harpercollins.com.

FIRST EDITION

Designed by Jen Overstreet

Library of Congress Cataloging-in-Publication Data

Names: Nelson, Dean, 1954- author.
Title: Talk to me : how to ask better questions, get better answers, and
    interview anyone like a pro / Dean Nelson.
Description: First edition. | New York, NY : HarperPerennial, [2019]
Identifiers: LCCN 2018040757| ISBN 9780062825209 (trade pbk.) |
    ISBN 9780062825216 (digital edition)
Subjects: LCSH: Interviewing in journalism.
Classification: LCC PN4784.I6 N45 2019 | DDC 070.4/3—dc23
LC record available at https://lccn.loc.gov/2018040757

23 24 25 26 27 LBC 8 7 6 5 4

To Paul Miller, my first magazine editor, who asked me, while I was still a college student, "Have you written any of this down?"

CONTENTS

TALK TO ME

More Than Instinct

Asking Better Questions, Getting Better Answers

HERE'S MY BEST EXCUSE: I was young and didn't know any better.

When I was in my mid-twenties, in my first journalism job in central Missouri, I saw a calendar listing that said a jazz musician was going to do a concert in my town. That was my beat, and I naively assumed he'd have some time to talk to me while he was here, so I called around trying to reach him. I ended up with a phone number for his record label and called it, blissfully unaware that I was calling California from the Midwest, and it was 7 A.M. there.

A groggy voice answered and I explained who I was and what I was trying to do. The voice mumbled that I could probably reach the musician at the hotel where he was staying. "And what hotel might that be?" I asked. He named the hotel in Boston. "And to whom was I speaking?" I asked. When he told me his name, I looked at the information I had about the record label. Yup—I had just called the head of the label out of a deep sleep.

As I said, I was young and didn't know any better.

So I called the hotel and, again, the phone rang a long time. Another voice answered. I guess I woke him up, too. It was 10 A.M. in Boston. What a sleepy bunch these music people were!

I told him who I was, and asked if I could spend some time with him when he was in my town in a few weeks.

"Sure, I guess that would be okay," he said.

"Is there any chance you could make that exclusive to me, and you don't talk to any other reporters?" I knew I was pushing my luck with that one.

"For that you'll have to pay me," he said. He was clearly waking up.

"I'm sure I can't do that, so I'll see you when you get into town."

I ended up spending the entire day with him as he gave high school jazz band workshops, and was backstage with him before and after his show that night. He wasn't the warmest person I've ever met, but it was fun to see this legend take the teenagers (and me) seriously. He walked slowly; his short, heavyset body was relaxed as he moved from chair to music stand at the high school. We talked off and on for hours. I made some mistakes while interviewing him, and even angered him at one point (note to self: Don't *ever* ask a jazz musician about the irony of coming out of a life of poverty and oppression and charging an enormous fee for performing). You would think that even a guy in his twenties would know better than to ask Dizzy Gillespie about something as personal as money. But back then, I was under the illusion that getting the perfect interview was 90 percent *getting the right person to interview* and 10 percent luck or instinct. I figured that once I got him to agree, the rest would take care of itself.

What I have learned over the last forty years as a journalist, working with publications such as the *New York Times*, the *Boston Globe*, the San Jose *Mercury News*, and multiple magazines and running the Writer's Symposium by the Sea in San Diego, is that there is *much* more to an interview than just getting the person to talk to you.

More than thirty years later, when I was back in that town and took my old editor to lunch, he brought up this event.

"I still can't believe you got that interview," he said.

We Have Questions; We Want Answers

I have learned a lot about interviewing since the Dizzy Gillespie event—first and foremost that interviewing is more common than most of us realize. We ask questions every day because we need to know something, or because we need information so our next decision will be an informed one, or we want to be able to share wisdom, or we want to avoid trouble, or maybe we are just nosy.

Mostly, we are trying to gain perspective on something.

If we depend solely on our own thoughts and observations and don't take into account the thoughts and observations of others who are not just like us, we run the risk of coming to inaccurate conclusions and possibly taking harmful actions. Other perspectives reveal our own biases and assumptions. And think of what could have been accomplished (and avoided!) in our history had we just asked a few more questions. Asking good questions keeps us from living in our own echo chambers.

Think of the questions we have heard or have asked—questions as simple as: "What is the secret to your chocolate chip cookies?" "What happened at school today?" "Did you think about the consequences?" "Would you like to have dinner with me?" "Will you marry me?" "Why is the coffee always gone?" On the one hand, those are simply questions. But they can lead to other questions and become conversations that will draw out personalities and understandings. They can become a kind of interview.

The questions that surround us may be simple and obvious; they may be cosmic and profound. But they all serve a function. Consider the following scenarios from everyday life—in this case mine:

There is a plate of spaghetti on the floor, and the dog is eating it as if he had been waiting his entire life for this moment; his tail is wagging hard enough to spin a turbine. I look at my young son. He is standing, frozen in place, hands outstretched, eyes as big as the plate that is upside down on the floor directly under his hands. I look at my daughter, who is three years younger than my son. She is at the kitchen table, silently crying. Not because of the lost spaghetti or the stained carpet, but because she thinks I am going to punish the dog.

"What happened?" I ask.

That's an interview question. It's a dumb interview question (more on asking dumb questions later), because it's obvious what happened. But it's an interview question nonetheless. Maybe a better question would be "*How* did this happen?" And then "What do you think is *about* to happen?" But we'll talk about that more in Chapter 6.

I CALL THE BANK BECAUSE I'm having trouble with my account. I always call customer service people with a certain dread, because I assume they won't know anything.

"How can I make your day better?" the voice asks.

That's an interview question. I answer, and she follows up with another question. She's trying to help me figure something out.

THE FLASHING LIGHTS IN MY rearview mirror could mean one of two things: 1) The highway patrol is going to nail that guy who blew past me a few seconds ago. Cool! I love it when they get the guys in the BMWs; or 2) The highway patrol is coming after me for blowing past the Buick a few seconds ago.

It's me. I pull over to the shoulder and roll down my window. The officer swaggers up and leans toward me.

"Do you have any idea how fast you were going?"

That's an interview question. Sort of. It's a bit rhetorical—he doesn't really need an answer before he writes me a ticket.

THE SNOW IS MARVELOUS, AND today feels like a good day to try something new. I head down a trail I have never skied before, assuming it couldn't be that difficult on a day with such glorious powder conditions. I'm not a great skier—I'd call myself adequate—so when I see the trail sign with double black diamonds as I speed past, I get a little concerned. Too late. I'm suddenly on a super-advanced slope. Now I am airborne. I wipe out in a spectacular manner, skis and poles flying in various directions. My shoulder and helmet take most of the impact. I stay in a prone position, taking mental note as to whether I can feel all four limbs, all ten digits. This crash was performed beneath a breathless audience on the chairlift passing above. Several cheer. Someone from the lift leans forward and down a little.

"Are you okay?" she asks.

It's an interview question—for a very brief interview—to determine whether she needs to call the ski patrol.

THE THERAPIST WELCOMES ME TO his office, points to a chair for me to be seated, and sits behind his desk. We look at each other in silence for a few moments.

"Why are you here?" he gently asks. It's an interview question. It's how a lot of counseling sessions begin.

I LISTEN ENTHUSIASTICALLY TO A jazz band at a club, and during a break I walk up to the pianist and ask, "Did I hear a little Thelonious Monk buried in that last song?"

That's an interview question that endears me to the band.

Everyone Is an Interviewer

Insurance adjusters, social workers, lawyers, nurses, teachers, investigators, therapists, podcast hosts, customer service representatives, bankers, and police officers spend a good part of each day asking questions. And that's what an interview is: a purposeful series of questions that leads to understanding, insight, and perspective on a given topic. What these people do next depends on the quality of the answers they get. And the quality of those answers has a lot to do with the quality of the questions.

I once had a doctor who never looked up from his computer screen when he asked me questions. I had visits in his exam room for a torn rotator cuff, skin cancer, migraines, and annual physicals. I could barely describe him to you, because all I ever really saw was his hairline over the screen. He asked questions and pounded on those keys like he was trying to smash a scorpion under the keyboard.

In that same clinic I had a doctor who asked me questions other than just what my symptoms were and how often I was going to the bathroom. We talked about our joint love for the lakes in Minnesota, and our joint lament over the quality of journalism in the country. The second doctor's visits didn't take much longer than the first. But guess which doctor I was willing to be more open with? Guess who was better able to help me figure out some of my physical issues?

Doctors are under lots of pressure from insurance companies to spend as little time with patients as possible and to document everything. I get it. But even medical journals write that the interviewing skills of doctors can be key to developing adequate diagnoses and therapies for their patients. Good doctors do more than order lots of tests. They ask questions. They listen. They evaluate. They follow up. They *interview*.

Once I recognized the intentional line of questioning, I appreciated what the second doctor was doing. He wasn't just getting to know me in a casual sense. It wasn't like we were going to go out for drinks later. He was gathering information so he could develop a plan. He was, in an informal way, taking my medical history, which is a term doctors use for conducting an interview. It was a conversation, but directed toward a specific goal.

Other careers depend on quality interviews, too. A social worker I know told me that how she works with a client depends on what that client tells her. And what that client tells her is a direct result of the questions she asks: "The interview is everything." Same story for human resources, where the interview is the time you can look past that mountain of near-identical resumes and find out what really sets a candidate apart. Law? A deposition is an interview. Jury selection is a series of interviews. So is a trial, when lawyers ask witnesses questions. Financial planners? I have never been asked more personal questions than when I talked to a financial planner. He was interested in my family's goals, our definitions of success and comfort and security. Those were all interview questions.

Journalists, of course, ask a lot of questions. It's their job. Most of their careers depend on their ability to conduct a good interview. As a journalist I have interviewed people who were overjoyed, and those who were overwhelmed. Successful, and gutted. Winners and losers. Interesting and dull. Saintly and corrupt. Heroes and antichrists.

Virtually every profession depends on getting people to talk to you, and the good news is that conducting a great interview is something you can learn. We see doctors, lawyers, police officers, and journalists on television or in movies, and it seems that they have a poised, professional, confident manner when they conduct interviews. They look like naturals. The shows give the impression that conducting a great interview depends entirely on your being an extrovert with insatiable curiosity. We get a stereotype in our minds about interviewing, that we're just born with the interviewing gene or we're not. But I don't think that's the case at all. Remember, *everyone* is an interviewer. Every profession has its times where we need to ask questions of strangers. Boisterous and confident people can be great interviewers. Marc Maron is very good at this. He gives off an air that says, "It's so cool that you're talking to me on my podcast, but of course you wanted to talk to me in the first place." For

Maron, it's a combination of little-kid wonder and arrogance, and it works for him. But shy and insecure people can be great interviewers, too. Some of the best interviewers I have seen are tentative, noncombative, soft-spoken people. Their personalities put people at ease and make them easy to talk to. They know their subject well, and they know that their source can help them gain even more understanding, and they are okay with being vulnerable. I heard the journalist Katherine Boo describe how she got people in Mumbai to be so open with her in her book *Behind the Beautiful Forevers*. She said that she showed up so often that people sort of forgot that she was there.

Good interviewers are simply themselves. They're not acting. They're curious. They know how to be quiet and listen. The authentic ones who ask good questions are the ones who extract profound answers instead of clichés, and who get past the surface and into something that rarely gets explored.

Asking good questions in a good order that leads you to greater understanding will enhance any job, and any life. I have seen it happen with virtually every personality type, in virtually every professional context.

Why Other Perspectives Matter to Writers

Becoming skillful in the art of the interview *as a writer* will add a tool to your writing toolbox that will set you apart from everyone else because very few people think through what they want the interview to accomplish. They depend too much on the hope that the source will say something interesting, and not enough on the preparation that will draw that source out. If you can master the art of asking good questions, you'll be able to describe which part of the sky the moon was in, what those waves sounded like as they hit the cruise ship, what that person thought about as he tried to escape the hotel fire, what happened to that mom's soul when that baby was set on her chest within seconds of being born, why that homeless person returned that wallet, or why that businessperson hurt that Cub Scout. You'll be able to capture *how* a person said it—the cadence, the accent, the catch in the throat—in addition to *what* was said. You'll be able to make the interaction more human, more believable, more artful, more inspiring, more beautiful.

Whether you're just getting started writing your personal memoir and you haven't written anything since high school composition class, or you're at the top of the literary food chain in fiction, journalism, essays, columns, and short stories, your creative work can always use perspectives from others. Getting those perspectives takes a certain kind of skill. Getting those perspectives is why we interview.

As writers, most of the time we're not at the scene when something happens, so we have to talk to people who were. That's how we get informed in order to inform others. For example, when I came upon the site where two small planes collided and crashed onto a golf course, I talked to the people who were on the fourteenth tee when the crash occurred. They told me about hearing the planes approaching the nearby airstrip, hearing an engine sputter, then looking up in time to see one plane clip the tail of the other, then watching them both crash into the fairway right in front of them. Their description helped my readers visualize what happened.

Fiction writers need to be able to talk to people, too, in order to capture local lore or the description of a setting, or a chain of events. Not everything you write will come completely out of your own experience or out of other written accounts. You're going to have to talk to strangers every now and then.

Sometimes we interview others because they're such interesting people, or they have accomplished something significant, and we want to glean some insights into a person's mind and practice. They may not be celebrities, but they have experience in life that is different from ours. We might view something differently as a result of their perspectives. They might challenge our way of thinking and give us new approaches for how to operate in this world.

This is what I have been doing with great writers about their work and about writing in general. The series I started is called the Writer's Symposium by the Sea, and for more than twenty years I have conducted interviews with journalists, poets, playwrights, screenwriters, novelists, songwriters, essayists, and others. Interviews in this series have been seen live by thousands of people; they have been viewed or downloaded online approximately four million times.

Some interviews in this writers' series have gone very well, and some have not. Some of those I interviewed were delightful and entertaining, while some were prickly and evasive. The interviews have given great insight into the writing world and into each person's approach to becoming a writer. They show the audience how much work, frustration, joy, and satisfaction can come from writing well. Mostly, though, the interviews show how different everyone is when they approach the craft. Some see it as a mysterious, spiritual thing, while others see it as a much more mechanical endeavor. That's why the interviews are so valuable—they show such a variety of perspectives on the same topic, and they give a glimpse into the personalities of those who create such great art.

I talk to people every day. Whether I'm conducting interviews as part of the Writer's Symposium, or in my roles as a journalist and author, I am constantly interviewing.

You talk to people every day, too.

Whether you're interviewing famous writers or golfers who are witnesses to a tragedy, the kinds of questions you ask in each circumstance will have a direct impact on whether you will glean anything interesting or important. Your questions will determine whether you will capture a true glimpse of the person or event or will perpetuate the carefully protected persona and point of view the person wants to project. Your questions might be the difference between getting the truth and getting propaganda.

Remember, good interviews are more than just having the source say yes to your request and hoping that the interview gods will smile upon you. The more you are aware of what goes into an interview, the better result you'll get.

I LOOK AT CONDUCTING INTERVIEWS the same way I look at writing stories. Ultimately, a good story is a controlled release of the narrative. This leads to that, which leads to something else. It doesn't tell everything—it reveals only what's necessary for the story to develop. It has a beginning, a middle, a climactic point (usually), and an end. With an interview, you generally want to have one question lead to another, in some type of order, with a sense that it is heading somewhere. I'll get into the particulars of this later, but writing stories and conducting interviews are also similar in that you may think the story—or interview—is going in one direction, when it veers off into another direction. Improvising, following up, and paying attention are parts of both endeavors. Like a story, a good interview has a beginning, a middle with a climactic point, and an end. And hopefully a few surprises.

Good interviews reveal information, but great interviews reveal so much more. They reveal humanity, struggle, victory, joy, grief, and sometimes a glimpse of transcendence.

But great interviews don't just happen. It isn't all charisma, coincidence, and chemistry. You have to be intentional about what you're after. And you have to get past your own self-doubt.

Beverly Lowry, who has written novels, short stories, and nonfiction crime books for decades, depends a great deal on getting strangers to talk to her so that she can tell an accurate story. She said she often goes into the interview process with some self-doubt, but proceeds anyway. "Walking up to a rank stranger who probably doesn't want to talk to you, introducing yourself cold, then making certain at every turn that you're the one in charge and what you're conducting is not a friendly conversation but an interview—these are not natural, or even particularly friendly, ways to behave and not a piece of cake to perform," she wrote.[1]

Lowry says that interviewing is part instinct, combined with a need to know. Instinct will get you only so far, though.

I have had plenty of experience in approaching people who I assume don't want to talk to me. Sometimes I'm surprised. If I ask them good questions, they often warm to the occasion. It's uncomfortable to talk to strangers. But just because it's uncomfortable doesn't mean you should avoid it. Writers learn to realize that they need to be able to talk to people more than they need to be comfortable. And you can mitigate a lot of your discomfort by how you approach the interview in the first place.

We have all seen athletes who seem "natural" in their sports. But the reason they are so good is that they pay attention to other things, too. Tony Gwynn, the Hall of Fame hitter for the San Diego Padres baseball team, had a beautiful, natural swing. It looked like the most effortless thing in the world for him to step into the batter's box and, smooth as silk, smack a fastball, curveball, changeup, slider, or knuckler into the opposite field and drive in a run. What did he do when he wasn't hitting or fielding? Was he just waiting for his next turn at bat? Hardly. What he did when he wasn't batting was study video

---

[1] Carolyn Forché and Philip Gerard, eds., *Writing Creative Nonfiction* (Cincinnati: Story Press, 2001), 98.

of pitchers and his own swing. He was researching. Preparing. Practicing.

On game day, it looked like he was operating on pure instinct. But he took that instinct to record levels because of the preparation and behind-the-scenes work he did before he ever put on his uniform.

Instinct will get you part of the way toward a successful interview. But becoming consistently good at it is the result of paying attention to the craft of it behind the scenes.

This book will give you surprising new methods to consider when talking to people. It will show you:

- How to decide whom to talk to and how to get them to agree to it

- How to prepare so that the course of the interview won't be left to chance

- What questions to ask and in what order

- How to conduct the actual interview

- How and when to ask the tough questions

- How to ensure accuracy

- How to keep from getting sued

- How to get past your ego when you interview idols and idiots

This book is a collection of wisdom from some of the greatest writers in the United States, along with insights of my own as the one who interviewed them, and as one who has interviewed hundreds of others in my forty-plus years as a journalist for some of the top news organizations. This book is about talking to strangers and getting them to talk to you at a level that goes way beyond the surface, where the interview may even create an insight that surprises you, your source, and your readers or viewers.

Interviewing is at the root of inquiry, of knowing, of sharing information, of sharing experience.

It is at the root of storytelling.

Being young and not knowing any better won't last long. Eventually you'll need to take steps so that luck and instinct aren't your main resources.

What follows is what's really behind the phrase when you say to someone, "Talk to me."

CHAPTER 1
It Starts in Your Head

Deciding Whom to Interview and Why

IF YOU TRY TO WRITE a story about whatever comes out of your head at the moment your fingers hit the keyboard, it may come across as interesting stream-of-consciousness creativity, but it also may read like the rants of a lunatic. You may be the next Ken Kesey, or the next Ted Kaczynski. But it will be difficult for a reader to stay with you very long. Even still, I see many of my students write stories exactly this way. They have an assignment, the deadline is upon them, so they write before they think. Some of them can make this work—their creative juices kick in and organize while the words appear on the screen, as if some Invisible Hand (thanks, Adam Smith!) is guiding them toward meaning—but as much as I wish differently, that is not how it works for most students. They need a prompt, an idea, a guiding thought before the starter's pistol can go off.

The stories that don't have some kind of guiding principle

are like a roulette wheel spinning, and you hope as you read that eventually the marble will drop into a slot so the stories will make a point. I've read some stories where there wasn't a marble at all.

Good interviews, like stories, must have at least a marble.

In my early days in journalism, I wrote a story about a man who was walking across the state of Missouri. The story was full of facts, wisdom, and passion. I turned it in, poured myself some coffee, and waited for my editor to drop everything and alert the Pulitzer committee. Instead, he wrote across the top, "Why was this story written?" and handed it back with a grimace on his face, as if he had just stepped in a turd and it was my fault. I stared at that note for the longest time and then reread my story. Yes, there were facts. There was some passion, too. Less so on the wisdom. There was definitely no point.

No matter how finely tuned the language or interesting the topic, my article was just a collection of words. It wasn't really *about* anything. I had typed the story, but I hadn't *written* it. My editor was right. It was my turd he stepped in.

The same thing happens in interviews all the time. We blithely assume that talking to someone is interesting in and of itself. Just think of the hilarious *Saturday Night Live* sketch where comedian Chris Farley interviews musician Paul McCartney. What makes it funny (besides Farley's physical humor) is that Farley is so starstruck that he has no idea what to do with the interview. Some of his questions begin with, "Remember when you were with the Beatles?" McCartney is polite in his responses, but he can see (as can the audience) that

the Farley character has not thought past who he was interviewing. Farley repeatedly looks at the camera and mouths the
words "This guy is awesome!"

I have seen a lot of interviews that struck me the same way,
only they weren't meant to be funny. After watching them I
have wanted to channel my old editor and ask the interviewer,
"Why was this interview conducted?"

The reason I wanted to interview Tracy Kidder at our
Writer's Symposium was that I thought he was a significant
writer who had contributed a great deal to the world's understanding of business, technology, humanitarianism, craftsman-
ship, aging, education, the human spirit, and many other topics
through his books and his journalism for the *Atlantic* and the
New Yorker magazines. I thought he would be able to talk to
us in depth about his works in specific and about the craft of
writing in general. The audience included writers at all levels.

As I read Kidder's books in preparation, such as *The Road to
Yuba City* (a book he hated), *The Soul of a New Machine* (which
won the Pulitzer Prize), *My Detachment* (a memoir about his
time in Vietnam, another book he wasn't crazy about), *House,
Home Town, Old Friends, Mountains Beyond Mountains, Strength in
What Remains, Among Schoolchildren,* and *A Truck Full of Money,* a
theme started to emerge in my head. I'm not particularly interested in architecture, but Kidder made it interesting in *House.*
I've never been particularly intrigued by the tech world, but
his books about computing and software held my attention.

Kidder's books were the embodiment of what Don Hewitt
said when he described the success of *60 Minutes,* the popular

television newsmagazine. "I don't care about issues," he said. "I care about how people are *affected* by issues." *60 Minutes* segments always focus on a main character and point to a bigger issue. That's the approach Kidder took to his books. His stories were about people, and how they were affected by something bigger. He found the stakeholders.

But something more fundamental struck me as I read Kidder's books: I was amazed at the access his sources gave him. In *Old Friends* he describes conversations in rooms in a nursing home. In *Among Schoolchildren* he describes the teacher grading papers at her kitchen table at night. In *The Soul of a New Machine* he describes the morning routine of a project manager when he wakes up. In *Mountains Beyond Mountains* he describes the main character's conversations and habits when treating patients in Haiti. Since this was nonfiction, I knew he didn't make this up. He saw it so that he could describe it.

How did he get people to let him into their personal lives like that? I decided that my interview with him would hinge on that question. We would talk about other things, too, of course, but at least I knew we would explore the issue of access. That became my "why." Sometimes that's all you need to craft the rest of the interview.

Finding the Stakeholders

What I'm talking about here is trying to identify the stakeholders in every story. Who are the experts? Who are the people most affected? Who can provide insight? Who can educate me and then, by extension, my readers and viewers?

Stakeholders are the ones who can put an issue into human terms. They humanize an incident, data, or an idea. Hearing their voices means the reader/listener/viewer can relate to the story. Stakeholders make the story believable.

We interview people for at least one of these four reasons:

1. To get a perspective on a specific issue or event from a participant, authority, expert, or witness. Who saw it? Who can describe it? Who organized it? Who can speak with credibility about it?

In 1957 Larry Lubenow was a twenty-one-year-old journalism student and freelancer for the *Grand Forks Herald* newspaper in North Dakota. The great jazz musician Louis Armstrong was in town, and Lubenow landed an interview with him.

It was probably enough of a "why" to get an interview with Armstrong simply because he was famous, and he was in a town that didn't attract many famous people, let alone famous black people.

But any good writer would have known that the interview would be better if there was an even deeper purpose. A theme.

Just two weeks before the concert, nine black children in Little Rock, Arkansas, had been denied entry to the high school in their neighborhood, despite a judge's ruling that the school be desegregated. President Eisenhower had been un-successful in getting the Arkansas governor to comply with the ruling and open the school. The judge who made the rul-ing was from Grand Forks, a town that had a very small black population. It seemed unlikely that Lubenow would get much from Armstrong regarding the recent events, since the mu-sician was known for not speaking publicly about race. He was the Michael Jordan of his era—he was one of the best in his field yet completely silent on social issues. But Lubenow thought that Little Rock might be a fresh angle for the fre-quently quoted musician.

When the young reporter started the interview,[1] he and Armstrong talked about music. Then Lubenow asked Arm-strong about Little Rock, Eisenhower, and being a black man in America. Because of the current events, his timing was perfect. Armstrong's heated and often profane responses to Lubenow's questions surprised the young journalist, but he immediately knew he had a "why" to his story. The theme presented itself, and Lubenow was ready for it. Armstrong had strong words for Eisenhower's inability to enforce the law and had to come up with a printable euphemism for the Arkansas governor, Orval Faubus ("uneducated plow boy" is what they agreed on). Armstrong described the difficulty

---

[1] The way Lubenow even got the interview is more interesting than the way I got Dizzy Gillespie. I'll tell you how he did it in the next chapter.

of being a goodwill ambassador for the United States around the world when blacks were treated so badly. He even went so far as to sing a version of "The Star-Spangled Banner," with his own obscene lyrics. Remember, this was about sixty years before Colin Kaepernick ever took a knee before a football game.

At first Lubenow's editor and the Associated Press editor in Minneapolis didn't believe that Armstrong really said these things, and made Lubenow go back to the musician for him to verify it—which Armstrong did. Then the story went around the world.

One week later, President Eisenhower ordered U.S. troops to escort the nine students into the school in Little Rock.

The Armstrong interview would have been fine simply as a "celebrity comes to town" story. But it became a great interview because the writer connected it to a bigger theme. He had a "why."

2. For human interest, or "color." Who can put the subject in human terms? Who can make it more interesting than just reciting facts? Who can provide details or expressions that take it out of the ordinary?

Richard Preston, a writer who focuses on infectious diseases (his book *The Hot Zone* is excellent), said he looks for a certain kind of source when he is gathering information for a story. And he looks for a certain kind of theme.

"I look for characters who embody the paradoxical interaction between the public figure, who has very important public responsibilities, and the private person who is dealing with the mundane reality of American life," he said.[2]

That kind of paradox is interesting. It helps us understand how humanity works—or doesn't. That's his "why." Paradox is always worth exploring, in my opinion, because it shows that human beings are never entirely this way or that way. Every fundamentalist has his caveat. Every liberal has a conservative exception. The paradoxes are what make us so uniquely human—flawed, unpredictable, surprising. You want to get at those apparent contradictions so that you avoid clichés and stereotypes.

3. To become more educated about a topic. Who can provide some big-picture perspective? Who can give you some context?

Before I get too far into a complicated story, I usually try to find an expert who can explain big concepts to me in layman's terms. Before doing a story on a world-class physicist, I asked a physics professor to explain the difference between Newtonian physics and quantum physics. I obviously could not write extensively about this topic just from that conversation, but it helped me frame in my own mind what the issues were.

Sometimes, though, you need the subject to provide that deeper education. Your source can explain the variables of the

---

[2] Robert S. Boynton, *The New New Journalism* (New York: Vintage Books, 2005), 306.

subject. And there is a good chance you had no idea those variables even existed.

I talked to a social worker recently about her interview process, and she said she is always looking for the big picture when she interviews a client. For years she worked in a neonatal intensive care unit (NICU). For her, it wasn't enough just to find out what the family needed and what was wrong with the baby. She wanted to know the context this baby was in. Until she knew that, she said, she couldn't come up with a useful plan to help the family.

Over the years her interviews have revealed some disturbing beliefs, which she then has to address in how she works with the clients.

"Many times a parent believes that the child is in the NICU because of something the parent did in the past, and now is being punished for," she said. "I hear 'This is all my fault' more than you would imagine."

If this social worker didn't have that information, her plan for the family wouldn't be nearly as effective. The "why" of her interview is to get past the surface of the baby's immediate medical condition and into the real stuff of the family's life.

4. To portray the impact or consequence of an event. Who is affected? Who will benefit from this? Who will pay the biggest price? Who wins? Who loses? Often, the best way to answer that question is to think about the Three *E*s: Eyewitnesses, Experts, and Explainers. Eyewitnesses can give you the drama of what happened; Experts can give you the official version and authority; Explainers can give you background and put it in context.

When I covered a school shooting in San Diego, I talked to all three categories: I talked to representatives of the police and Red Cross (Experts); neighbors of the boy who killed the others, school psychologists, and teachers (Explainers); and, I had to talk to the ones who were most affected: the other students (Eyewitnesses).

Unfortunately, school shootings are getting more common. They are important stories, though, and they point to an aspect of life that we don't want to get used to—at least I hope we don't get used to it. So how do we provide insight and shared humanity when we cover these stories? By not settling for easy answers, clichés, and tired arguments. When we interview Experts, Explainers, and Eyewitnesses, we are really trying to understand ourselves and our nature.

You Know What They Say About Assumptions . . .

One thing that all interviewers must confront is that we all carry assumptions about people we talk to. It's unavoidable. Even good scientists make assumptions as they go into an experiment. Good scientists take note as to whether their assumptions were correct, and adjust accordingly. Good interviewers must be aware of their biases as they head into an interview and must be equally ready to abandon or at least adjust those assumptions as the interview progresses. To return for a moment to my interview with Dizzy Gillespie, I made the assumption that his coming to town was sufficiently interesting to get my editor to give me the assignment. I assumed Gillespie would make a good interview by virtue of having a recognizable name. So far so good. My editor agreed. But then I needed to dig a little deeper about *why* I wanted to interview him.

Why do we want to interview famous people? What do we assume about them? What could we ask that hasn't already been asked a thousand times? What could we offer that isn't already out there? What could we ask that won't just perpetuate the clichés or myths? (*People* magazine, are you listening?)

The world would be a better place if more reporters pondered those questions before rehashing what we've all heard a million times.

To be fair, it's not always easy to get past the surface. When a celebrity comes to town, it is usually a tightly managed event to keep the public from seeing anything other than a carefully cultivated image.

That's how it was when the famous radio DJ Wolfman Jack came to town, and I was assigned to interview him at his hotel suite. Wolfman Jack was immortalized in the movie *American Graffiti,* and I looked forward to talking with him about rock music and his career. I was hoping to even get him to howl at the moon the way he did on the radio. If you've never heard of him, watch *American Graffiti* and you will see what an icon he was for years.

But when I got to the hotel, I was ushered by his handler

into a room that had at least ten other journalists and fans (I couldn't tell the difference). We waited in the living room of the suite for close to an hour, then the celebrity came out of one of the bedrooms a little bent over, doing a Groucho Marx impression, pretending to smoke a cigar. When none of us laughed (it was more weird than funny), he straightened up and criticized us for being boring. It never got better than that. It was a group interview, and everyone got to ask one question and have him autograph a photo of himself. Then he left in a huff.

He signed my photo, "To Dean, Da Bean!" followed by his name.

I hadn't been called "Dean Da Bean" since junior high.

A celebrity was in town. But there wasn't really a reason to write about it. There wasn't a bigger story to report. We ran a photo and a long caption instead. Dean Da Bean. Whatever.

WITH GILLESPIE, ONCE I GOT him to agree to the interview, a low-level panic began to build. What could I possibly ask him that was new? And, from an ego perspective, how could I avoid looking like an idiot? I was in my twenties. He was in his sixties. I knew a little about jazz, and when I started backgrounding him I realized that he actually changed jazz with his style called bebop (thus the title of his autobiography, *To Be or Not to Bop*). Anyone who had watched him play knew he played a trumpet with the bell pointed upward instead of in a straight line away from the mouthpiece, and they knew his cheeks bulged out like a blowfish. Neither of those facts was something to ask about, I felt, because *everyone* had asked him about those two items.

This kind of thinking ahead of time will be the difference between a useful/interesting/revealing/important interview where you truly engage the person in a deep, meaningful way, and a routine ho-hum/I've-heard-all-this-before/why-are-you-wasting-my-time exercise where a semi-trained orangutan could have done the interview just as well.

Multiple Voices Matter

As I said earlier, an interview is a form of storytelling. What makes it tricky is that it's storytelling you do with another person. You might have just a sketchy outline of your story—such as, "I want to write a story about someone who discovers she was adopted and then sets out to find her birth parents." Or, "I want to write a story about wanting to punch that TSA agent in the face." That is enough information right there to get the writing process started. A poet might want to describe a darkening sky over the horizon, or a darkening melancholy in his own spirit. Like Robert Frost, a writer could explore why a particular experience gave him a lump in the throat. It could be something as simple as that.

Most of the time we just need someone's perspective or eyewitness account. Sometimes we write about events and we don't have time to do backgrounding or internet searches, or reflect on the purpose. Sometimes we write about something just to tell readers what happened. Even so, we still need to be able to locate people to talk to, and ask them good questions. Without those other voices, we're writing a report, not a story.

Decades after writing the Dizzy Gillespie story, I did a different kind of jazz-related story. A big church in downtown San Diego had been doing a jazz vespers service on Saturday evenings for the past few years, and since I like jazz and I sometimes like church, I decided to check it out. It sounded like an interesting mash-up of incongruent forces, and incongruity, paradox, even conflict, always set off my story-worthy radar.

During the service, everything struck me as interesting. The black-and-white slides of Lionel Hampton and Miles Davis and Billie Holiday and Mose Allison that were projected onto the front wall, the talent of the jazz trio (seriously—the pianist played keyboard with one hand while he worked the saxophone keys with the other hand. Never seen that before. Other nights of the week this same trio plays the best clubs in San Diego), the earnestness of the preacher, the diversity of the small congregation (homeless folks from off the street and highly educated jazz experts)—all screamed to my soul, "There's a story here!"

I did some reading about jazz vespers services that have been conducted in other parts of the country (Duke Ellington, Wynton Marsalis, and Dave Brubeck have all done them), and I saw that this was one of the few that was conducted every week. Another reason to do the story—it was unusual.

So I made a list of the people I would need to interview (i.e., identified the stakeholders) and wrote down why I needed them. Turns out there were three big reasons (remember the three *E*s from earlier?). Let's take them one at a time:

1) I needed the official perspective. It seemed to me that the pastor of the church would be the voice of authority. He could tell me the purpose of this kind of service, what the church's objectives were, how he reconciled the perception of jazz coming out of smoky, boozy rooms where people definitely didn't sing from a hymnal with putting that kind of music into a hundred-year-old chapel with stained glass windows, pews (not tables), a cross at the front, and bread and wine for the Eucharist. What was the official version?

Your purpose in interviewing the expert or the official in a story is so that there is a voice of authority that can explain the events. You want that authority for the accuracy of the story, but you also want it so that your story can have credibility with readers and viewers. It wouldn't make much sense to ask just random people what they think about this mash-up (although it seems that television journalists do this all the time. What does the average person at a mall in Dubuque think about the European Union? Who cares?). Keep in mind, that official version may ultimately prove to be incorrect. The officials might be lying, or the accounts they got from witnesses may be faulty. But you need to start somewhere.

As Bob Woodward said, the goal is to get "the best obtainable version of the truth at the time." That "best obtainable version" usually means getting multiple perspectives, and the official perspective is one of them.

2) My story needed more than just the facts. I already knew how the service got started from the church's website. I knew that the church was one of the original churches in San Diego as the city was being developed. I knew about how people had moved out of the city and attendance at that church had dwindled, but now people were moving back into the city and there was a chance to redefine the church. Those were the verifiable facts.

Now I needed emotion, details, color, joy, or pathos. I needed humanity.

So I talked to the piano player. He was one of the best jazz musicians in town. He could make any lounge swing. How does a guy go from playing a souped-up version of "Nobody Knows the Trouble I've Seen" as people line up for the Eucharist to "What'd I Say" just a few hours later in an alcohol-fueled club? Why was he willing to associate with a mainstream church? How did the pastor find him and convince him this was a good idea? Including details of human interest is what helps readers picture the events and care about them. Details make your stories believable.

I also talked to guest musicians who appear in these services when they are in town to play in San Diego clubs later that night. One of them had never been in a church before, and wondered if snakes were going to come out of somewhere. None did.

3) So far, though, my story was missing the most significant stakeholders: the congregants. Joe and Joan Plumber. How did the people who came to mass each week experience this jazz/ Jesus mash-up? Why did they come? Here are the responses I got from them: For some, it's the only good church experience they've ever had. For others, it's the best jazz in town (which it may be!). For others, it's a chance to hear a sermon and some music in an unusual setting. For at least one person that I talked to, it was a way to redeem a terrible childhood church memory that was full of abuse and hypocrisy.

I can't stress this enough: Your story is incomplete until you have talked to the people on whom your topic has the most impact.

If you're a fiction writer, you'll want to interview people for some of these same reasons. If your novel is about the Iditarod dogsled race in Alaska, your research will include interviewing people who have some knowledge about the race—experts. You'll want to talk to people who have done the race so that you can better describe the fatigue, the frostbite, and the euphoria of finishing without being eaten by their dogs. And, of course, you'll want to talk to as many people involved as possible, just to get educated on the topic, to learn the unique language of the race, to hear about issues you never would have otherwise considered. Ideally you would want to get a perspective from the ultimate stakeholders—the dogs—but not everyone speaks their language.

DO YOUR HOMEWORK

I'll get into the nitty-gritty of this in Chapter 3, but research is crucial at every stage of the interview process. Maybe you don't like the word "research" because it makes it sound like you're in a laboratory, or brings you back to high school group projects. Call it what you will—backgrounding, preparation, homework, saving yourself from humiliation—you must educate yourself even just to get the interview. Preparation will help you figure out whom you need to talk to, and inform what you think you can learn of them. It might be as simple as reading articles published by that person, interviews she has given before, articles written about that person, even conducting some preliminary interviews with people who know that person. My go-to method is to alert a reference librarian about a topic I'm working on. I cannot overstate how valuable librarians are for both basic and complex research. A few hours of work ahead of time will be the difference between a good interview and a great one.

Developing Sources: Sometimes It *Is* Rocket Science

Janet Malcolm, in her book *The Journalist and the Murderer*, claims that what journalists do involves trickery, betrayal, and lying in order to get sources to talk to us. In the book's opening two sentences she states: "Every journalist who is not too stupid or too full of himself to notice what is going on knows that what he does is morally indefensible. He is a kind of confidence man, preying on people's vanity, ignorance, or loneliness, gaining their trust and betraying them without remorse."

Later on that same page she says, "The disparity between what seems to be the intention of an interview as it is taking place and what it actually turns out to have been in aid of always comes as a shock to the subject."[3]

We're liars and betrayers, according to Malcolm.

Joan Didion said something similar to this in *Slouching Towards Bethlehem:* "My only advantage as a reporter is that I am so physically small, so temperamentally unobtrusive, and so neurotically inarticulate that people tend to forget that my presence runs counter to their best interests. And it always does. That is one last thing to remember: writers are always selling somebody out."[4]

---

[3] Janet Malcolm, *The Journalist and the Murderer* (New York: Vintage Books, 1990), 3–4.

[4] Joan Didion, *Slouching Towards Bethlehem* (New York: Farrar, Straus, and Giroux, 1968), xvi.

Obviously, I disagree. Do we always mislead when we get sources to talk to us? Of course not. I have had conversations with people that became interviews, but I didn't betray them or trick them.

When my kids were little, my wife was often the one who would walk with them to their elementary school, and I would meet them at the end of the day to walk them home. One day, as I waited in the schoolyard, I found myself standing next to our neighbor. We knew each other mostly because our kids were friends. My neighbor and his wife had moved to San Diego after working with NASA on rocket programs, but the company that hired them and relocated them to San Diego had abruptly closed its rocket division and moved out of town. These neighbors were both unemployed. It was a bit of an enigma to me. I mean, what household can claim that they have two unemployed rocket scientists?

"How are things?" I asked, while we waited for the bell. I was not interviewing him in a formal way.

"We're making it," he said. "I'm trying to stay busy."

"Doing what?" Still not.

"I have a couple of inventions I'm working on. One of them is getting some traction."

"Cool. Can you tell me about it?" Hmm. Beginning to get curious.

What he told me was fascinating, and we ended up walking with our kids past his house.

"Wanna see it? It's in my garage."

Duh. I'm a reporter. Of course I wanted to see it.

He opened his garage door, and on his workbench were dismembered dolls and a bunch of electronic equipment. It looked like the butcher cover of the Beatles' *Yesterday and To-day* album, without the blood.

A few months before, he and his wife had been watching a PBS program on teen pregnancy, and how health and human sexuality classes in high schools had students (almost exclusively girls) carry around a bag of flour to simulate the weight of a baby, or an egg, to simulate its fragility, in order to show students what it's like to care for a newborn.

My neighbor commented to his wife, "The problem is that a bag of flour or an egg doesn't wake you up in the middle of the night."

Her reply: "So invent something that does."

The rocket scientist husband accepted the challenge from the rocket scientist wife.

He recorded their daughter's crying. "That cry that could peel paint," he said, laughing. As their neighbor, I could verify this. He put the recording on a microchip, connected it to a small speaker, and inserted it into one of his daughter's dolls, which made it seem like the doll was screaming. It dawned on me that perhaps the reason his daughter was always crying was that her father was doing surgery on her dolls. But I filed that point away for later.

With the newly wired doll, the only way to get the screaming to stop was to hold it in a feeding position and insert a key, holding it there for several seconds. He programmed the chip to scream at random times throughout the day and night. The chip also measured how long the screaming went on before the doll was "fed," and whether it was treated roughly.

"Who else has seen this?" I asked, my reporter persona now fully engaged.

"I have a few prototypes out there in health clinics and a local high school. I'm calling it 'Baby Think It Over.'"

I arranged for a time to come back and interview him more formally. I didn't trick him. I told him what I was interested in, and he agreed to it.

I wanted to know more about his motive. He was adamant that I not think he was doing this for moral reasons related to teen sex, or to the social problem of unwanted pregnancy. "This is not about altruism or morality," he told me. "I am trying to feed my family." I wanted to know how the electronics worked, how he was getting the prototypes assembled, what his plans were.

But I also knew that I needed other perspectives. Whom did I need to talk to, and why? Who were the stakeholders? Once again, I made a list of the experts (in this case, my neighbor), the eyewitnesses (participants—students who could describe the experience of babysitting this screaming doll), and the explainers (teachers, social scientists who could provide context).

I needed to know how big the issue of teen pregnancy was and whether something like this screaming doll would have a deterrent effect. I interviewed the high school teachers and reproductive health clinic workers who were using the prototype. And, most important, I interviewed high school students who had to be responsible for this doll for twenty-four or forty-eight hours, when it would scream at unpredictable times, regardless of whether the student was on a date, at work, at a concert or movie, at a restaurant, or asleep. ("I'm never having sex," one high school girl told me.) It was the high school students on whom this product would have the most impact, so of course I needed their perspective.

By getting all of those voices in the story, and knowing the purpose of each kind of voice, I was getting the best available version of this story at the time. No trickery, betrayal, selling out, or shock when the story appeared.

I did this story for the *New York Times,* and within a day of publication, news trucks and reporters from around the world descended on my neighbor's house.

His screaming baby doll, conceived in his garage, is now used around the world. Seems like sometimes it does take a rocket scientist to keep kids from getting pregnant.

For any story I work on, I create a list (sometimes on paper, on my phone, or just in my head, but the first two are better) of who all I need to talk to in order to have the most perspectives.

I literally put words like this on a piece of paper:

"Who are the experts?"

Then I just brainstorm all possible types of people (actual names if I know them, but most of the time it's categories of people. For the jazz vespers story I listed groups such as "Church leaders," "Other leaders who have done this," "Decision makers," "Historians," "Music/Church researchers," etc.).

"Who made this happen?"

Next, I try to find out who all was involved, from the person in charge to the administrative assistant. More on this later, but administrative assistants[5] are some of the best sources in the world. They tend to know everything.

"Who are the participants?"

Then I list all the people who might be doing whatever the story is about. In the story about the screaming baby doll, this was primarily the husband and wife in my neighborhood.

"Who is affected?"

I list everyone I can think of who is affected in ways big and small.

"Who can provide the human element?"

That person will probably be one of the people listed above.

This is similar to the process Ira Glass of NPR's *This American Life* described when he was working on a story about immigrants from Mexico working in an American meatpacking plant.[6]

"What we were looking for were the exact participants," he said. "People who worked in those jobs in poultry plants when Mexican workers arrived, and the Mexican workers themselves who are still around. We wanted the people who were there, and the people who managed those plants, and

---

[5] Put them up there with librarians as people to call on. Most of them like being helpful.

[6] I lightly edited his comments for tense and clarity, since they came from a podcast.

specific politicians who fought over this as the years went on. We imagined a little map of the story and asked, who would be interesting to hear from? And then we just started going out and reporting it—calling people, and literally knocking on doors."[7]

As I mentioned earlier, I covered a school shooting in San Diego, and on my way to the school I made my own little map in my head—a mental list of the participants I would need to interview. A fifteen-year-old boy brought a gun to school and killed two people and wounded thirteen. Those were the facts I had going in. I knew I needed to talk to police and other emergency responders, school officials, teachers, eyewitnesses, students who knew the boy who opened fire, and students who knew the victims. I knew there would be other perspectives, too, but those were at least the "have to" sources. Those were the stakeholders I could identify at first.

When I got to the school, many of the people I needed were in the same vicinity behind police tape. I was able to talk to most of them within the first hour or so. Then I tried to broaden my scope. Who else? I noticed that there were some groups praying, so I talked to members and leaders of school faith groups. Then I thought about the neighbors of the boy with the gun. I had his home address, so I went to his apartment complex and talked to as many in the area as I could.

---

[7] Ira Glass, "Q&A: Ira Glass on structuring stories, asking hard questions," interview by Jesse Thorn, *Columbia Journalism Review*, June 22, 2017, https://www.cjr.org/special_report/qa-ira-glass-turnaround-npr-jesse-thorn-tal.php.

After a few hours, though, I felt my body sag. I hadn't eaten since about 6 A.M. and my blood sugar was way down. I found a Jack in the Box nearby and ordered some tacos. Looking over my notes, I realized I didn't have much of a perspective from students as to the impact this had on them. I was considering whether to return to the school when I saw a group of about five teenagers and two adults walk in. The teenagers' faces were blotchy red and streaked with tears. They were carrying stuffed animals that still had the tags on them—they looked brand-new. I figured the students had just come from some kind of grief or trauma counseling at the school.

I watched as they ordered their food and sat at a table. Then I went over to them and introduced myself to one of the adults.

"I'm a reporter working on a story about what happened at the school today. Would it be okay to talk to the students for just a moment?"

The adult nodded to the teenagers and said, "It's up to them."

They talked to me about what kind of school it was before the shooting, and what they perceived would change after today. "And what about you as individuals?" I asked. "What changed today for you?"

One of them clutched the teddy bear she was holding and said, "I grew up too fast today."

I ended my story with that quote.

There was one other kind of source the *New York Times* wanted me to get for that story, and I tried. Sort of. The editor wanted me to check on the status of the victims still in the hospital with gunshot wounds and get comments from friends and relatives who were waiting on the surgery floor. I went to the floor and talked to a nurse to confirm who the hospital was treating and their condition.

I stood outside the waiting room where friends and relatives had gathered, and when people came down the hallway to go into the room, I identified myself and asked if they would ask anyone in the waiting room if there was someone willing to talk to a reporter out in the hallway about the shooting. Most of the people said they'd ask, but no one came out. I thought it would be tacky, insensitive, and invasive to go into the waiting room myself.

I asked the nurse if she'd be willing to ask people in the waiting room if anyone would be willing to talk to me, and she said, "Absolutely not." So I told my editor that we'd have to do without that perspective.

The most important dimension of any interview is to know why you're talking to people in the first place. Knowing your purpose will directly impact whether you get anything useful, and it will tell you how hard you need to work to get your sources to talk to you. In the case of the hospital, readers could easily imagine the horror and grief the families were feeling, and ethically I didn't think their perspective outweighed their right to privacy. So I didn't spend any more energy on getting them to talk to me. They would have added an interesting emotional and human dimension, but, in opposition to Janet Malcolm's and Joan Didion's proclamations,

I wasn't willing to be the kind of person it would have taken to get those interviews.

Your own humanity matters as much as the humanity of your sources.

Whom do you want to talk to? Why? The more articulately you can answer those questions, the more prepared you'll be for the next step.

Where "Clueless" Meets "Reckless"

David Greene from NPR Interviews Chrissie Hynde from the Pretenders

Broadcast on October 6, 2015

THE BEST WAY TO LEARN about interviewing is to watch or listen to interviewers in action. Just as you would deconstruct a story to see why it works well or doesn't, it is useful to take interviews apart and examine them. You can tell how well prepared the interviewer was, how nimble, how willing he or she was to improvise, how well she stuck to her purpose (and whether there even was a purpose), how open she was to reading the vibe of the person she was interviewing, and how the interview was structured. This interview between David Greene and Chrissie Hynde on NPR's *Morning Edition* is a classic. If you aren't already familiar with it, I highly recommend that you read or listen to the full interview since I'll be focusing in on specific moments here, and paraphrasing the rest.[1]

---

[1] You can find it here: "Chrissie Hynde: "I'm Just Telling My Story,'" interview by David Greene, on *Morning Edition*, produced by NPR,

The interview was panned by many listeners and critics, but others felt that it revealed the amazing personality of Chrissie Hynde. No matter how you feel about it, their conversation is an example of an interviewer not paying attention to his source. Hynde didn't just hint that she didn't want to continue a certain line of questioning—she came out and said it. And yet he persisted. Maybe Greene felt strongly that the topics he raised were more important than her comfort level, but it didn't feel that way when I listened to it. He just struck me as tone-deaf to what she was saying.

So why did Greene want to talk to her? Well, Hynde had just published her memoir, *Reckless: My Life as a Pretender.* This is the reason the interview is taking place. But remember earlier in this book I said you have to know *why* you are doing this interview? If it was just to promote a book, then the publisher should buy an ad. She has a new book, she's a rock star, and she made some people uncomfortable with some of the things she revealed in the book—all good reasons to get her on air. But at no point does the listener get a sense of the purpose of this interview. As we know, It's the interviewer's job to look beyond a book-promotion obligation and get at something deeper.

There are many moments in Greene's interview that are problematic For one, any time you have to start the audio with the caveat that "I'm just going to say it—Chrissie

---

streaming audio, 7:16, https://www.npr.org/2015/10/06/446083413/chrissie-hynde-im-just-telling-my-story.

Hynde is a really tough interview," you know you're in hot water. And then he describes her as a "Midwestern girl," even though she was sixty-four when they did this interview.

He begins by recounting some of the things she described about how much she loved rock and roll as a kid. In her book she said she saw the Rolling Stones and wanted some tangible token from the show.

> **GREENE:** I loved reading about how you sort of took some of [Rolling Stones] staging off to take it with you almost as a souvenir.

I understand what he's doing here, and I have done similar things (to varying success), but there is a huge risk of referring to something a source has said or written without asking a question. It's a hope that she will pick up on the cue and go into more detail. As you see from her response, it sort of blows up on him.

> **HYNDE:** Yeah. Do you want me to repeat the story? So I don't know if that's a question.

She is clearly not interested in going over material that is in the book. Since he didn't make it clear whether there was a question, she puts him on the defensive.

> **GREENE:** Yeah, I'd love you to. No, I'd love you to. What . . .

Again, I have been in this situation, and what Greene is doing is trying to regain some rapport, some friendliness, and get her to tell more about her love for the Rolling Stones. It's not a question that is central to the interview. It's merely an attempt to show her personality. But she tells him she doesn't want to go over what's in the book. As she has said time and again, "I don't want to do a book reading, as it were."

A lot of authors being interviewed about their books have no problem repeating on air what they've already written as a means to get more people potentially interested in the book. More important, though, this is the second time Hynde has told Greene that she's not interested in retelling what she has already written. He should have dropped this topic and moved on to something else. A legitimate question—not for the interview—is why Hynde is even doing the interview in the first place. It's evidently a contractual obligation with her publisher as a promotion gig. She is clearly a reluctant participant. Eventually he changes the subject, but it doesn't improve the dynamic.

GREENE: (to Hynde) There is a story in this book about you ending up with a biker group. Can you tell me about the night where you ended up in an abandoned . . .

HYNDE: No, I'm not going to tell you stories that are in the book.

Again, I see what he's doing. He has picked up on some controversy that a section of the book has created. But if he had been paying attention to what Hynde had just said, he wouldn't have framed his question this way. He wouldn't have asked her to repeat something that was in the book.

Over the course of this first portion of their exchange, Hynde says no fewer than six times that she does not want to tell stories that she has already written.

Greene's best move at this point would have been to pivot into the bigger picture here instead of insisting on her recounting a salacious story.

Someone must own the interview, and it has to be the interviewer, but there is a difference between owning the interview and being clueless to what the source is saying.

To his credit, Greene tries to save it by suggesting she go into more detail than is in the book, but it's just awkward. I'm not a fan of the phrase "Say more about this . . ." or "Talk a little more about that . . ." It just sounds lazy. Ask a question. Don't make the source have to figure out what you want.

GREENE: I wanted to give you the chance to describe what happened . . .

HYNDE: Well, I'm not going to describe it because I've written about it in the book. But what I can say is I never said I was raped, and I've never used the word, and it's not in the book.

GREENE: I mean, I can certainly read a couple lines from the book if that—if that would be better?

He seems fixated on this. Maybe it's his "why" for the interview. It seemed insensitive to me. Still, quoting directly from the book is a reasonable move. He's not interpreting or speculating. He has picked out a key, provocative statement for her to amplify and explain.

Soon after that exchange, they have the opportunity to talk about something in a productive manner, but instead they take a rocky turn:

GREENE: I just think there was one comment you made in an interview about the book to the *Sunday Times* of London.
(reading) If I'm walking around in my underwear and I'm drunk, who else's fault can it be?
HYNDE: So what are you getting at? Why are you asking me this?

At this point Hynde sounds confused, annoyed, and bordering on enraged. Is this an interrogation? Is she being asked to defend her point of view? Or speak on behalf of all women? This is officially a disaster now, because she already said she didn't want to repeat stories from the book, but he goes ahead anyway, and now he's putting her on the defensive for a comment that seemed to minimize sexual assaults, and it is even more unclear why this interview is taking place. This could have led to a bigger conversation about social media commentary, public shaming, and asserting your right to tell your own story as you see it. Instead, he has lost control of the interview. They never get back on track.

Hynde made it clear from the beginning that she wasn't going to get personal with Greene. Had Greene been more aware, he could have gotten her perspective on bigger issues. She also made it clear that she wasn't going to go for the charade of just a couple of buddies yakking in the studio. It sounds like that's what Greene was hoping for. But for Hynde, it was clearly a contractual obligation. It was a painful interview to listen to.

Had Greene prepared himself better, he would have realized that Hynde wasn't going to be his buddy. Had he listened more closely to her answers, he would have dropped his focus on the sexual assault and moved on when Hynde made it clear that she wasn't interested in how the world was interpreting that scene. Had this been Donald Rumsfeld being evasive on why we invaded Iraq, or Bernie Madoff not copping to the fact that he ruined thousands of lives with his pyramid scheme, then Greene by all means should have dug in and not let them off the hook. But this was a rock star who described a sexual assault in a manner that was counter to the modern definition of assault, and she clearly didn't want to say anything beyond what she had al-ready said in the book. Why bet the farm on staying with that topic? She's a rock star who wrote a memoir. It's not *The Brothers Karamazov*. You can't make it something that it's not, and you can't make her something that she's not. He needed a better "why" for this interview.

CHAPTER 2
Then It Goes to Your Hands and Feet

Hunting and Gathering Your Sources

INTERVIEWS DON'T JUST HAPPEN. YOU have to go out and get them on purpose. Once you have done some thinking about whom you should be talking to and why, then you have to put that thinking into action. The first point to consider is this: Most people aren't going to agree to an interview just to do you a favor. You have to show them why they should.

Very few people wake up in the morning and say, "I wonder who wants to interview me today?" and then adjust their days to accommodate the interviewer. The ones who do think that way are typically politicians, public relations professionals, and the occasional CEO. You'll need those kinds of people sometimes, but the majority of the people you need to talk to are not those who factor "giving interviews" into their daily routines. We're usually an interruption in someone's day. An intrusion. People have to move things around in order to work us in.

The journalist Ray Suarez said that in order to get people to talk to you, a transaction needs to take place, and it rests on whether you are trustworthy, and "that you are not going to try to trap them or screw them or deal dishonestly with them. . . . You are entering into a very intimate transaction. . . . These are not people who want to talk to you, and you have to present yourself to them, tell them who you are, and then get them to do the last thing they want to do in life, which is talk to you."[1]

As the interviewer, you're the one who has to do much of the accommodating in order to get worked into your sources' schedules and commitments. It's hard enough to get someone to talk to you; it's nearly impossible if you make it difficult for them to do so. Many times I have been contacted by a television station wanting to interview me about some news media issue, and they have wanted me to "swing by" their studio downtown or in a part of the city far away from where I am. Simply put, the answer to that request is always "No." I have a regular day job, I have commitments, and I have a personal life. If the interview is important to you, dear television reporter, then you come find me while I am doing what I do. I'll work you into that. But I'm not going to spend an hour driving to your place, paying for parking, sitting down with you for a few moments, and then getting back to what I was originally doing.

As a reporter, I have gotten up at 4 A.M. in order to have

—————————
[1] Ray Suarez, "Q&A: Ray Suarez on holding the powerful accountable," interview by Jesse Thorn, *Columbia Journalism Review,* August 4, 2017, www.cjr.org/special_report/qa-ray-suarez-on-holding-the-powerful -accountable.php.

a phone interview with someone on the East Coast at 7 A.M. The sports broadcaster Howard Cosell went into a locker-room shower fully clothed with his tape recorder running just so the athlete would keep talking to him.

If you want people to talk to you, make it as easy on them as possible to do what you're asking them to do. Pay for the laundry service on your clothes if you have to.

Some will need you to make an appointment. Don't ask for an hour (nothing takes an hour, and no one has that kind of time anyway). Ask for fifteen to twenty minutes. If they let you have more, great! Take it. There are exceptions, but assume for the most part that you will get a minimum amount of time, not a maximum.

Sometimes It's Easier Than You Think

There is a myth out there that the only people who can get sources to talk to them are the hard-charging extroverts, the people who exude confidence through their pores, who have no trouble walking up to strangers and getting them to say things they wouldn't say even after the fourth waterboarding treatment. It's simply not true. There are some people who see no stranger danger, but most of us are a little more reluctant. Most of us know full well that it takes a willful suspension of discomfort to interview a stranger.

All of us need to leave our comfort zones sometimes in order to get to the heart of what matters. St. Francis of Assisi said, "Start by doing what's necessary; then do what's possible; and suddenly you are doing the impossible." That's not a bad mantra for interviewing.

That was how I approached a story assigned to me about a serial killer who was on the loose in Southern California.

In the 1980s a serial killer terrorized California. Known as the Night Stalker, he would break into people's houses late at night, then torture, rape, and sometimes kill the occupants. Occasionally he drew satanic pentagrams on the mirrors before he escaped.

I was doing freelance work out of San Diego, and when the Night Stalker attacked a couple in Mission Viejo, a community less than two hours from my house, a news desk called and asked me to get up there. In this specific instance, one of the victims was brutally attacked and raped but managed to escape.

"We already know what happened," the editor said. "We want a story about what happens to a neighborhood after something like the Night Stalker happens. What is that area like now, with everyone knowing the guy is still on the loose?"

I confess I was skeptical that I would be able to do a profile on a terrified neighborhood. Who would talk to me—especially when they knew the bad guy was still out there? The experience taught me several lessons about the interviewing process.

Consider what to trust—your knowledge, discomfort, or instinct

Okay, I'll grant you that some of good interviewing is instinct, but a lot of it isn't. Many interviewers wrestle with the tension between what you (or your editor) know you should do and your own level of discomfort. Reluctance to talk to certain people, or certain kinds of people, often comes from personal experiences, assumptions, stereotypes, and a desire to not bother people. My experience, though, has made me not trust my discomfort most of the time. Obviously if the person is grieving or ranting or trying to comfort a loved one, I won't interrupt them. But my observation—and especially my experience with this Night Stalker story—is that most people don't mind the intrusion of a sensitive, truth-seeking reporter. It may feel uncomfortable to you at first, but that doesn't mean you shouldn't approach those you need to. It's okay to show your discomfort. That's part of our shared humanity.

Driving up to Mission Viejo, I wondered whether my editor had any idea what he was asking me to do. He was on the East Coast and this neighborhood was on the West Coast. Those are different worlds. Did he think people would just drop everything and talk to me? Did he have any sense of the fear gripping the region? I generally trust editors, because I think they have a sense of what readers are interested in, and they often see the big picture better than I do. But I wondered in this case whether this was going to be a day of doors slamming in my face.

Based on the news accounts, I had an idea of where the last attack took place. I saw a postal carrier, identified myself, and asked if he knew the specific house. He pointed at it a few houses away. I made a quick list of the stakeholders I thought I needed for this kind of a story. I didn't need the official account—the paper already had that. I needed the local voices: neighbors, mostly, and those who try to make neighborhoods places of refuge.

My initial sense was that knocking on neighbors' doors would be at best a waste of time, and at worst an invasion of the neighbors' privacy. Maybe it wouldn't be an invasion in the legal sense, but in the ethical sense. Was I being a voyeur, or perpetuating sensationalism? Would I want to talk to a reporter if this had happened in my neighborhood? But the knowledge part told me that my editor had a good point. Fear is a universal emotion. Sometimes naming it, describing it, embracing it, bearing witness to it through a story can have a universal connection to the reader. Maybe I could help readers understand themselves better with this story. Maybe.

Getting their perspectives was the only way I could get at the truth of the story. What was really happening to this neighborhood? I didn't want some theoretical explanation. I knew I could only get the raw material by engaging the raw material.

How do you get people to talk to you? A therapist may need to share a personal anecdote in order to get a client to open up. A doctor may need to admit to not knowing everything but be willing to keep searching. A journalist may need to accept his discomfort and knock on a stranger's door. It is in that risk that we often get past our assumptions about what the other person will say or do. I assumed that no one would want to talk to me. But my boss was telling me to do it anyway.

Ultimately, I trusted my editor.

Think through your introduction

When someone knocks on my door or calls me—usually to sell me something—I give that person about five seconds before making a judgment as to whether to let that person continue. Those five seconds have to be convincing. They are almost always interrupting me from something I'd rather be doing, and they are almost always trying to sell me something I don't want. I'm polite (usually), but I almost always tell them thanks but no thanks.

One exception was when a kid who I guess was about twelve said, awkwardly, as soon as I opened the door, "I am going to try to sell you something." I was hooked. I listened to his entire routine and bought whatever he was selling. I didn't want it or need it, and I can't even remember what it was. All I remember was that this kid was authentic, and it worked.

As Ira Glass said, "It's better if you just show up and you're a human being standing in front of them who looks sort of normal."[2]

SO WHEN YOU TRY TO get a stranger to talk to you, how do you do it? You could imitate others, I suppose, and fake some confidence. But my suggestion is to be authentic and tell the person right off the bat who you are and what you want. Strangers smell phonies and rehearsed friendliness from a mile

---

[2] Ira Glass, "Q&A: Ira Glass on structuring stories, asking hard questions," interview by Jesse Thorn, *Columbia Journalism Review*, June 22, 2017, https://www.cjr.org/special_report/qa-ira-glass-turnaround-npr-jesse-thorn-tal.php.

away (thanks, Jehovah's Witnesses!). I recommend rehearsing your introduction. Say it out loud. You'll discover right away if it sounds clumsy or too long, or if it sounds like you're trying to sell them insurance or Jesus or candy bars.

For my Night Stalker story, I figured the simpler my introduction the better. Don't be too specific; don't be pushy. Be considerate; don't argue if they tell you no. Remember, no one is obligated to talk to you. In my case, these people were probably afraid. How could I respect them yet convince them that it was a good idea to talk to me—a total stranger? From one perspective, there was nothing in this for them.

No one really trains you for that kind of an interview. You don't want to play a role. You want to be authentic and caring. And also persistent. You have a job to do.

Finally, I came to this: I decided to throw myself at their mercy, just like that little kid at my door.

I went to the front door of the house next to where the attack occurred and knocked. No answer. More time for self-doubt.

I went to the house on the *other* side of where the attack occurred and knocked. An elderly woman opened the door a couple of inches—the width of the chain across it. I could barely see her through the heavy screen-door mesh. I tried to be friendly, but not overly so.

"Hello, I'm a reporter with the *Boston Globe,* and I'm wondering if I could talk to you about the aftermath of what happened here the other night?"

The woman answered quickly.

"No." And she began to shut the door.

"I understand, and I'm sorry to bother you," I said. "Do you have any idea of who might talk to me?"

The door paused and the woman's eye reappeared in the gap. "Don't think of *Jurassic Park,*" I thought. She pointed across the street.

"They might talk to you," she said. "That's the house the woman went to when she escaped."

Then the door closed.

I went across the street and rang the bell. I thought I could sense that someone was home, so I waited several moments. Then I rang again and knocked. Yep, I definitely heard activity. A few moments later, a woman appeared in a robe with her hair wrapped in a towel. I went through my same routine, with a few additions.

"Hello, I'm a reporter with the *Boston Globe,* and I'm wondering if I could talk to you about the aftermath of what happened here the other night? I understand the victim came to your house? I don't want to intrude—would you have a few moments to talk to me out here on your front steps?"

"The *Boston Globe*?" she said. "All the way out here?"

"I'm based in San Diego," I said. "They're interested in what happens to a neighborhood after something like this. It seems to me you must have been a good neighbor, if the victim came to you."

The woman didn't hesitate.

"I don't have time to come out there and talk—as you can see, I just got out of the shower, and I am preparing a dinner for friends. But if you want to come inside and sit at my kitchen table and talk to me while I make dinner, that's okay with me."

Be ready to improvise

Frankly, I was stunned by her response. The Night Stalker was still out there. How did she know I wasn't that guy?

But this is how interviews often go. You think you know what's next, but the person you're interviewing throws you off balance. This is why interviews are like stories. You start out writing one way, but the story takes off in a different direction. If you want it to be a lively, vibrant story, you go where it leads, as long as you get the pertinent information in there somehow. If you stick to the rigid ideas you started with, it won't be nearly as interesting, and it will read like propaganda. Interviews rarely go the way you think they will. More on this later, but for now think about conducting an interview the way jazz musicians play: with keen attention and infinite flexibility. They start playing a song, but, depending on what the soloists do, or even how the crowd reacts, they may take things in an entirely different direction.

I had just a second to decide whether I could improvise with this interview. I figured it would be safer for everyone if we stayed out in the open, in public. But she was inviting me inside.

"It's okay with me," I stammered, "if you're sure you're okay with it."

She opened the door and headed for the kitchen. I was there

for almost two hours. She even fixed me lunch! It was clear that she really wanted to talk about what happened. She hadn't fully processed the events, the terror, the aftermath, and I was a willing listener. She gave me a lot of facts, emotion, philosophy.

I got to see the experience through her eyes. She thanked me when we were done. And gave me a hug. Yes, it felt very weird, but I was grateful for her honesty, trust, and humanity. She was also a very good cook.

Give sources a chance to bear witness

Getting her to talk to me was easier than I thought. As I have observed in other difficult situations, people often *want* to talk about what happened. They want to bear witness.

The notion of bearing witness taps into something Ray Bradbury told me in an interview. He said that we owe it to the universe to "bear witness to the miraculous." Good interviewers give others the opportunity to give voice to what they observe, experience, ponder, question. Good interviewers help us understand ourselves and others because they draw out these dimensions. In this Night Stalker story, I was able to help others put into language the unarticulated emotions they were experiencing. That has value.

And to paraphrase the poet Mary Oliver, sometimes the most important things we do as human beings is pay attention and bear witness.

Interviews help us tell about it.

Here are some of the other stakeholders I talked to that day:

The librarian at the neighborhood library, who filled me

in on the local history, and found resources for me to read about the area. Remember what I said earlier about librarians. They're gold.

A local hardware store owner, who told me about how sales for window and door locks and motion sensor lights were way up.

A clerk at the gun counter of a local sporting goods store, who said sales of guns were way up.

A local Lutheran pastor who was trying to prepare his next sermon, knowing that his parishioners were facing a lot of fear after being confronted with senseless brutality and violence, and that they were more heavily armed than before.

All of these people seemed happy to talk to me. They could see that I was trying to bear witness to what happened, and they wanted to give me their perspective.

Getting the Famous and the Almost Famous to Talk

One of the best movies about interviewing doesn't appear at first to be about interviewing at all. *Almost Famous* appears to be about rock music and its effect on musicians, their entourages, and fans. It is a tribute to music and being a fan.

But I watched it again several years after it first came out, and I was struck by the interview style of the fifteen-year-old protagonist, William Miller.

At the beginning of the movie, William wants to write about the rock band Black Sabbath for *Creem* magazine but is rebuffed by the bouncer at the backstage door. It appears that there is no convincing this gatekeeper to let him in.

Then the opening act, a band called Stillwater, arrives, and William tries to engage them.

"Hi, I'm a journalist. I write for *Creem* magazine," he says, holding a copy of the magazine in the air.

"The enemy!" one of the musicians yells. "A rock writer!"

"I'd like to interview you or someone from the band," William says.

One of the band members dismisses the young journalist with a pointed expletive. Another takes a condescending tone and says, "We play for the fans, not the critics," and waves goodbye.

William, however, has come prepared, even for Stillwater.

"Russell. Jeff. Ed. Larry," William says to the band members, instantly gaining credibility. "I really love your band. I think the song 'Fever Dog' is a big step forward for you guys. I think you guys producing it yourselves, instead of Glyn Johns, was the right thing to do. And the guitar sound was *incendiary*."

William gestures with a fist.

"Way to go," he says. Then he turns and walks away from the door.

The band members look at each other.

"Well don't stop *there*," one of the musicians yells.

"Yeah, come back here!! Keep going!" another exclaims. "I'm incendiary, too!"[3]

Then the backstage door opens and they pull him in with them.

The rest of that movie is a clinic on what to do and not do when interviewing celebrities. I recommend it. William started out thinking his interview was going to be with Black Sabbath, but he was able to improvise and appeal to Stillwater. As Stephen Stills so aptly sang, "If you can't be with the one you love, love the one you're with." William knew the band's work, appealed to their egos, and threw himself at their mercy.

Getting famous people to talk to you has its own set of challenges. Unless they are promoting a movie, a book, a diet, a candidacy, a cause, or a fragrance and they want you to do the equivalent of an infomercial, they don't need you. You need them. So you have to do a kind of jujitsu move and use their energy to your advantage. You have to appeal to what *they* are interested in, not necessarily what *you* are interested in. And there has to be something new or fresh in there to make it unusual.

This involves appealing to the person's self-interest. And it involves preparation.

Why should this person talk to you? That's what you have

---

[3] Fugit, Patrick. *Almost Famous.* Theatrical release. Directed by Cameron Crowe. Los Angeles: DreamWorks, 2000. Paraphrased from http://www.dailyscript.com/scripts/almostfamous.html, p. 26.

to show them. You have to get them on board with the "why." And that "why" typically can't just be something that pops out of your head in the moment. Craft a convincing argument. Show them that you're prepared enough to ask them questions they haven't been asked a thousand times.

When I invited Kareem Abdul-Jabbar for an interview at our Writer's Symposium, I decided my approach would be that I would first emphasize what we were *not* going to talk about. I wasn't interested in basketball, I told him. Actually, I told this to his manager (more on dealing with gatekeepers later). This wasn't a basketball symposium, I said. It was a *writer's* symposium. I wanted to talk to him about writing. More specifically, *his* writing. I said I wanted to talk about his op-ed pieces in the *Washington Post* and *Time* magazine about race, Islam, politics, and police shootings, and about his books for young readers, and his sci-fi books, and his black history books, and his new book about his friendship with UCLA coach John Wooden. I wanted to talk about reading and writing, and why his voice mattered.

I figured a lot of people have approached him, so they could ask him about his historic basketball career. And maybe his awesome role as a copilot in the movie *Airplane*. I bet he was tired of talking about the same things from his past. And a lot had happened in his life in the decades after basketball.

Now, Abdul-Jabbar doesn't need to talk to me. He doesn't crave attention. An interview with me isn't going to advance his career. I'm not paying him the big bucks. But I figured he didn't get to talk about reading and writing that often. I figured that he would *want* to talk about it. And I was right.

One writer in particular had been on my radar as someone who I felt would be a great person to interview, but anyone I mentioned this to told me I'd never get him. He just didn't do these kinds of things very often, they told me. I finally found a way to reach him directly (it's always better that way), and gave him my best pitch. Our Writer's Symposium is always in February, so I asked this particular writer about a date in February of the following year. "Sorry," came the reply. "I never do more than one event per month, and I have commitments for the next few Februaries."

He thought he had gotten rid of me.

I wrote back to him immediately: "What is the next open February for you?"

Five years away, he said. Now he was *sure* he had gotten rid of me.

"I'll take it."

He came five years later, and he was awesome. We still keep in touch.

In addition to self-interest and persistence, it helps if you make your request personal. Not as in making it personal to you, the interviewer (although that can help at times, as long as you don't come across as needy). Make it personal to the person you want to talk to. I do enough preparation just to do the invitation that I can appeal to each writer specifically. I will address that person's work, the impact, the uniqueness. In my invitations to writers, I've included a baby gift for a writer whose wife had just given birth, had a faculty colleague include a personal note since he had been a professor where the writer's wife had gone to college, had a friend of the writer's (and mine) deliver my invitation to her—anything I could think of to make my request personal. Then I'm not just this nameless institution needing to fill a calendar date. They know they are being pursued.

Larry Lubenow, the young reporter I mentioned in the last chapter who interviewed Louis Armstrong, got that interview by convincing the hotel staffer who was going to deliver dinner to Armstrong's room to let Lubenow be the room-service guy. Once Lubenow was in the room, he told Armstrong who he was and asked if he could interview him.

I'm not an advocate for deception and impersonating others, but sometimes it does serve a purpose. Maybe Janet Malcolm was onto something after all.

Usually when I ask a writer for an interview, I try to find something that person has written and connect it to a current event or some experience I had. This is a way to make the invitation personal.

When I invited Bill Moyers to our Symposium, I knew I was asking a lot for him to come from New York, where he lived (although San Diego in February is a bit of an incentive!), and I knew that I couldn't pay him what other places paid him. But I knew that he was from the South, and that he had a love for southern writers. While I was thinking about how to make this trip appealing to him, I ran across this line in Flannery O'Connor's book *Mystery and Manners*:

"[The Christian writer] does not decide what would be good for the Christian body and proceed to deliver it. Like a very doubtful Jacob, he confronts what stands in his path and wonders if he will come out of the struggle at all."

I told Moyers that this line made me think of the journalism, books, and speeches he gives the world. I wouldn't have known about all of those stories, books, and speeches had I not been preparing for my invitation. That's the preparation part.[4]

When you're trying to find that little nugget of a connection to a famous person, pay attention to what is going on around you, to what you're reading, hearing, observing, experiencing, and use that as a way to communicate your readiness to engage.

The great sportswriter and broadcaster Dick Enberg was one of the few people who got the baseball legend Ted Williams to talk to him. How? He was prepared, persistent, and creative. Ted Williams was Enberg's idol. When Enberg was the play-by-play announcer for the California Angels in 1969, Williams was the manager of the Washington Senators. Part of Enberg's job was to do the pre- and postgame shows, and he was determined to get Williams on the pregame show.

The problem was that Williams hated people in the media and almost never did interviews.

Enberg went through Williams's autobiography to see if

---

[4] As it happens, Moyers wrote back and said he would cut short a vacation in Mexico to come to the Symposium, and he told me later that it was the O'Connor quote that appealed most to him.

there were any nuggets he could draw from, and then he went to the *Baseball Register,* and there it was. In 1941, Ted Williams pitched an inning and two-thirds against Detroit. That was Enberg's hook. He'd ask Williams about *pitching,* not hitting.

During batting practice, Enberg approached Williams from behind. He introduced himself and told him that he wanted Williams to be on his show. Williams ignored him and kept looking at his players on the field. Enberg then said, "I promise I won't ask you one question about hitting."

Williams looked at Enberg, and Enberg continued: "I want to talk to you about the time you pitched for the Red Sox against the Tigers and struck out Rudy York."

Williams put his arm around Enberg's shoulders and agreed to the interview. They remained friends the rest of their lives.

"He wouldn't have wanted to talk to me if I wanted to ask him the questions everyone else was asking him," Enberg told me years later.

There is at least one other approach to getting famous people to talk to you, but it's risky, and a little counterintuitive. If you do it you have to commit to taking the long view. That tactic is this: Ignore the person.

That's what the sportswriter Jackie MacMullan told us she did in regard to interviewing the basketball star Patrick Ewing. MacMullan, who was a basketball star herself in college, covered the NBA for *Sports Illustrated,* the *Boston Globe,* and ESPN. She knew the game better than most writers, and whenever she covered the New York Knicks, she noticed that all of the other reporters surrounded the team's famous center Patrick Ewing for postgame quotes, regardless of whether he was much of a factor in the game.

MacMullan took the opposite tack. When she was at our Writer's Symposium, she described how she approached virtually everyone else on the team for a quote, but not Ewing. She was also visibly pregnant during one particular season.

When a new season started, she continued her same approach to talking to almost all of the players in the locker room, and after one game she said it was as if the light was suddenly blocked from behind her. She turned around and there was the seven-foot Ewing.

"What did you have?" he said.

"What? What are you talking about?" MacMullan said.

"Last season you were here in the locker room and you were pregnant. Did you have a boy or a girl?"

MacMullan said that this was the beginning of a significant writer/subject relationship. She ended up doing a profile on Ewing for the *Boston Globe* and won an Associated Press Sports Editors national award for it.

One other point about getting famous people to talk to you: Make it easy for them to do this. With famous writers, I try to make it easy on them just by virtue of making their appearance an interview. That means they don't have to prepare a talk or a reading. If they want to do that, too, they can. But I assume they are busy and that they don't need another task. If they can just come and answer questions, that's easier. Sometimes the difference between getting an interview and not getting it is in how easy you make it for the person. That was part of the appeal when the podcaster Krista Tippett agreed to appear. She interviews people for a living. And now I was inviting her so she could answer questions instead of ask them? That was extremely appealing to her.

Occasionally you'll be surprised by an individual's desire to help you. If you ever assume that someone won't talk to you because you're young, you're not famous, or you don't have much of a sales pitch, take this example to heart. I had wanted to get Ray Bradbury to our Writer's Symposium for years but didn't have the courage or the connections to ask him. Breaking my own rules from Chapter 1 about establishing a specific purpose for an interview, I didn't have a "why" other than that I was a fan and I knew he was passionate about writing. That was enough for me.

I heard him speak at a writers' conference and my heart pounded because I was in the same room. "It's now or never," I thought. "Today's the day to ask him." But what if he said "Why should I?" or "Never heard of your symposium," or "Stop wasting my time"? Could I handle the humiliation in front of all the others?

So I stood in a book signing line for more than an hour just so I could ask him the best way to invite him to the Symposium. He wrote down his fax number, handed me the piece of paper, and said, "You need but ask!" Then he turned to the next person in line. I faxed him the next day, and he immediately accepted.

But even if I had carefully constructed my purpose for the interview, it wouldn't have mattered. None of the traditional interviewing rules applied to him. Within the first few minutes of our televised interview, he hijacked it and went in whatever direction the levers in his pinball attention span wanted.

He ranted, he raved, he implored, he inspired, he entertained, and he instructed.

As the interviewer, I was the most irrelevant person in the auditorium.

And it was the best interview ever.

What About the Not-So-Famous, or the Reluctant?

But what about when you're trying to get people to talk to you just because you need their eyewitness account, their expertise, their perspective on something? How do you get the average citizen to talk to you? This was what I faced when working on the Night Stalker story. The people I needed weren't famous. Which was the point. I was trying to paint a picture of a neighborhood.

When trying to get a layperson's perspective, the best way to do it is to acknowledge their unique point of view. Every person has a vantage point. Every person has a unique experience. The more particular you can get with a person's account, the more human it is going to be, and the more universal it is going to be. That's why we try to get witnesses, bystanders, participants. They help us see a version of events that is more than the official one.

When the Witness to War project started recording interviews with World War II veterans, filmmakers contacted my dad about his experience at a weather station on the Arctic Circle. He was assigned there with four other soldiers for a year, where they gave hourly weather reports so the Air Force could plan their bombing runs in Europe. My dad was ninety when the filmmakers came to his house to talk, and he was thrilled to talk about it. He showed some of his uniform patches, the ivory carvings given to him by the indigenous people, and lots of photos. It's a topic he loved to talk about, and he didn't get many opportunities to do it in his later years. He was retired and had the time. He wasn't General Patton or General Eisenhower. He was a kid living among native people. That was the point. He was a layman who could give a unique perspective.

But sources aren't always this willing.

They don't always have time; they don't see what's in it for them; they aren't very verbal; they don't see the point of talking about it; they don't want to incriminate themselves. Or they just plain don't feel like it. What's an interviewer to do?

Simple answer: Keep trying. Lawyers and judges have subpoenas, which are court orders to make you talk to them. Even then you don't have to, if you don't mind getting fined or going to jail (thanks, Judith Miller!). But for the rest of us, reluctant sources take more effort. Maybe it's just personal pride, but I never like to give up on reluctant sources unless they give me a reason. I will go to great lengths to make them finally say no. But ignoring me isn't going to make me go away. I want to hear you say "Go away." Then I will. Usually.

Reluctant sources might be more willing to talk to you if

you tell them why they have a unique perspective, and why it matters to understanding the big picture. I have used phrases such as "You're in the best position to comment on this . . ." or "No one else has the knowledge you have on this, and the public would benefit from hearing your perspective . . ." or "You are uniquely situated to help us understand this complex issue." Is it flattery? Sure. Is it *too much* flattery? Not if it's true.

I once waited outside a hospital administrator's office for more than three hours, just to get a "no comment" from him. I had to at least get that. His assistant told me that he would eventually have to leave his office to go to the bathroom, so I sat in the waiting room between his office and the bathroom, with plenty of reading material, hoping he wasn't wearing a catheter. I needed to show my readers (and my editor) that I gave him a chance to give his perspective on the story I was writing. When he came out of his office and saw me, he had his chance, and I had the satisfaction of having him look me in the eye and say he would not talk to me. That's better than my having to tell readers (and my editor) I wasn't able to reach him. When I read an important story that leaves out a crucial piece of it with a line like "Repeated efforts to reach So-and-So were unsuccessful," I am rarely convinced that much effort was put into reaching So-and-So. You may have sent them an email or two, or called them after hours. Make them tell you no.

Sometimes it is just plain persistence and truth-telling that will get you the interviews you desire, even when the people you want to talk to think you're the enemy.

When the investigative reporter Steve Weinberg tried to get people to talk to him about the biography he was writing about the industrialist Armand Hammer, he found that most of Hammer's associates were reluctant to participate in a book they thought was going to be critical of their boss. Hammer had even instructed his associates not to talk to Weinberg.

"I sent letters, examples of my previous work, explained what I wanted to cover and why I was doing it without Hammer's blessing," Weinberg wrote. Weinberg said that when you share some of the information you know, it might impress the source that what you are working on isn't just going to be a hit job. Lines such as "And last week, when I was checking all the land records . . ." will show your sources that you're serious about research and accuracy.

In the letter he wrote to Hammer's associates, Weinberg explained that Hammer was one of the most important people in the history of business. All of the associates ultimately cooperated with Weinberg's book.[5]

If you're a young person, you may be able to use your age to your advantage. I have seen students say, "I'm a student reporter—can you help me out here?" And even, "You remember trying to get started in your career, don't you? I could really use your help." Almost no one refuses that approach.

---

[5] Missouri Group, *News Reporting and Writing*, 12th edition (Boston: Bedford/St. Martin, 2017), 44.

Gatekeepers Rule (the World)

But sometimes we can't share humanity, information, exchanges of ideas, because something is standing in the way. More precisely, someone. That someone is a gatekeeper. A gatekeeper is the person whose job it is to protect your source from people like you.

A gatekeeper might be the source's administrative assistant, public relations person, agent, bodyguard, bouncer, spouse, lawyer, or other kind of representative. Their job is to put their client's best foot forward, to keep their image unsullied, to minimize damage, and to keep their client, boss, or loved one from getting harassed by people like you.

You absolutely must be nice to them. They will ultimately decide whether you will have access to the person you want to talk to. You should be nice to everyone, of course (thanks, Mr. Rogers!), but you should *really* be nice to assistants, secretaries, receptionists, and anyone else who can get you connected. If they can get you connected, that also means they can keep you from getting connected.

The way to get through the gatekeepers (around them is best, but sometimes you do have to go through) is with the same approach you would take if you were in direct contact with the person you want to talk to. You have to put your request in such a way that it is in the source's best interest to do this interview, that the source is the best one to talk about this topic, and that the world's understanding of the topic will be enhanced with this person's perspective.

Often, it simply comes down to whether the gate-keeper likes you and sees that the interview will help advance what the source represents. The way to convince gatekeepers to "open the gate" for you is through your professionalism, preparedness, trustworthiness, demeanor, and ability to briefly express why you want to talk to this person.

I once had a corporate CEO's assistant finally take pity on me when she realized her boss was avoiding me. I had called several times and left multiple messages, and it became clear the CEO thought that if he ignored me long enough I would give up. (That person clearly didn't know many journalists. Being ignored merely amps us up.)

After repeated attempts on my part—all made in perseverance bathed in politeness—the assistant gave me the CEO's cell phone number and said that between 1 P.M. and 3 P.M. that day he would be stuck in traffic on the New Jersey Turnpike. When he answered his phone and I identified myself, he said, "Oh God." He wasn't happy to talk to me, but he did. I sent his assistant flowers.

I had another gatekeeper take pity on me when I was trying to get a famous writer to consider coming to our Writer's Symposium. I knew I couldn't afford his fee. I asked his assistant for advice on how to appeal to him.

"Well, he does like to play golf, and he can almost never get on Torrey Pines in San Diego," she said.

She didn't even need to finish that sentence. I got us a tee time at Torrey Pines, and he even brought along his buddy

Brian Doyle-Murray, who cowrote the golf comedy *Caddy-shack*. Hole in one.

IT TAKES PERSEVERANCE, PATIENCE, AND kindness to get people to talk to you. It takes perseverance, patience, and kindness to get gatekeepers to let you inside in the first place.

Occasionally it takes shame.

Shame may not be a good parenting technique, but in journalism it can occasionally work. I rarely use it, because it seems so arrogant, condescending, and morally question-able. And if a person is already inclined not to talk to you, shaming that person isn't much of an incentive to change her mind. It never works with gatekeepers, by the way. It only strengthens their resolve and their opinion that you are a jerk.

Essentially, you resort to shame when your source won't respond to logic, self-interest, altruism, and a plea to "please help me out."

The only time I think it is a legitimate tactic is when you can reach the actual source with your request, and frame it in a way that says the refusal to talk to you is a violation of some kind of public trust or responsibility.

San Diego Magazine hired me one summer to investigate who was really running the city: San Diego was in colossal disarray, and it seemed that no one knew who was really in charge. The city council thought it was in charge, and re-peatedly hobbled and criticized the mayor; the city attorney was a firecracker who sensed a power vacuum and assumed it was his God-given right to fill it; the mayor was the former police chief, and he couldn't understand why people didn't just do what he told them to do. He had made some big mistakes that made him look like he was a stooge for the real estate developers in the city. The city council, the city attorney, and the mayor's office were constantly peeing on each other very publicly. So who was really running the show?

The city council members were happy to talk to me. They had strong views on everything, and they were angry. Getting interviews with them was easy because it gave them a chance to criticize everyone and thump their chests. They were mixed in their views on the mayor, but the one thing they seemed unanimous on was that they hated the city attorney. One city councilperson described the situation between the mayor and city attorney this way: "It's hard to score a touchdown when your running back keeps tackling your quarterback."

The city attorney was a little less agreeable when I contacted him about wanting to do an interview. He wasn't quite as eager as the city council, but I learned a lesson from my time with this Napoleon. I learned to be patient. As interviewers we typically want our information right now. This guy decided to test me, to test the depth of my desire to do this story. It took time, patience, and humility on my part, but it was worth it.

He suggested I come to his office downtown just so I could observe the manner in which he operated. He didn't officially agree to an interview, but said I could at least be in the same room. Sure, it was a power move on his part (and he had a considerable ego), but I complied. Sometimes you have to put your own ego on the shelf for a while.[6]

I sat in his office for hours, watching him conduct business and meet with staff members, listening to his side of phone calls, watching him grandstand on my behalf, and receiving his Al Pacino–esque speeches directed at me about the news media, the city of San Diego, and his own greatness. When I would begin to ask a question, he'd hold up his hand and say, "I still haven't decided whether to let you interview me." As I said, he had a considerable ego.

I could have called bullshit on all of it and walked out, but what would that have proved? That my ego was as big as his? That I wouldn't allow myself to be made small? And then what? A call to my editor explaining that I didn't have a story because this bully didn't respect me? I decided to wait him out.

At the end of this very long day of one-way communication (him to me), he said I could come back the next day and we'd have the interview. Now he trusted me, he said. I saw it as short-term pain for long-term gain.

The interview the following day was outstanding. He was a reporter's dream. He was a loquacious quote machine. He had passion, insight, and history and seemed like a cheerleader for the common man. In fact, when I rode down in the elevator with him to go to lunch and the elevator door opened, people in the lobby saw him and applauded. He was their hero!

---

[6] I address this more fully in Chapter 11.

It was also apparent that he hated the mayor.

While I was having success getting the movers and shakers to talk to me, there was still one person who kept ignoring my calls: the mayor. But it wasn't the mayor himself. I wasn't convinced that he even knew I was trying to reach him. He had a gatekeeper who would have made J. D. Salinger proud. I tried phoning several times per day, hoping the gatekeeper's assistant might let me slip through if I called when I knew the gatekeeper was gone. I tried personally going to the mayor's office, but was always sent away. "He's too busy," was the mantra. "He wishes you luck on your story." I went to events where the mayor was scheduled to appear, but he always made his appearance brief and was whisked away.

One day, when I was in the elevator at City Hall after another blistering interview with a city council member, the elevator stopped and a young man got in. I knew this guy. He was an alum from the university where I teach.

And he worked in the mayor's office.

After we exchanged pleasantries, he asked what I was doing at City Hall. I told him and followed it up with, "It's too bad that this story is going to seem so stacked against your guy, though. I've got the city council complaining about him, and the city attorney *really* complaining about him, but since he won't talk to me so that I can get his perspective, the story is going to look pretty one-sided. I'll show how many times I tried to reach him and how many times your office declined to let me talk to him. Too bad. He's going to look like a coward."

The elevator doors opened.

"Have a nice day," I said.

"What's your cell number?" he asked. I gave it to him and walked to the parking garage.

Before I was even to my car, my phone rang, and the former student said, "Can you come in tomorrow at nine A.M.? The mayor would like to talk to you."

When I got to the mayor's office he was gracious, friendly, and very apologetic.

"I had no idea you were trying to reach me," he said. "I'll have a word with our communications director after this."

The interview was marvelous. He seemed honest, forthcoming, and prepared with good information. When we were done, he told me that he was leaving the next day for a family vacation in Hawaii, but gave me his cell number and told me to call him directly anytime.

Specific Strategies

As you can tell from the examples above, there is an art to getting the interview. Later on I will show you that there is an art to *conducting* the interview, too. But for now, let's focus on how to get people to talk to you.

Here's the SparkNotes version of how to get people to talk to you:

1. Appeal to self-interest: Remember, very few people have to talk to you, or even want to talk to you. It's

your job to make them see why they should, and why their specific voice matters. Remember what I said before: The world doesn't run on altruism. It runs on self-interest.

2.   Prepare: In order to appeal to a person's self-interest, you have to have done enough homework to figure out what kind of an appeal would work best.

3.   Persist: What is the difference between being persistent and being a pest? I have no idea. Maybe when the person simply stops responding to your emails, phone calls, and letters and you keep sending them anyway, you have reached the level of pest. (There is a famous writer who I hope is reading this paragraph. And yes, I am talking about you. I would even try to shame you if I could.)

4.   Find your shared sense of humanity: The best interviews, in my opinion, come from this element, whether it is an eyewitness, an expert, a gadfly, or a celebrity. When sources reveal even just a glimpse of their humanity, they stop being "types" of people and become simply people. When that happens, others can relate to them immediately.

Appealing to the shared sense of humanity is what I was trying to do in getting people to talk to me for my Night Stalker story. There wasn't a lot of preparation I could do for that story, other than have the facts of what happened.

This approach takes vulnerability on your part. And you have to be sure you aren't just using that humanity to manipulate people. Many reporters start their request with, "I have a problem, and I'm hoping you can help me understand it." Then they explain why they want that person to talk to them. It becomes a favor. The source is helping you. I have done this very thing, but only when I really had a problem or was confused about something. Some reporters use that approach all the time, and while it does appeal to a person's shared humanity—we all just want to help each other, don't we?—it can come across as phony or manipulative. This approach is effective, and you can use it, but only if it's true.

There is another level of shared humanity that I'm talking about, though.

I'd love to tell you that I taught this student the trait of shared humanity, but I confess that she came up with it on her own. Maybe she taught it to me. The situation at our university newspaper was a delicate one. It was homecoming weekend, and for a big variety show, one of our alums played his saxophone and brought the huge crowd to its feet. He lived in Phoenix and had flown in with his dad in a private plane the day before. The show was on Friday night. The alum and his dad flew back to Phoenix on Saturday.

But something happened, and the plane crashed, killing both the former student and his father.

It was a story—a tragic one—and I discussed the approach with our student reporters.

"Someone needs to call the house in Phoenix," I said. "We need to get a family member to tell us how they are coping with this news."

No one wanted to make that phone call.

Finally, one of the students said, flatly, "I'll do it."

"Don't be pushy," I said. "Just ask if they want to say something to our readers."

When I read the story, I couldn't believe how beautifully done it was. There was an extensive interview with the alum's sister—she had just lost her father and brother. The story was heartfelt and deep.

"How did you get her to talk to you?" I asked the reporter.

"I called the house, very nervous, hoping no one would answer," she said. "When someone did, I identified myself and said I was doing a story on the tragedy. I asked if she would be willing to talk to me about it."

The sister, understandably upset, asked, "Why would I want to do that?"

The reporter hadn't thought about how to answer that question, but she said this:

"I have a brother that I adore. And I love my father very much. I know that if something like this happened to them, I would want the world to know how wonderful they were."

There it was—an invitation to share the humanity, the grief, the remembrance. To bear witness.

The story went from focusing on the details of the crash

to the kinds of men the passengers were. Readers had a deeper sense of what it meant to love, to lose loved ones, to be part of the human experience.

We're human beings before we're interviewers and sources. That's a good place to start.

Giving readers a glimpse into shared humanity is my favorite kind of story to write. We all need stories that tell us what happened in the world today, but we also need stories that remind us that we all share some fundamental experiences, that all over the world we have at least a few similar values. That's why stories about life in a refugee camp help us understand the human toll of failing economies or war or epidemics of disease. Stories that show us life in the slums of Mumbai, or the projects in Watts, or the ranches of Montana, or the Iron Range of Minnesota, or the deportation detention centers in Texas, show us that mothers and fathers all over love their children as much as you love yours. They show us what binds us, what separates us, what motivates us, what breaks our hearts, what brings us simple joy.

Just for a moment, when we read stories of shared humanity, we drop our defenses, stop thinking about others as "other," and see ourselves in a bigger story.

I tapped into that "bigger story" with an assignment about a natural disaster on the West Coast. Early one summer morning the national desk of the *Boston Globe* called (again!) and said they had a story they wanted me to do. Forest fires had been raging in Northern California for weeks, and it looked like they could rage for weeks or months more.

They wanted a similar kind of story to the Night Stalker assignment, in that they didn't need the number of acres burned, or structures lost, or a dollar figure for the damages so far. They had all that from the Associated Press.

These "bigger" stories are important. Since we have access to the immediacy of the facts of the breaking news, we sometimes get removed from what these facts mean in the long run. Are there bigger themes these stories can connect us to? Do they reveal personal and cultural similarities to other populations? Do they show us how loss and grace are usually experienced simultaneously? Do they deepen our understanding of our attachment to things and to one another?

"Find a group of firefighters who have been working nonstop for a long time," the editor said. "Show us what it's like to face the elements they're facing with no letup in sight. Show us the human cost of fighting these fires. But keep in mind we need a quick turnaround on the story."

"Great idea," I said. "When do you want it?"

"The end of today," she said.

"You realize this will cost you a lot of money," I said. "I'll have to fly to Northern California, rent a car, find some firefighters, write the story, and fly home tonight. I don't want to be gone overnight."

"How long would it take you to just drive there?" she asked.

This is when I realized that people in New England have no idea how big California is.

"About eight hours."

"If I drove eight hours north of Boston, I would have gone

through four states and would be well into Canada," she said. Pause. "Well, you'd better get to the airport."

I drove immediately to the San Diego airport, bought a ticket to San Jose, was there in a couple of hours, rented a car, and drove toward the smoke in the mountains. I found a National Guard–run base camp for the firefighters. It was like a major military outpost, accommodating firefighters from all over the United States and hundreds of jeeps, trucks, bulldozers—and a few helicopters.

I found the person in charge and told him about the story I was working on. He radioed several groups, and to my good fortune he found a group of volunteer firefighters who had been working for a few weeks but were now dug in at a mountain town where their own homes were about to be overcome by the fires.

He pointed to a road that led up a mountain.

"You can't miss them," he said.

I drove for thirty or forty minutes, hoping the commander was correct, and I finally came to a clearing where a group of exhausted and filthy men were sitting on the ground. I identified myself and asked if I could talk with them. They were too tired to say no.

When I asked them about the homes they were trying to save, they got emotional. They told of building these homes with their parents and children, about the years of planning, of putting all of their life savings into these mountain retreats, of the joy these homes had brought them, and the anguish at the thought of losing them. The dominant emotion that came through, though, was determination. That's what I tried to capture in my story.

I spent a few hours with them, watched them work, took lots of notes, then drove back down to the base camp. I wrote my Man versus Nature story sitting at a picnic table and sent it in.

It was early evening and there was still some light left in the day. I went to the National Guard officer to thank him for his help, and he asked if I wanted to see the fires from the air. He pointed to a Vietnam-era helicopter that was just getting its rotors moving.

I wanted to ask, "Shouldn't it have sides?" It had a top, with the rotors, and a bottom, with wheels, a nose, and a tail. But no walls. You could see right through from one side to the other. It looked like a transparent shipping container with propellers.

"We're taking up a county land assessor and a television crew," he said. "You're welcome to join them." He handed me some earplugs and walked away.

I decided this was not the time to confess to him that I was going through a phase where I tended toward airsickness, particularly in small aircraft. Just a few years before, I had fouled the cockpit of a friend's private plane when he asked me to take aerial pictures of his new property. I was doing just fine until he abruptly banked the plane with the wings straight up and down so that I could get an unfettered view. I got the shot, but lost my lunch.

My seat on the helicopter was directly across from the assessor. Once we were airborne and got over the fires, the news videographer put on some straps and suspended himself outside the helicopter to get a better shot. I felt the nausea rise with the smoke. I couldn't appreciate the spectacle of seeing an entire mountain in flames. I had an internal volcano I was trying to cap. I kept looking at the assessor, trying to gauge how I was going to tell him that he was directly in the line of my own fire. I looked out the side of the chopper and wondered if I could survive a leap.

When I got home that night I told my wife about the helicopter and how I nearly puked on an assessor. That's when I told her an insight into my future.

"If you ever hear that I fell out of a helicopter, I just want you to know the truth," I said. "I didn't fall. I jumped."

And If They Are Still Reluctant

If preparation, persistence, and an appeal to self-interest don't work, you can resort to flattery, but you don't want to get weird with it. There is a difference between flattering sources and just blowing sunshine up their dresses.

When I try to convince someone to talk to me, I am trying to convince them that they have a unique perspective that the world should hear, and that if they let me interview them, they will be in good hands.

Still, it raises questions about the ethics of flattery. How much is enough? When does it become pandering just so you get what you want? When do you cross the line from being authentic and personal to being King Lear's daughters who tell him how awesome he is? When do you go from being Cordelia to being Goneril and Regan?

When does it seem like the prayer scene in the Monty Python movie *The Meaning of Life*?

CHAPLAIN: Oh Lord . . .

CONGREGATION: Oh Lord . . .

CHAPLAIN: Oooh you are so big . . .

CONGREGATION: Oooh you are so big . . .

CHAPLAIN: So absolutely huge.

CONGREGATION: So ab-solutely huge.

CHAPLAIN: Gosh, we're all really impressed down here I can tell you.

CONGREGATION: Gosh, we're all really impressed down here I can tell you.

CHAPLAIN: Forgive Us, O Lord, for this our dreadful toadying.

CONGREGATION: And barefaced flattery.

CHAPLAIN: But you are so strong and, well, just so super.

CONGREGATION: Fan-tastic.

HEADMASTER: Amen.[7]

I DO NOT RECOMMEND THIS extreme approach no matter how desperate you are, even if you are trying to score an interview with God himself.

---

[7] John Cleese, Terry Gilliam, Eric Idle, Terry Jones, and Michael Palin, *Monty Python's The Meaning of Life*, 1983, transcript by Screenplaysfor

You want to be complimentary, but you don't want to come across as a sycophant. Most people have a pretty good crap detector, and they know when you're slinging it. You want to be real and be taken seriously. If it doesn't pass your own smell test, it isn't going to pass your source's, either.

How would *you* like to be treated when someone wants something from you? That's not a bad guide.

Being persistent and personal means you also have to be ethical.

And speaking of ethics, a situation occasionally comes up where sources ask to be paid for their information.

If we're journalists, we don't pay them to talk to us. Or usually we don't. Historically there has been an ethical taboo on journalists paying sources to tell their true stories. The thinking has been that a financial incentive might invite sources to tell a juicier, more exaggerated story in order to justify the payment. But the *National Enquirer* pays sources (they had the best intel on the O. J. Simpson trial and broke the story on presidential candidate John Edwards's love child this way), and other news organizations have had to hold their noses and publish sentences like "As first reported in the *National Enquirer* . . ." because they didn't have insiders on the payroll. But the *Enquirer* also gets a lot wrong when they pay sources. They also pay lots of money to settle libel cases.

Ever wonder why jailhouse informants give information

to cops that later gets thrown out of court? Often it's because the informants feel pressure to come up with something worthwhile, whether it's true or not, in order to get the reward or have their sentences reduced. Paying for information can be an incentive for a source to give you only what you want to hear. It can encourage sources to come up with information that is bizarre and sensational. There's already enough of that out there.

It is still a reasonable expectation in journalism that people will give you information because it is interesting or important to the public. Hopefully it's both. But typically it is not for sale. Paying sources for their insight for a news story can taint the public's perception of the credibility of that information. It may get the person to talk to you (money is a self-interest). If you do it, though, you should also tell the public that you paid for it, and let them decide how seriously they want to take it. Be transparent about what you've done.

When I interview writers for our Writer's Symposium, I pay them an honorarium for coming to our school, meeting with students, sharing meals with students and faculty, and sitting down with me for a televised program. Some do it for free, but not many. Unless they are Stephen King or J. K. Rowling, they aren't making *that* much money on their books, and this is a legitimate way to supplement their income, in my opinion. But even if the writer is very successful, I'm not against paying an honorarium. It shows that you have some skin in the game and that you're taking the event seriously.

Paying an honorarium is not the same as paying for information.

Dick Enberg faced the dilemma of whether to pay or not to pay when he was trying to score an interview with Leo Durocher, a baseball manager even crabbier than Ted Williams. Enberg told his producer that he planned to get Durocher on his show, and his producer told him it would never happen.

"Durocher always demands that you pay him if you want an interview," the producer said. "And we don't pay for interviews. Period."

Enberg did a little digging and pursued Durocher anyway. It started out similarly to how Enberg approached Williams. The broadcaster found the manager at the backstop, watching his team take batting practice.

"Mr. Durocher," Enberg started, "I'm Dick Enberg, announcer for the California Angels, and I'd like to interview you for our pregame show."

Durocher kept looking out on the field.

"It will cost you a thousand dollars," the manager growled.

"Well, since I make only forty-five hundred a year, that's not going to happen," Enberg said. "But I am willing to buy you a bottle of whiskey for your trouble."

Durocher smiled and agreed to the deal.

Now that's what I call appealing to a source's self-interest!

How do you get people to talk to you? Do your homework. Appeal to their self-interest. Throw yourself at their mercy. Persevere. But try, regardless of what you assume they'll say.

As I learned on the steps of the house in Mission Viejo, Ray Bradbury's comment is true most of the time: "You need but ask."

CHAPTER 3
Then You Dig

What You Don't Know Will Hurt You

NOTHING MAKES OR BREAKS AN interview more than preparation. As I mentioned in the last chapter, it is preparation that will get you the interview in the first place. You have to convince the person that this interview is in his or her interest, and you can do that if you know how to approach the person. If you're prepared, most people will talk to you.

Likewise, it is preparation that will get your sources to give you something worthwhile once the interview begins. Not only will they talk to you, but they will also give you insight that goes way beyond the basic facts of the topic you're discussing. If your sources know that you're prepared, they'll be far more willing to go into depth, provide you with their insight, and give you anecdotes that will illustrate their points. They will reveal their personalities, which is what you want. You will not get that level of quality and personal perspective if your sources feel that they need to stick to the basics and educate you on a topic when you could have educated yourself. It's not because people are rude, necessarily (although some are). It's because they don't have time.

I've said it before but it bears repeating: Good interviews do not just happen. They can seem spontaneous, and sometimes real surprises occur. But if it's a good interview, it's because you were ready to conduct that interview. You did your homework. You practiced. You were prepared.

Preparation will do at least two things during the interview: One, it can put the person you're interviewing at ease, knowing he or she is in good hands, which makes the person relax. Two, it can put the person you're interviewing on notice that you've done your homework, so he or she had better tell you the truth, since you probably know it anyway.

There's a great exchange in the movie *The Company You Keep* that illustrates this. Ben Shepard, a reporter played by Shia LaBeouf, is investigating the arrest of Sharon Solarz (played by Susan Sarandon) after she had been a fugitive for decades. Shepard does some digging, uncovers a connection to a local farmer, and drives onto the property of Billy Cusimano, a farmer played by Stephen Root, so that Shepard can interview the apparent accomplice.

SHEPARD: Billy Cusimano? My name's Ben Shepard, from the *Albany Sun-Times*. I wanted to ask you a few questions about the Sharon Solarz arrest?

CUSIMANO: You can, but why would I comment about that?

SHEPARD: Well, you know her, don't you?

CUSIMANO: No, I don't.

SHEPARD: Quick search of police records shows you and Sharon together in Mendocino in 1971.

CUSIMANO: I've never been to Mendocino.

SHEPARD: That's not true, is it? You were dealing hash there for an outfit called the Brotherhood of Eternal Love. Which is a great name, by the way.[1]

At this point Billy Cusimano knows that he can't buffalo this reporter. Billy knows that he needs to either tell the truth or end the interview. He chooses the latter. Shepard doesn't portray a prosecutorial tone, but he lets Cusimano know that he knows what he's talking about.

Preparation lets the person you're interviewing know that you're ready, and that this isn't your first rodeo (even if it is).

If you are interviewing a high-ranking person, an expert, someone well-known, a client, a customer, or a potential employee, you should know many if not most of the answers before the interview begins. You're probably not interviewing them for answers or specific information, anyway. You're interviewing them for insight, details, complexity, color, per-

---

[1] LaBeouf, Shia, and Stephen Root. *The Company You Keep.* Theatrical release. Directed by Robert Redford. New York City: Sony Pictures Classics, 2012. Paraphrased from https://www.springfieldspringfield.co.uk/movie_script.php?movie=company-you-keep-the.

spective, in a manner that elicits an interesting way of saying something. If you're asking the same questions as everyone else, then it's a waste of everyone's time. But if you can reveal to your source that you already have the facts, then you can leapfrog the obvious parts and get right to the good stuff. The source will probably be more engaged and maybe even grateful. At least with the Billy Cusimano exchange, Billy knew that he had to change his tactics in dealing with this reporter.

You're trying to write something that hasn't existed in this exact manner before. Just as when you go to a jazz club, these songs probably haven't been played in exactly this manner before. Interviews can bring something new into the world.

But only if you're prepared.

When I was getting ready to interview Tracy Kidder, I found out that he disliked his first published book so much that he tried to get it removed from Amazon, Google, and libraries, so I made it my mission to find that book and read it. What could have been so bad about it that he didn't want it digitized or stored in any database? Wouldn't most writers *want* their work forever immortalized? It was definitely something I wanted to ask him about.

A dogged librarian at my university who knew the intricacies of the interlibrary loan process tracked down *The Road to Yuba City* in a little library in Montana and had it sent to me. It was Kidder's account of following the trial of Juan Corona, who was convicted of murdering several migrant workers in Northern California. And while I felt that his other books were better (*Mountains Beyond Mountains* is my favorite of his), I didn't see why he would go to such lengths to have it removed. He addressed the issue in some of his essays, saying that it wasn't interesting, and that it was obviously just a lengthier version of his story on the same topic in the *Atlantic,* so I had a general idea of what was behind his decision. But there was a lot more he could have said. I made a note to bring it up eventually. I knew he didn't like the book—there's the preparation. But why? There's the improvisation.

I was warned about being prepared as I got ready to interview the CEO of a major international corporation. The last time this CEO was interviewed by a member of the news media, the interview lasted just under five minutes. The CEO had mentioned something about the company's stock, and the writer said something to the effect of "I've always wondered about the difference between stocks and bonds. Can you explain it to me?" When the CEO realized he was being interviewed by someone without that fundamental knowledge, he ended the interview. My interview with him was a good one, but it was because I tried to know a great deal about his business before I walked in his door.

I wanted him to feel as if we were already in the middle of a conversation, rather than one where we had a steep mountain of education to climb. It's not his job to educate me on the obvious things—just the ones where his perspective was unique. Note to budding reporters: If you're going to interview the CEO of a major international corporation, know the difference between stocks and bonds before you arrive at the CEO's office. I promise he or she will want to talk about the company's stock.

Preparation is crucial no matter what you do or whom you're interviewing. Social workers need to be familiar with the issues they are going to be discussing—what kind of environments are best for people with certain challenges? Lawyers need to know legal options, ramifications of decisions, case law, before talking with their clients. There is a scene in the Amazon Prime Video series *Goliath* where the main character, a public defender played by Billy Bob Thornton, is talking with the mother of a young man in jail. It is clear that Thornton has no idea what the case is about, or even the name of the young man he is representing. When it dawns on the mother that she is dealing with an unprepared attorney who allegedly will be giving excellent legal counsel to her son, she loses control. And she should. If the lawyer isn't prepared for an interview with the people he is representing, it's time to find a different lawyer.

Preparation is a little like mining for gold. You start to pursue a particular region of ground, assuming there is something valuable under those rocks. While you are unearthing that gold, though, you might find some other veins that are of interest—they might be even more valuable than the gold you were pursuing. Backgrounding a subject is a pursuit of a certain line of inquiry, but the astute explorer will also be open to what else that pursuit might reveal. When you're doing your preparation, dig for the gold, but keep your eyes open for the zinc and the arsenic.

For example, if you're getting ready to do a story about an apartment complex that is pushing out its low-income people in order to charge higher rents, you will want to read everything you can about real estate, housing density, the local economy, the impact of gentrification, the pluses and minuses of rent control, and the impact on social services, to name just a few topics. That's the broad preparation. That's the gold. You'll also want to find out as much as you can about that particular landlord, the property owner, tax records for the property, tenants who have been there a long time, tenants who have been there a short time, neighbors, and local businesses, just as a start.

Those are the other veins of your exploration. You're getting both the big picture and the smaller pictures. And hopefully, while you're doing this work, you'll meet people who can give you that personal perspective to illustrate what you're discovering.

Start with the Obvious

In the age of the internet, there is no excuse for not doing your homework before an interview.

A quick internet search on any topic or person will reveal articles, videos, research papers, photos, archives, blog posts, and on and on. They are easy to access. They also easily mislead. As with any other fact, you must verify that what is posted is accurate. But still, the internet is a good place to start.

I read Wikipedia as much as the next person, but I don't

stop there. Much of the value of Wikipedia is in the footnotes and links that the site provides. And those links usually lead to other links. It's not always wise to count on Wikipedia's site itself, since the information provided comes from the general public, and it depends on the public to make eventual corrections. But I do spend a lot of time looking at the links, and those sites are often trustworthy.

Internet searches are useful at so many levels. You can find little nuggets of details (such as Tracy Kidder's dislike for his first book), as well as the more obvious facts (such as the year he won the Pulitzer). If I see several references to the same information, I skim past it. It can't be that interesting if everyone has mentioned it already.

Occasionally I will watch interviews with my subjects on YouTube, or watch TED Talks the subject has given. The value of seeing the person interviewed or seeing the person giving a speech is similar to my point about common points elsewhere on the internet. The videos help me see what topics to avoid. If the person has already discussed this publicly, and it's accessible online, then why would I go over the same territory? Besides, the subject is probably tired of talking about it.

The other objective in reviewing what a subject has said on record previously is that I'll find an idea in those videos that I can ask the person to expand on. Internet backgrounding is a mining expedition. You're looking for something—a nugget would be great, but you'll settle for a pebble.

Sometimes it helps to watch interviews with your subject, because they will give you an idea of how other interviewers handled this particular person or topic. But I typically don't anymore. I thought it was harmful to my preparation. When I watched interviews, I realized that I would make up my mind as to whether the person being interviewed was interesting, was boring, avoided tough questions, rambled, was evasive, lovable, or detestable. I didn't want all of that in my head when my interview began.

And it made me very judgmental about other interviewers. Occasionally I was intimidated by how good the interviewer was, and maybe even tried to imitate that person a little. Neither emotion is helpful, so now I just don't do it.

The internet is obviously a great place to gather information as you prepare. Type a person's name into Google, and you can find virtually everything written about that person—everything from published materials to blog posts to TMZ videos of them leaving Dunkin' Donuts. From wild praise to scorching criticism, it's all there. If you want to know something more specific about that person, such as how many times she has been sued, then type the person's name, followed by "AND lawsuits." The more specific you are in the search, the less overwhelmed you'll be by all that's out there.

There Is More to Research Than Google

But if you can find it quickly on the internet, everyone else can find it as quickly as you did. That's why it's important to go beyond Google. If you just cover the same material as anyone else who has access to the internet for five minutes, then why is your interview going to stand out? You don't want your audience saying, "I already knew that." So you want to go beyond what is at the very top of the internet search. Call it going "old school," or applying shoe leather, or whatever other metaphor you want, there are effective ways to prepare that don't always involve an internet connection. Here are some of them:

What are those things called again?
Oh yeah—books!

If I am getting ready to interview a writer, I read as many of that person's books in chronological order of their being published as I can. It helps me see how they think and how they have evolved as writers. But reading books by and about someone also provides some of those nuggets I mentioned earlier. When I interviewed Kareem Abdul-Jabbar, and asked him when he realized he was a good writer, he told me about having his essay read in English class at UCLA.

"What was the essay about?" I said. (I already knew the answer to this because I had read his account of it, but I wanted to hear him tell it.)

"It was about going to a jazz club in New York and what I experienced there."

"It was the Village Vanguard, wasn't it?"

This seemed to surprise him.

"How did you know that?" he said.

"Dude—I do my research!"

Then he seemed to relax and told the rest of the story.

Just that little nugget of knowledge on my part drew him out more, and, I believe, made him think he was in good hands. I was ready for him.

It's the same as when I travel to a different country. I try to read some of the literature that comes out of that region, across different periods of time.

Getting ready to go to Haiti to work on a book project, I read a lot of Zora Neale Hurston, which paid off almost immediately in an interview I hadn't even planned on doing.

On that trip I was there to write about how certain communities were forming civic groups to solve their communities' problems. Each community group had representatives from local business, government, schools, and churches. And among the church representatives was always a local voodoo priest. I had expected to see a parish priest from the Catholic Church, and a pastor from one of the local Protestant churches, but I was curious about the voodoo representation.

Hurston and other writers exposed me to Haitian history, literature, and culture, and you can't read about those things without reading about voodoo.

After one gathering of community leaders, I approached the woman who introduced herself as Madame Brigitte—the local voodoo priestess. I asked if I could sit down with her later in the week and talk to her. She graciously invited me to meet her at her temple.

I didn't know a lot about voodoo, but I knew that it was more than just the kitsch you can buy when visiting New Orleans gift shops on Bourbon Street. Because of the books I had read, I knew we could talk beyond just what it is and why so many people are afraid of it.

When I arrived at Madame Brigitte's place a few days later, she had set up plastic chairs in the shade under a big tree in the courtyard where a lot of the ceremonies take place.

I asked her if she became a priestess because it was the family business. Were her parents voodoo priests? Her grandparents? I figured this was the case, because my understanding through my reading was that this was how many voodoo priests became voodoo priests—it was passed down from generation to generation. She seemed pleased that we started there, and I sensed that she was relieved that I seemed to know at least a little about voodoo's history and significance. She told me how far back this practice went in her family, back to her ancestral roots in Africa. Our interview lasted a few hours.

When we were done I asked if she would show me around her temple and explain the artifacts, the paintings, the icons, and even about the stereotypes we have in the United States about voodoo priests putting hexes on people and sticking pins in dolls to make others suffer.

Interestingly, the Haitian translator I had hired would only stand in the doorway of the temple and yell his translations to us. He wouldn't set foot inside. I asked him why once we got back in the car, and he simply said that his church had taught him to stay out of places like that.

As Madame Brigitte hugged me goodbye, she invited me to a ceremony in a few months and even offered to give me some training as an apprentice (maybe a new family business for me in San Diego?). I'm certain that she was open with me because I had at least some baseline knowledge. Had I started with "So, what is voodoo, anyway?" I'm certain our interview would have gone in a far more stilted direction.

Again, preparing for an interview is similar to preparing to write a story. If you were going to write about any topic, whether it is gold mining or cooking or home repairs, you would do a lot of research on the topic so that you had something intelligent and trustworthy to draw from. The same goes for preparing for an interview.

Reference librarians

Some of my favorite resources are reference librarians. When I tell librarians that I am getting ready to interview someone and want their help in getting background information on that person, I can almost see the pools of saliva forming in the corners of their mouths. This is how Pavlov would have done his experiments on librarians: Instead of associating a bell with food, he would have associated it with a research problem. I'm going to make some huge generalizations about librarians here, so understand that these conclusions are based solely on my experience with them.

In a word, they are amazing. But they are also mostly bored. Many of them have advanced research degrees—I call them MFS degrees—Masters in Finding Stuff. Yet once they leave grad school they rarely get to put those skills to use. So when you present them with a research problem and ask for assistance in your preparation for an interview, don't be surprised if they dive in wholeheartedly. They love doing this kind of work.

Many times I have had a librarian find an obscure fact or quote from a person I am researching, and email it to me. When I look at it, I realize it was sent in the middle of the night. The note usually begins with "I had a little insomnia last night and was searching for information on your topic, and came across this. . . ." And then they attach something from a little journal out of Canberra, Australia, which is like a gold nugget. This is what librarians do when they can't sleep.

If you don't have access to reference librarians, or other researcher types, you can use interns. I know, I know, internships in many organizations are just a form of indentured servitude, but until that changes, my feeling is to use them for tasks like this. It doesn't matter what your profession is— there is some young person needing some experience. They're probably more adept than you when it comes to computer searches. Here's their chance to impress you.

I used a nugget from a librarian who found an obscure article as I was preparing to interview a well-known theologian. I learned that the theologian was conceived when his father was home after a stint in jail and just before his next stint in jail. It wasn't a central part of my interview, but I thought it revealed something interesting about how he arrived in this world. About halfway into my interview I asked him about whether he viewed struggling people with more compassion, since he had a story that was similar to so many people who struggle. I briefly described his upbringing, and included this point about his conception. When I did, he seemed stunned. Then he turned to the audience and said, "This guy does his research!"

It's one of the highest compliments someone can pay an interviewer. The other great compliment you can receive as an interviewer is when your subject says, "No one has asked me that before." That means you made them think past their cliché responses. This is presuming, of course, that the question you asked wasn't just a bizarre one about owning a planet or something.

Conduct interviews before interviews

Asking other people questions is a great way to formulate a plan for your main interview, because you will often get information that is nowhere on the internet. You'll get anecdotes. Nuggets. Topics to explore with your source. These are background interviews (I get into the specifics of these later), and they give you insight into your source that you won't find on the internet. You get a much more human, much less cultivated sense of your source's personality. With this kind of background information you can quickly get beyond the facts of the person and get into his or her character. These kinds of background interviews help you get past the clichés of who the person is.

Early in my journalism career I got an assignment from *Mpls. St. Paul Magazine* that put this approach to the test. The magazine wanted me to do a profile on the famous college football coach Lou Holtz when he made the bold move to leave his very successful program at the University of Arkansas and go to the very unsuccessful program at the University of Minnesota. He was leaving the world of Razorbacks (aggressive wild hogs with an underbite that display life-threatening tusks) for the world of Gophers (mice with stripes). Holtz was known to be somewhat impatient with ignorant or lazy reporters, so I wanted to make sure my time with him would be well spent.

That commitment was even more significant when his secretary told me I would have twenty minutes with him.

"This is the cover story of the magazine," I whined. "I'll need more than twenty minutes."

"That's the most he gives anyone," she said. "Take it or leave it."

What that meant was that I needed to be *so* prepared that every one of those twenty minutes would count.

I started the background phase with the sports editor of the newspaper in Fayetteville, the Arkansas university's hometown.

"What should I know about this guy?" I asked when I called him. "What questions did he leave unanswered when he left Arkansas? What do you wish you could ask him now?"

I got some excellent information, and he referred me to several stories that the paper had done on Holtz. That editor suggested other people I could talk to. This is another avenue you won't find in an internet search. My favorite part of this kind of backgrounding is when the person I'm talking to says, "You know who you should really talk to?" And the person gives you some obscure person who knows almost everything, but is way under the radar. Background interviews almost always beget more background interviews.

I also talked to members of the Arkansas football team who played for Holtz. I talked to the athletic director of the school, assistant coaches who worked with him, the athletic director of the University of Minnesota, and members of the team who would be playing for him next season. Then I talked to his wife and kids. All of this was done on the phone. I didn't plan on using much, if any of it, in my actual story. This was all preparation for the interview.

Somewhere in my preparation I read that his favorite book was *The Magic of Thinking Big,* so I bought the book and skimmed it. I also discovered that he took his Christian faith very seriously. And that he liked to do magic tricks when he talked to large groups. I learned that he was speaking to a Rotary Club in Minneapolis, so I attended the speech.

For an interview like this, I wanted to feel as if I already knew him very well before I actually met him. The interview went well because I was ready for him. I was prepared.

Avoiding clichés

When I do background interviews, I often ask people what they would ask if they were conducting the interview. If several people say the same thing, I have to consider it from two angles. One is that there are some things unanswered in this person's life that the public wants to know about, and whatever has been said before hasn't been satisfactory.

Another way to look at it is that there is a good chance

the person has been asked this many times and is probably tired of addressing it. How many times could George Plimpton address what it was like to be one of the only people to have interviewed Ernest Hemingway? What would that add to the discussion? A good interviewer will try to avoid asking the obvious questions. I'm happy to ask a tough question.[2] But I'm not going to ask the one that's been asked by everyone else. Nobody needs to ask Kareem what it's like to be so tall.

When I was backgrounding Dizzy Gillespie for my interview with him, I read a lot of references to the way his neck swelled up when he played. I watched videos of his concerts, and he looked like a balloon inflating to a dangerous size. He had been asked about that unusual style most of his life. Asking him about this wouldn't have provided anything new. Besides, this wasn't an interview about physiology—it was about passing down his wisdom to the next generation.

Asking obvious questions are like using clichés in your writing. The sportswriter Rick Reilly told me that he tries to never use the first simile or metaphor that comes to mind when he writes. If he is talking about the speed of a runner stealing second base, he might be tempted to use a phrase "he ran as fast as lightning." But that's a tired comparison, and readers don't engage with it because they've heard it so often. A better phrase, Reilly said, would be "he went faster than rent money."

It's the same with interview questions. The first questions that come to your mind are probably the least interesting ones,

---

[2] More on this in Chapter 7.

and your subject has probably been asked them many, many times. If you want engagement, thought, complication, color, humanity, don't ask the questions everyone else is asking. If you ask a question and your subject says, "I get asked this all of the time," that's a double curse. One, they are telling you that it is obvious you haven't done your homework, and two, they have answered this question so many times that they're bored and won't give you a very interesting answer. Worse still, you have lowered this person's expectations of how the rest of the interview is going to go. They're already thinking of how soon they can get away from you and what they're going to do next. They're already daydreaming about their fishing trip next month.

If you do ask a question everyone else is asking, at least make sure you're asking it intentionally, and not out of laziness. Maybe you'll get the straight answer once and for all.

Barbara Walters did this effectively in 1984 when she interviewed Mike Wallace of *60 Minutes* fame. She opened her interview by saying that when she told people she was going to interview the intrepid and feared Wallace, they all told her she should ask him a certain question.

"Why does he dye his hair?" he guessed. And he was right. On national television he acknowledged that many people thought he dyed his hair, but he was adamant that, though he was sixty-six at the time, his jet-black hair was still that of a much younger man. Naturally.

The other reason this was a strategic question is that it put him at ease with Walters, and gave him a chance to talk about his father and growing up.[3]

When I interviewed the writer Gay Talese, it seemed that everyone who had ever interviewed him focused on one particular story he had written for *Esquire* magazine back in 1966, called "Frank Sinatra Has a Cold." It really is a magnificent story, and *Esquire* to this day says it is one of the best stories they have ever published. But I was interviewing him in 2008, more than forty years after the story appeared. There might be more to say about how he did that story, but I doubted it.

My interview was in the evening, in an auditorium in front of an audience, on his birthday, and it was being televised. To help promote the event, he was scheduled for a radio interview earlier in the day. Wanna guess what that interviewer focused on for most of the radio program? That's right: "Frank Sinatra Has a Cold." Talese seemed bored during that program, and I didn't blame him. I was equally bored. He had answered these same questions hundreds of times. I vowed to make him perk up when it was my turn. If the Sinatra story came up, fine—I wouldn't avoid it. But Talese had done amazing work since then, and I knew we'd have plenty to discuss. I even found a sentence in one of his stories that was probably the longest sentence I had ever read. I diagrammed it and saw it as perfectly constructed. Exquisite, even. It was like Einstein's $E = mc^2$, only longer. I figured Talese would be more

---

[3] More on the strategic order of questions in Chapter 4.

interested in talking about that than a story he'd been asked about over and over. So I read the 426-word sentence to him, where he describes himself sitting in a restaurant.[4]

He seemed amused by my wondering why this sentence had to be so long, and when I was done reading it out loud, he reached over and shook my hand. It gave us a chance to talk about the craft of writing.

Maybe there really is more to say about "Frank Sinatra Has a Cold." But I doubt it.

Don't perpetuate myths

If you *are* going to go over familiar territory with your source, make sure you have correct information. Nothing gives you away as lazy or a rookie more than repeating something that might have struck you as interesting but is in fact not true, or was reported as true at one time and has since been disproven. Preparation means you not only did your homework but also made sure your homework included the most correct information available. Your credibility suffers when the person you are talking to says, "Actually, that's not quite it anymore," or "You're not totally up-to-date on this."

It's not that hard to stay up-to-date; neither is it that hard to verify urban legends, gossip, or assumptions. Again, in the

---

[4] I won't include it all here, but if you're curious, you can find it beginning on page 71 of his book *A Writer's Life* (New York: Alfred A. Knopf, 2006). It's impressive.

age of the internet it is irresponsible and inexcusable not to double-check your so-called facts.

At a forum at Syracuse University in 2009, the great writer Ken Auletta did an interview with prominent journalists Barbara Walters and Steve Kroft that showed even the great ones take a hit when they're sloppy in their preparation:

> **AULETTA:** Barbara, what's the dumbest question you ever asked that you wish you could just call back?
> **WALTERS:** *(looking perplexed)* The dumbest question I've ever asked?
> **AULETTA:** Start with "tree"?

Auletta was referring to a widely circulated story about Barbara Walters asking Katharine Hepburn, in a televised interview, "If you were a tree, what kind of tree would you be?" The story made Walters the butt of many jokes, and she was derided for it for years.

The problem is that she never really asked that question of Hepburn, and she took the opportunity at the Syracuse forum to set Auletta straight. She explained that she had just said to Hepburn that the actress was a legend, and that Hepburn replied, "I'm like an old tree." Walters, as any good interviewer would have done, followed up on that statement and improvised with, "What kind of a tree?" Then Hepburn described why she was like an old oak tree.

Somewhere along the line the lore left out the original

Hepburn comment, and it became simply a way to make fun of Walters because she asked dumb questions like "What kind of tree would you be?"

When Walters was done explaining the misleading anecdote, Auletta, to his credit, said, "So that should be in the category of *my* dumbest question."

It may not have been his dumbest question, but better preparation would have saved him some embarrassment.

Just because a story has been told many times doesn't mean it's accurate.

How do you know when you are sufficiently prepared? A good indicator for me is when I start seeing the same information from multiple sources—reading, videos, librarians, interviews. You are probably not ever going to be completely comfortable with how well you have prepared. There will always be one more obscure person or journal to check out. You cast the net out widely—eventually you have to reel it in. Sometimes I stop backgrounding when I run out of time. But remember, some backgrounding is always better than no backgrounding. You want to know the material well enough to wander away from the main point, but not too far.

Your interview might start in Tunisia, go to Belfast, Dubuque, Bogotá, Havana, Naples, Arusha, and Reykjavík. But you have to start by knowing where Tunisia is in the first place and how to find your way back.

CHAPTER 4
Now You Make a Plan

Pick a Structure, but Be Ready to Abandon It

JUST AS IT IS WITH a story, the structure of the interview is crucial. All life forms, I have been told, crave some kind of order. Even people we interview. You want to communicate to your subject (the same way you would to a reader) that these questions are going somewhere—that you have thought this through, that there's a plan. If you are conducting the interview in front of an audience, as I typically do, then you want to communicate that same sense to the people watching.

I think we have all heard someone tell a story that, to the storyteller, perhaps had meaning or significance, but to the people around the dinner table, it had no purpose or resolution. It was just an anecdote. In grammar terms, it was a modifier that didn't modify anything. Then when the story is done we sit around in silence until someone says, "Cool story, bro."

You don't want that to happen to your interview. It needs

to happen in a context, in a space, in a time, in a direction, where everyone can see where it's headed.

But even if you are interviewing someone and it's just you and the other person, you want to be able to communicate that you have given some thought to this exchange and that one piece of information is intentionally leading to another piece of information. If the source senses that this is just a haphazard exercise in pinball conversation, he or she will have an unease about the experience and, I predict, will give you shorter answers in order to end the conversation more swiftly.

If you are in a profession where talking to others is part of your routine, you can see why this is important. A doctor will ask questions of a patient, assess the immediate symptoms, back up a little and ask about personal history, family history, environment, and then move toward a course of action. Human resources professionals will have a structure to interviewing candidates, often moving from a candidate's history to traits of good employees, understanding corporate culture, and where the candidate sees herself fitting in. Even when I call a help desk for a problem with a phone or computer, if the person on the other end of the line is skillful, she will ask a series of questions that will lead both of us to a resolution.

Your Story Starts Here

The interview should have an interesting beginning, it should appear to head somewhere, there should be a culminating question or topic where the person being interviewed is forced to think seriously about the response, and then there should be a "cooldown" set of questions leading to a conclusion.

Taking this approach to an interview is similar to telling a story, because a story's arc usually goes from an interesting beginning to rising and falling action, then a critical or crisis point, then a falling-off of the action toward a resolution. Good interviews often follow that same pattern, and you create that order in the way you organize your questions. You don't want to start a story with all of the climactic action. If you do that, your interview could run out of steam within minutes. You want to build up to it and create a sense of expectation both in the person you are interviewing and in the audience. A story-like structure to the interview allows the source to build from previous points, to increasingly trust the interviewer, to increase the level of comfort and intimacy in the conversation. Good conversations (remember, that's what this should feel like) usually have a focus. The structure helps you keep that focus so that you or your subject isn't like some cat suddenly intrigued by a ball of yarn. You have a destination in mind.

A lot of the writing students I teach spend too much time setting up their stories and essays before anything actually happens in those stories. They give paragraphs of background and history, their own personal biographies, before any action occurs in the stories. Countless times I have drawn large Xs in the first several paragraphs (and sometimes pages!), drawn an arrow to a paragraph where some kind of action takes place, and written in the margin, "Your story starts here."

Unless you're Ken Follett and you're writing a thousand-page novel set in the third century, you don't need all of that throat clearing before the action begins. Your story has to look interesting from the very beginning.

Similarly, I have watched a lot of interviews over the years where it seemed like the interviewers got rolling in their introductions, and had no idea how to stop talking and let the sources in on the conversation. The introduction had so many layers, and the interviewer was so enamored with his or her own brilliance or cuteness, that I wanted to shout, "SHUT UP ALREADY!!!" Believe me, I have watched some of my own interviews and have actually shouted at myself, "SHUT UP ALREADY!!!" It's as if I had a lariat twirling over my head and forgot I was supposed to let it fly and rope a calf. I kept twirling and twirling.

Just shut up and rope the calf.

THE EXCEPTIONS

Some interviews will strictly be quick hits—asking a witness "What did you see?" or "From what direction did that meteor come?" or "Where were you when this happened?" or "What did you grab from your house when your neighborhood was evacuated?" or "What was the first thing you did when you found out you won a 'Genius Grant'?" I asked that last question and the answer was beautiful—"I got the Volvo fixed," he said. You still want to ask quality questions, but you won't always have time to give them a lot of thought or structure. It's impossible to have much of a structure if you are with a group of reporters and you're vying for position to ask your one question. Sometimes you really can only ask, "What happened?"

But for interviews that are arranged, where the purpose is deeper than an eyewitness account, serious thought needs to go into what questions you will ask and in what order you will ask them.

Structure Matters

A well-crafted interview gives both you and your source confidence. You know you're headed somewhere, and your source senses this, which will make your source more comfortable and will provide more thoughtful responses.

If I know that the interview is going to be in-depth, where we are going to explore a person's past, successes and failures, motivations, life lessons, influences, and other open-ended topics, then I will be methodical in the ordering of my questions. I don't want to get too personal, or too philosophical, or too gooey too soon. As the interviewer, you'll have to rely somewhat on a gut feeling of how soon to get into the deep stuff, but mostly I want to establish a comfort level with my source first. The more often you do this, the more you can trust your gut in how to order your questions.

Of the many writers I admire, John McPhee is at the top of the list. He can take the most obscure topics (geology, art, bark canoes, oranges) and make them fascinating. He's great at description and skillful at capturing that concrete and significant detail. But what I like about him most is his commitment to the structure of his stories. Here's how a *New York Times Magazine* piece described him in a profile: "McPhee is obsessed with structure. He sweats and frets over the arrangement of a composition before he can begin writing. He seems to pour a whole novel's worth of creative energy just into settling which bits will follow which other bits. The payoff of that labor is enormous."[1]

I'm with you, sir.

---

[1] Sam Anderson, "The Mind of John McPhee: A deeply private writer reveals his obsessive process," *New York Times*, September 28, 2017, https://www.nytimes.com/2017/09/28/magazine/the-mind-of-john-mcphee.html.

For interviews that are broad and far-reaching, I go through every note, every underlined passage from a book or an article, every question someone else told me I should ask, and I write them all out on a legal pad. Some can do this on their computer screens or their phones. I can't, because I am more comfortable flipping through pages than I am toggling through screens. If you can do the screen thing, knock yourself out.

At the end of all this note-taking I have pages and pages of questions, comments, and passages I want to explore with my source. I put those questions in groups. If some of the questions seem related to others, I put an *A* next to each of them. A different set of questions on a related topic get a *B*. I have seen people take a similar approach and use different-colored highlighters instead of using letters.

Then I look at each question or statement with an *A* and put them in order of how I want to ask the questions in that group. So each group is going to have *A-1, A-2,* etc., then *B-1, B-2,* etc. I try to determine that order according to a logic of what should come first, then what would be a good follow-up, then what would be another good follow-up.

Then I rewrite the questions and put them in order, almost as if I am putting together a puzzle. Interestingly, it's almost never chronological.

This method means I am writing out the questions at least twice—once to just get them on the page, and another time to put them in order. In addition to having them in order, a benefit of writing them out twice is that they are more lodged in your memory, and you will likely be able to remember what comes next without having to frequently look at your questions. The interview will feel more like a conversation, which is one of your goals.

A Little Planning Goes a Long Way

Terry Gross, whose interview program *Fresh Air* is distributed on NPR, does an excellent job with structure. The topics she discusses with her subjects are in an order that makes sense, and they seem to flow naturally from one to the next. She'll discuss the person's current project, then perhaps go into the person's background, then come back to the present, then go up ten thousand feet and discuss race or gender or religion or current events, then come back to the present. Her interviews have a direction. There is nothing haphazard about them.

But how do you determine the right order? Well, that depends on the purpose of the interview. If you are interviewing someone to get his or her history, as in a "How did we get here?" interview, following chronological order makes sense. If you are looking for insight, depth, understanding—anything that isn't concrete and quantifiable—then an order of easy, to more difficult, to even more difficult, might make the most sense.

No matter what, there are three easy questions that I use to guide me when I'm choosing the order for my questions: 1) What do I need to know? 2) What does my audience need to know? And 3) What's the most effective way to get my source to answer numbers 1 and 2?

Chronological approach

Most memorable stories don't start with the birth of the main character and then follow him or her until the end. (Except for *Superman*.) Many well-crafted stories have action, then a flashback or a setting, then a return to the present, then another revelation about the character's motive, then another return to the present. It's not a formula, but it's a way to keep the audience interested. Writers can (and do) follow a straight chronology, but they don't have to. And unless you are Gabriel García Márquez and you don't care if your reader is confused by the structure of *100 Years of Solitude,* each section of your story must logically follow from the previous section.

With interviews you have the same choices. You could start with the subject's beginnings, but you don't have to. For my interview with Joyce Carol Oates, I thought the chronology was the best approach because I thought her upbringing in a kind of isolation was important to understanding the writer she became.

Thematic approach

When I prepared for my interview with Mary Karr, I thought it was interesting that her real love was poetry and that she wrote a lot of it, but she wasn't known for her poetry; she was known for her memoirs. How she became a writer also got my attention, but I thought it would be *more* engaging for her if I started with the potential conflict between how she sees herself and how the world sees her. This struck me as a better theme to begin with than asking her about the first poem she ever wrote when she was a little girl.

But starting with conflict can be tricky. It can't be the kind of conflict where the very mention of the topic might end the interview abruptly.

Starting with this semi-conflict with Mary Karr didn't strike me as much of a risk, because it was really a compliment. She was very well-known for a certain kind of writing, even though she loved a different kind of writing even more. It gave her a chance to describe why she wrote those memoirs and launched us into a spirited discussion about storytelling. In other words, it was a good conflict. More of a paradox than a true conflict.

Usually, though, if the interview is going to involve a potentially contentious question, you don't want to lead with that. You want to get everything else that's important first, and then ask the difficult question.

Had I started with a serious conflict question when I interviewed a U.S. Border Patrol supervisor about a shooting at the border, my interview would have lasted about a minute. He still probably would have jumped across his desk and grabbed me, but that would have been the extent of our interview. I actually got something useful out of him before he had an aneurysm.

WHEN I WAS GETTING READY to interview the writer Dave Eggers, I knew that he didn't do many interviews and was reluctant to do this one with me. I got the sense that he didn't trust interviewers. He agreed to do an interview with me at our Writer's Symposium as long as it wasn't recorded. We could do it in front of an audience, but that was it.

Having the knowledge that he was suspicious, I decided to start with a question about a high school teacher who inspired him and made him want to become a writer. I wanted to make him comfortable, so I started with what I presumed would be a good memory for him.

In that case, I thought a chronology regarding his writing life made sense and put him at ease. It did. For a while.

Other Options

When I say that an interviewer needs to make a plan and create a structure for the interview, I do believe that. But the structure doesn't always have to come in the form of writing out the questions.

Years ago a columnist interviewed me and brought a stack of five-by-seven-inch index cards. She sat across from me and set the stack on my desk. She had one question written on each card. She would ask me the question on the card, then turn it over and write my response in her notebook. Several times before I was done answering (or at least I thought it was before I was done), she picked up the next card and looked at it. She had already moved on to the next item. I found that very distracting, and counter to the idea of an interview being a conversation. I considered telling her some big confession about an unsolved murder just to see if she was paying attention, but I didn't do it.

Every question doesn't have to be written out. But even if you do write down the questions, make sure you're listening closely enough to the answers that you can ask a follow-up. Being locked into the written questions can possibly keep you from something good.

Documentary filmmaker Errol Morris has gotten murderers, politicians, police officers, and average citizens to tell him amazing things. He doesn't write out his questions.

"I don't believe in lists of questions," he told an interviewer. "In fact, I think it's a real, real bad idea. . . . If you have a list of questions, it means you're not engaged in listening to what the person says. Say they say something that inspires a question that's not on your list. Then what do you do? You know? Pull the pin and jump on your hand grenade?"[2]

But not every interviewer has the time to just hang out for hours and hours the way a documentary filmmaker does.

MORE RECENTLY I WAS INTERVIEWED about the news media and democracy in Barranquilla, Colombia, at a large public forum. The interviewer, a magazine editor from Bogotá, had no notes with him. This piqued my curiosity, so while we were

---

[2] Errol Morris, "Q&A: Errol Morris on catching the interview bug," interview by Jesse Thorn, *Columbia Journalism Review*, July 14, 2017, http://www.cjr.org/special_report/qa-errol-morris-on-catching -the-interview-bug.php.

standing offstage, about to be introduced, I asked him if he had prepared questions or whether this was going to be all improvised. He was a seasoned and well-respected journalist. I wasn't worried—just curious.

"My interviewing style is that I know what my first question is going to be," he said. "Where it goes from there is up to how you answer that question."

I liked it. And the interview was fantastic. He knew how to pay attention, to follow up, to challenge, and to circle back if he didn't think I gave an adequate answer.

Not everyone is as quick on their feet as that guy. He was well versed in world politics, news media rights and abuses, current events, and big-picture ideas. He appeared to be in his fifties. He had experience. So it was probably a safe approach for him. My guess is that he used a more methodical approach when he was first starting out and learning how the world works. It takes a lot of confidence to approach an interview like he did mine. The risks are that the source might not give much of an answer at the beginning. What if the source says, "I dunno"? Where do you go from there? My guess is that this editor had done enough backgrounding on me to know that there are some topics I know something about, so he knew we'd be on good conversational ground. The reward was that it really did feel like a naturally evolving conversation. I complimented him later.

His approach can work if the purpose of the interview is to explore a topic more than a personality or a person's specific experience. He was interested in the role of a free press in a free society, just as the nation of Colombia was settling its decades-old civil war, and just as the United States' president, Donald Trump, was declaring the news media "enemies of the American people." The magazine editor knew the current events of both countries, and was more interested in a dialogue about those topics than anything else. When your topic is as open-ended as that, then knowing the opening question is like shooting a starting gun in a race and then just following the runners as they take off.

If the purpose of this interview was to understand my own personal experience with journalism and democracies, then this editor's approach would not have worked as well, because he wouldn't have been able to guide me through those topics in a meaningful way. It works when it's a freewheeling, wide-ranged wrestling match of ideas. It doesn't work if you're after something more specific.

I rarely work without a net like this guy did, but I don't always write out my questions, either. Sometimes it is enough to just list the topic areas you want to cover with a source. If that's the case, I write the topics at the top of my notebook page so I make sure I get to each of them eventually.

But even then, those topics need to be in some kind of order. One should logically lead into the next.

I was assigned by a magazine to write about a very contentious race to be district attorney of San Diego. After I prepared for the interview with the DA who was running for reelection, I didn't write out all of my questions. Instead, I made a list of topics I knew we needed to address. The list said:

- Successes

- What still needs to be done

- Why San Diego still needs him

- Criticism

- Specific cases where the DA's office has blown it

- Opponent

- What people in his office have said about the difficulty of working for him

There was no need to write out specific questions as long as we talked about these areas. But you can see that there is a structure to that list. The first three questions got him talking about the positives of his time as DA. The next four were about why others thought he should be replaced. If I would have started with the criticism, I don't think I would have gotten very far.

As it was, he did spin off in a rage (more evidence on why he needed to be replaced, perhaps?), but I couldn't use it. (More about that in the section on "Off the Record," page 335.)

Richard Ben Cramer took a completely different approach, and his approach worked well for books that had a lot of lead time. He didn't ask any questions. He just kept showing up and watching the person until the source was so comfortable with his being there that the source started talking to him—even confiding in him.

"And at *that moment* I've moved from my side of the desk to *his* side of the desk," he said. "That's the judo move I try to pull off, using *his power* to throw him where I want him to go. I'm *always* trying to be on his side of the desk. If I come in with my notebook and my list of questions, then I'm just another schmuck with a notebook and questions to be brushed off with the 'message of the day,' or whatever form of manipulation is in vogue.

"But if I don't *have* any questions—except for the basic one of *What the Hell is Going on Here?*—and I'm willing to hang around forever trying to see the world from his side of the desk, *then* I become something else entirely."[3]

The same goes for Richard Preston. But remember, both of these writers write books, so they have more time to commit.

"I don't usually write down any questions beforehand," Preston said. "I try not to come into an interview with any preconceived notions about what the person is going to say, or where it's going to lead. The interview is an organic process. I let the interviewee take over the interview and decide, essentially, what questions will be asked. This is extremely time-consuming and can turn what should be a one-hour interview into a six-hour interview. People generally want to talk about everything. It's a little bit like fishing. I'm there with a line in

---

[3] Robert S. Boynton, *The New New Journalism* (New York: Vintage Books, 2005), 39.

the water, pulling something out once in a while. It sometimes takes a long time to catch a big fish."[4]

Some interviewers ping from one topic to the next as if they are popping popcorn. To be fair, some do this intentionally so that the subject never gets a chance to relax. But nine times out of ten, it's because the interviewer didn't spend enough time thinking about structure.

There May Be Blood

It is possible that the interview will not go as well as planned. Reporters rarely want to interview people when everything is going right. No one is going to want to interview the head of the airport authority on the day all the planes landed safely, but we will want a word with the people in charge if a plane does not. Some interviews may not be an invitation for everyone to ride the peace train.

I mentioned earlier that a Border Patrol supervisor took offense to my line of questioning. Here's the background: I was in his office, which at the time was in a trailer, to talk with him about an incident a few days before where a Border Patrol officer standing on the U.S. side was hit by a rock thrown by an eleven-year-old boy on the Mexico side. The officer pulled out his weapon, dropped into a combat crouch, and shot the

---

[4] Boynton, p. 308.

boy, blowing out a portion of his midsection. This incident occurred before there was the wall that is there now. Back then, the division between the United States and Mexico was an imaginary line in the sand. Rocks and bullets could fly internationally without impediment.

Luckily for the boy, his buddies were on him immediately, picked him up, carried him onto the U.S. side, and then stepped back into Mexico. Their friend's blood poured into U.S. soil. The Border Patrol officer called for assistance, and a medical helicopter transported the boy to the children's hospital in San Diego, where his life was saved.

"You got bullets flying across the border down there?" my editor said, incredulous, on the phone. "Get down there and find out how the hell that can happen."

I arranged for a ride-along with the Border Patrol in that same area and brought a photographer with me. We signed the forms saying if something happened to us we wouldn't blame them. Then we climbed into the green SUV and began patrolling the border. The officer assigned to us struck me as a good man—seemingly honest in his answers to my questions. We didn't talk much at first, but then as the day went on, he became more open. His truck intercepted a group trying to cross illegally into the United States. It was five or six women and children, led by a man. I asked if I could talk to them.

When they saw the SUV pull up in front of them as they crested a hill, they didn't try to run. They simply put their hands in the air.

The officer got out of the vehicle and talked to them in Spanish.

"I'm not going to arrest you," he said. "I have a journalist with me and he wants to ask you some questions."

They nodded.

Stunned, I got out my notebook and asked where they were from, where they were headed, why they were coming into the country illegally, whether they knew of the danger from dehydration, the desert, bandits, and the risk of being arrested. They talked freely with me but kept an eye on the officer. We told them goodbye and drove off.

I have no idea if they were captured later, but I thought the incident showed a compassionate side of the officer.

Not long after that, though, his radio crackled and a chase was on. We bounced through the dirt and sand until we could see a group of men ahead. They were running, and when they saw our SUV in pursuit they started to scatter in several directions. But the Border Patrol had already dispatched a helicopter, and it roared over us and got in front of the men.

Then the helicopter did something I had never seen a helicopter do: It dropped until it was about fifty feet off the ground and turned sideways so that the rotor was up and down, directly in front of the men. This created such a tsunami of dust and sand and dirt that the runners stopped and covered their faces. Our SUV pulled up behind them and the officer jumped out—he pointed to me and the floor of the front seat and shouted, "Get down there!" I started to crouch to the floor, but my reporter-self kicked in. "Wait a second. I should see this. That's why I'm here!" So I got out of the truck and watched. A few more vehicles barreled up and officers got out with batons in their hands. Some of the runners put their hands up and were handcuffed immediately. Others ran or resisted, and they were beaten with the batons and then handcuffed. Then they were put in the backs of the vehicles and hauled away. The helicopter was long gone.

My ride-along officer saw that I had watched the whole thing. When he got back in the SUV, panting, covered in dirt, he swigged some water and said, "You may have noticed that it got a little rough out there."

I nodded.

"It happened because they didn't play by the rules," he said.

I wondered about the "rules," but decided to wait until I could talk to the big boss later that day.

Our border tour guide had gone from a compassionate soul to a Rodney King cop faster than rent money. Note to budding reporters: Compassion is not a bottomless well.

At the end of the shift I thanked the officer and promised to send him my story when it was published (which I did— another note to reporters: Always do this. Even if your sources don't like the story, they will appreciate the gesture and you will have a source for life), then went into the supervisor's office for my interview.

I didn't need a lot from the supervisor. The crux of my interview was on the kind of training the officers received, and how they were trained to deal with pressure, stress, anger, and, yes, being hit by rocks from kids with good aim.

I wouldn't describe the supervisor as cordial, but he was civil, and I sensed he was trying to tamp down his contempt for this reporter who had the nerve to question the actions of a brave officer who felt that his life was in danger.

I had a specific trajectory to my interview with this officer, and when I got to what I figured would be my denouement question, it turned out that I was correct, because he leaped at me and I thought he was going to crush my skull. I hadn't planned on that happening, but, as I said before, not all interviews go as planned.

The climactic point of an interview does not have to be rife with conflict. Not all interviews have that nature to them. But they should at least follow the trajectory, like a story, where the questions are leading to something.

Things Fall Apart

While the world, and our interviews, crave a certain kind of order, sometimes we still have to improvise. You will probably sense relatively quickly that the interview got off to a bad start, or that you were inadequately prepared, or that your source just isn't that into you. When I interviewed Kareem Abdul-Jabbar, I wondered throughout the entire interview why he wasn't loosening up, why his answers were so short, why he wouldn't follow up with an anecdote, even when I prodded him to do so.

I had already been warned by plenty of people that he was a "tough" interview, but this was more than tough. It was a struggle just to get more than a few words out of him.

I learned afterward that he had found out that a good friend of his had died while he was on the way to our interview. It's a mark of his character that he didn't cancel—lord knows many of us would have. You can't always know what's going on in the life of the person you're talking to, and sometimes the plan you worked so hard on just isn't going to work.

Interviews are organic things. You have an impact on the other person. So does the environment that you are in at that very moment. To presume that things will go as you planned them out is a rookie mistake. You have to hold on to your structure loosely. Even if you have a good order to your questions and are convinced you have McPheed them into perfection, you must be ready to abandon the plan.

That's what I did when I interviewed George Plimpton, one of the founding editors of the *Paris Review* and one of my favorite sportswriters. I couldn't wait to talk to him and had pored over my questions for weeks, perfecting the order to facilitate the best possible conversation. But as Plimpton and I walked from dinner toward the auditorium, things took a sharp turn. I was prepping him on the format of the interview when he stopped cold in the middle of the sidewalk.

"Interview? What interview?"

"The interview I am about to do with you right now in that auditorium," I said, trying to keep our momentum moving toward the hall.

"This is the first I have heard about an interview," he said, getting agitated. "I never agreed to an interview. I thought I was going to do a reading." He held up proofs of his new book.

"You're going to do a reading, too," I said. "After the interview."

He wasn't moving.

"You never said anything about an interview." He was boiling now. "What will you ask me? Are you going to embarrass me?"

"It was in my original invitation," I said, hoping I was exuding calm despite my internal desperation. "I'm going to ask you about your career, your craft, Hemingway. I'm not Mike Wallace. There won't be any 'gotcha' questions."

He glared at me. We were quiet for a moment.

"See that line over there?" I pointed to the crowd waiting to go into the auditorium. "Those are all people who came to see you and to see me interview you. We'd better get in there."

He moved with me toward the building.

"I did not agree to this," he said as we went in.

I knew then that I needed to rearrange my questions. They were in a good order for two people already comfortable with each other, as we were at dinner. But now we were temporary adversaries. I needed to find a question that would cool him down.

We sat in the front row until the audience was seated. He stared straight ahead at the two chairs on the stage. He was fuming. I was scrambling. I looked at my pages of questions, and while I can't remember what my original first question was going to be, I knew it had to be replaced. I found one that I thought would put him at ease right away, circled it, and wrote in the margin, START HERE.

Much of Plimpton's sportswriting was in the genre of what is called "participatory journalism," which meant he didn't just observe events and write about them, as most sportswriters did. He *participated* in the events. The Detroit Lions football team let him attend their training camp, practice with the players, live in the dorm, eat at the training table, and work out as a quarterback. They even let him run a play during a preseason game. His book *Paper Lion* was wonderful, and I used it as inspiration to do the same thing with my college alma mater's football team ten years after I graduated. I truncated the time, though. Instead of working out and practicing with the team during the preseason, I did it for the week leading up to the homecoming game—the biggest game of the year. Got my ass kicked every day.

Plimpton also worked out as a goaltender with the Boston Bruins hockey team, spent a month on the PGA tour, and boxed with heavyweight champion Archie Moore (who broke Plimpton's nose), and wrote about all of it. He was known for his great prose on these topics.

What wasn't as well-known was that he did something similar with the New York Philharmonic and played the triangle way in the back with the percussionists, under the direction of the legendary Leonard Bernstein. He had a funny story about this experience, so I figured he would enjoy telling it, which would get the audience immediately engaged, and then we could proceed as if we were both happy to be there.

Which is exactly how it happened. Once the audience got to laughing about the triangle and his incurring the wrath of Bernstein for screwing up, the rest of the interview went smoothly and I kept to the original structure. Plimpton never brought up this misunderstanding again.

KNOWING WHAT KIND OF INTERVIEW you're going to conduct (informal, informational, personality driven, thematic) will determine whether you write out your questions, have a general idea of where you're headed and improvise, or just pull the trigger on the starter pistol to see where it goes.

When you find yourself in a situation where you need to improvise (and I hope you do, because that means you're paying attention and maybe discovering something new), go with that rip current for a while, but never lose sight of the shore. You still need to satisfy the original purpose of the interview. Be ready to abandon some questions or topics and recalibrate the importance of your original plan, but don't forget why you are talking to this person in the first place.

As you saw earlier, this is what David Greene should have done when he interviewed Chrissie Hynde. His biggest problem was that he wanted to talk about a sexual assault that she described in her book, and she didn't want to, but he just forged on.

I witnessed a missed opportunity in improvisation when

I brought the poet Robert Pinsky to a public radio station where he was going to read some of his poetry and be interviewed by one of the local radio hosts. But Pinsky wasn't just going to read his poetry in the traditional way. He had three jazz musicians with him—all university students, who were going to play behind him while he read. They had practiced with him, and they created a very cool vibe of poetry and jazz. Before the interview was going to be recorded, though, they wanted to rehearse one more time—in the studio. Just as they were about to run through it, the host came into the studio and said she wanted to record her interview right then. She had her questions written out on a notebook in front of her. She seemed like she was in kind of a hurry.

But Pinsky is a pro. He has been interviewed thousands of times.

"Why don't you listen to our rehearsal, and then I can answer your questions," he said.

"I'd rather do the interview right now," she replied.

"I think you'll have a better idea of what to talk about after you hear this," he said.

Then he turned to the musicians and they started to run through their arrangement.

The host turned to me, exasperated, and said, "I'm going to ask the same questions whether it's before the rehearsal or after. Why can't I just do the interview now?"

"Because he thinks you'll see something you'll want to ask him about," I said. The music and poetry in the background were amazing. Beautiful. Transcendent. Inspiring. They should have created an entire world of questions on their own.

"Well, he's wrong," she said. She turned her back to the artists and spent the rest of the time looking at her phone. She never heard a word or a note.

When the musicians and poet were done, Pinsky turned to her with an expectant smile.

She launched into her questions and never acknowledged that something new had just been created. You could tell in Pinsky's demeanor and answers that he gave her the same pat responses he has already given a thousand times. But here was a chance for something new—a follow-up to something amazing that had just happened. Oblivious, she was done in ten minutes and stormed out.

What a lost opportunity. Something magical had just happened in the studio, and she missed it. She had come in with an average interview in mind, and that's exactly what she got. It could have been artistic, and she blew it by not paying attention.

Having a plan is crucial. But so is being ready to adjust it on the fly.

INTERVIEWING ISN'T JUST ASKING A bunch of random questions to random people. It's a guided conversation. Sometimes even a seasoned river guide has to say, "Oh wow—let's see where this goes!" Every river has twists, turns, hidden rocks, rapids, and fallen trees, and experienced guides know where most of those are. That doesn't mean the ride will be smooth and easy, necessarily. But good guides know how to prepare the riders; they know where the best place is to start, how to be confident during the unexpected developments, and how to guide the boat to a peaceful landing.

You're the guide.

CHAPTER 5
Just Before You Start

A Few More Considerations Before the Questions Begin

KNOWING WHOM YOU ARE GOING to interview and why and planning out the questions and putting them in a coherent order are crucial components of conducting a worthwhile conversation. But there are still a few elements—some more subtle than others—that will have a direct impact on the quality of responses you get.

Consider my interview with the former president of Mexico Vicente Fox. Spoiler alert: I committed a tactical error.

I had already interviewed him once in San Diego, in a lounge at a hotel. We had a great informal discussion there and found many similar interests, particularly our shared appreciation for Ignatius of Loyola, the sixteenth-century priest who started the Jesuit Order of the Catholic Church. It's an obscure point of connection, I know, but it made the conversation much richer.

When our relaxed interview ended, he suggested I come visit him in his hometown of San Cristóbal, Guanajuato, Mexico. His presidential library and family ranch are there.

"At my place we will have some real enchiladas," he said.

A few months later I was there on an assignment from *San Diego Magazine,* sitting at a conference table with him in his office at Centro Fox. I thought I had prepared well for this interview. I had a clear purpose, knew his story backward and forward, and had prepared the order of my questions carefully.

But he seemed uncomfortable, awkward, forced—nothing like the friendly vibe we had in San Diego. I felt like I wasn't even getting straight answers from him. Was he evasive? Cagey? Bored? Annoyed? I couldn't really pin it down.

I struggled to get us into some kind of a groove. Improvising, I gestured to the room we were in, and asked him about the important decisions he still makes in this office.

"This office—where we are right now?" he said.

I nodded.

"I don't make any decisions in this office," he said. "I don't even like to be in this office. I'm only in here now because you suggested we do the interview here."

That was my mistake.

Remember when I said that interviews are usually an intrusion into a person's schedule? I assumed that he would be working in his office on the day of our interview, so I suggested we meet there. I also knew that his office would be a better location for the video recording. There would be fewer visual and audio distractions. The technical quality would be higher.

I didn't think of how it would affect Fox's demeanor and the quality of the interview itself.

Location, Location, Location

Where the interview takes place is crucial to the level of the interview's success, and it takes some strategic thinking on your part to conduct it in a place that will get the best results—not just the best technical results.

What's that cliché about real estate? Oh yeah—location, location, location.

"Where do you want to do this, then?" I said.

"Anywhere! I like to walk around. This is too confining."

I stood up and asked the videographer, Carlos Solorio, if he could unplug and move with us. He nodded.

"Then let's walk around!"

We walked through the displays at the library, past his ornate saddle collection, past the banners of his heroes such as Lech Wałesa, Mother Teresa, Mahatma Gandhi, Nelson Mandela, Marie Curie, and Martin Luther King, Jr. We paused under each banner and he told me why each made an impact on him. He even got a little theatrical as he pretended to walk on a tightrope, describing the challenges of young people who were tempted to get involved in drug cartels so they could

make money. Then he went outside so he could show me
the broccoli ranch that has been in his family for generations.
We walked to the church across the street from the home
where he grew up and had authentic enchiladas in the dining
room where he had his meals as a child.

The videographer and I were able to improvise, and the
interview was eventually great.

Knowing whom you are going to interview, why you are
interviewing them, and what you're going to ask them may
make it seem like you're ready to have the greatest interview
ever. But you're still not ready. The location of the interview will always have an impact on the quality of the interview. You must consider where it will occur in order to
get the best results. Out of all the details that came together
for that Fox interview to occur, I had overlooked a major one.

If you're a therapist, you don't have a lot of choices on
the location. You're going to meet in an office so that it's away
from the client's distractions or triggers. But even in an office
setting, a therapist is looking to create a space where the client
will feel safe and can be his or her genuine self.

That's what any interviewer is looking for—a place where
truth can thrive.

Some writers like to interview their subjects in their
homes, some at restaurants, and some while riding in the car,
the way Jerry Seinfeld does for parts of his interviews in his
series *Comedians in Cars Getting Coffee*. Some do it between
two ferns. You can get some great quotes and insights from

sources when it's a little less formal, and there are the distractions of traffic or food. Running errands with a source can be a gold mine. When it's just you and your source looking at each other, it can feel a little intimidating. If you're going somewhere together, or there are other things to look at while you're talking, you usually get a better level of discussion. The silences aren't as awkward.

The writer Ted Conover said that the only bad place to interview someone is a site that doesn't feel natural, like a sterile office or a conference room.[1] Writer Richard Ben Cramer didn't like to interview people in their living rooms.

"People don't talk well in living rooms," he said. "The living room is the place where you sit with your hands folded in your lap." If he found himself in the living room with a source he'd say, "Could we do this at the kitchen table? . . . The conversation is *so* much better in the kitchen."[2]

For Cramer, it was all about getting the person comfortable with him before the interview officially could begin. He said he would take a source to dinner several times and not write anything down. Eventually they'd go to a restaurant and he would fill several notebooks with notes.

"At a *certain* point you've got to get it down. But only at the point where he and I are building the boat together. I say,

---

[1] Robert S. Boynton, *The New New Journalism* (New York: Vintage Books, 2005), 20.
[2] Boynton, 49.

'The stuff you've told me during these six dinners is *fabulous*. But I don't know it well enough to tell the story. So now you're going to help me understand it well enough to tell it.'"[3]

When we had people over to our house for dinner, my wife and I used to suggest we move the conversation from the dinner table to the living room, assuming it would be more comfortable. Whenever we did that, though, the conversation died. At the table we were having a raucous time. In the living room we got boring. So we stayed at the messy table, and kept the lively conversation going there amid the visual chaos.

THE LOCATION OF THE INTERVIEW should make the source feel comfortable. But some locations serve a different purpose. They awaken memories in the sources that you otherwise would not have gotten. I wrote a book about John Polkinghorne, a world-class physicist who, when he was in his forties and at the top of the physics game at Cambridge University in England, decided to leave academia and become an Anglican priest. For the next several years he wrote more than thirty books about the relationship between faith and science. He was eventually knighted by the Queen, inducted as a member of the Royal Society, and made president of Queens' College at Cambridge.

I interviewed him for several hours at a time at his home, but I sensed that he was growing weary of just sitting and talking, and he didn't seem as free-thinking in his sitting room

---

[3] Boynton, 48.

as he had been when I interviewed him in coffee shops or pubs when I first met him in the United States. So each day I suggested we go to different places of significance and do our interviews there. He didn't see the point, but he trusted me (or at least hoped I had an idea of what I was doing). We sat in the living quarters of the current president of Queens' College (he was out of town and the administrator let us in); in the faculty lounge at Queens'; in the Senior Combination Room, where they had plenty of refreshments and the walls were covered with portraits of former college presidents (it was kind of cool interviewing John Polkinghorne underneath a portrait of John Polkinghorne); in the chapel where he participated in the Eucharist when he was in seminary; in pubs all over town. And then we drove to Blean, a community not far from Canterbury, where he was the parish priest for three years.

We talked as we walked the familiar path from his former home to the church, to places where he would reflect on his work in his parish, to the altar where he prayed.

Each location brought back memories that he would otherwise not have retrieved. Sitting in the chapel, we talked about the process of becoming a priest. Sitting in the church in Blean, we talked about the people he baptized, married, and buried. He remembered one particular time on a cold Sunday morning when they were about to baptize a baby and they removed the stone lid to the baptistery and poured in warm water. But since it was a cold morning, and the baptistery was cold, when the water hit the stone basin, steam surged up.

"The parents looked horrified and turned their backs to the baptistery," Polkinghorne said, laughing. "It was as if they thought, 'My God, they are going to scald our baby!'"

Would I have gotten that anecdote sitting in his living room in Cambridge? Maybe. Probably not.

We also walked through the back buildings of Trinity College, where he studied and taught. He told stories about famous Trinity students from history such as Erasmus and John Cleese, and visits from Albert Einstein and C. S. Lewis. The first time he ignored the signs that told the general public to keep out, he saw me hesitate before following him. "I'm not the general public," he said.

Each place where we stopped and talked, he would say, "I hadn't thought about these things in years."

Bingo.

Interviewing him several times over a period of months created a level of comfort with Polkinghorne that I don't always get to experience. If you're working on a magazine piece, you usually get one interview and maybe a follow-up with the source. A book provides multiple chances to delve deeply into a variety of subjects. A bond can develop—maybe even a context for humor.

Before the book was published, Polkinghorne came to the United States for a series of lectures. I thought it would be interesting to create some cognitive dissonance, so I took him to the Creation Museum in Santee, a town outside of San Diego. It is a site that claims proof that the world was created in six twenty-four-hour days, that the world is six thousand years old, that evolution is a hoax, and that it is a small step from Darwin to Hitler. Polkinghorne takes an emphatically different view on all of those topics.

He is so reserved and controlled in his demeanor that I thought this would get him charged up a little. I even tried some good-natured needling as we stood in front of exhibits that showed dinosaurs and humans living in harmony.

"Aren't you a little ashamed of yourself, sir?" I said as we stood shoulder to shoulder looking at a display that contradicted much of what Polkinghorne believed. "Don't you feel badly that you have misled thousands of people when the answers are all right here? Why did you have to make things so complicated, when it's all so simple?" I wasn't serious, but I was trying to goad him a little.

This is a third kind of location for conducting interviews— a location that might cause some discomfort. You have to be strategic and intentional if you do this. You don't want to put the source in a place that will frighten or anger him or her, or bring back memories of a trauma. But create a little tension? I'm okay with that, if I have a good reason for doing it. You never know what kind of responses you'll get.

There is a certain strategy of conducting an interview— even an informal one—in a place that might create some tension in the source. A place that stands for a kind of science that directly contradicts the kind of science that Polkinghorne, Einstein, Newton, and others practiced allowed me to go right to some of the conflicts of faith and science. I would have gotten theoretical answers had I asked about this in his living room. Here, the contradiction of views could not have been more clear. And even though I was goading him in a good-natured way, I thought the location and the questions created a deeper discourse.

If you go to a place of tension with your source, you won't need any warm-up time when you begin your questions. If you're in the belly of the beast, it doesn't make sense to start by talking about the weather.

The first couple of times I needled Polkinghorne about leading people astray, he acted like he didn't hear me. Finally he turned from the wall of shame (Darwin, Pol Pot, Goebbels, Mengele, Hitler, and others) and faced me.

"I'm afraid my British reticence will not allow me to rise to your American baiting," he said. Nowhere else could I have gotten a quote like that!

On a different book that I wrote, I had a series of interviews with the former chaplain of my university. He was known as one of the deepest and most memorable thinkers in our school's history, and he was living in retirement in San Diego. A publisher wanted me to revisit the themes in some of his more famous books, and see what he wanted to say about those themes decades later.

We started out talking at his house in the study where he still wrote. We tried to talk in his living room, but that attempt only proved Richard Ben Cramer's point. Nothing happened in the living room. And his wife kept interrupting us.

We ended up spending a lot of mornings at the Denny's by his house. But even there I soon sensed that we'd hit a wall.

Everything I was getting seemed to be coming out of his head. I wanted a deeper sense of authenticity. I wanted to get things out of his heart. So we drove to Pasadena and sat together on the stage where he used to give his chapel talks to the student body.

Being in that location opened up capillaries in his memory that hadn't been opened in years. He remembered details, conversations, emotions. He remembered moments in history that he felt needed to be addressed in his sermons, such as student protests of the Vietnam War.

Location matters.

Making Do

If you're on a tight deadline, or work in other professions, you may not always have the luxury of choosing your location. Doctors and nurses interview their patients in tiny rooms with examination tables, bright overhead lights, and cabinets full of gloves, needles, and sutures. Sitting on an examination table in a flimsy gown surrounded by instruments of pain isn't going to put anyone at ease on its own. But if you ask good, thoughtful questions, you can help your patient ignore the surroundings.

Lawyers often take depositions in sterile conference rooms that defy meaningful conversations. I have a lawyer friend whose expertise is in mediation, and while he usually has to conduct his sessions in a conference room, he also brings in food that his wife has made just for that day. So while the room looks stark with its windowless walls, it smells like soup, or homemade calzone, or pumpkin bread. It puts everyone at ease.

Very few writers have the kind of time or the opportunity to visit multiple settings. Still, even for a magazine piece or a short news story, or background for a novel, the *where* of the interview can have a significant impact on the *quality* of the interview.

No matter the constraints you're working with, all interviewers can be intentional about location. Take some extra time and think it through. You want to find a space where the person and the discussion can be as authentic as possible. Where can the person be comfortable and real and not too distracted? That's what you're after.

Some of the best places I have found are a library's study room, a coffee shop, a park, a car, on a walk, in a hospital waiting room, or in a person's kitchen.

Sometimes, though, you have no say as to where an interview takes place, and you may be one of many people who want to interview the person. We've all seen press conferences where it appears that chaos reigns and everyone just yells their questions. I'm not convinced that anything useful comes out of those, but if the person being interviewed has been evasive or impossible to pin down, then I suppose it's an important last resort.

Thankfully, most group interviews aren't the boisterous mosh pits that we see on television and in the movies. Most abide by a certain order. The downside to these, of course, is that you don't have the source's undivided attention, and you will be able to ask just a few questions—or one. If that's the case, be strategic in where you situate yourself so that you can have direct eye contact with the person you're asking. Get close enough that you can sense a real exchange between you. If you're part of the White House press corps, you get closer to the person being interviewed as a matter of seniority. For everything else it's a matter of getting there before the others, having some thoughtful questions prepared, and intentionally placing yourself where you can't be avoided.

Once you have thought through the location, there are a few more intangibles to consider if you want to make this interview the best it can be.

Arrive Early

Wherever the interview is going to take place, make sure you aren't just on time. If it's a coffee shop, get there in advance so you can stake out a relatively private table, or at least one that isn't next to the cappuccino steamer; if you're at an outside table, try not to be under the flight path of the local airport or next to the construction workers jackhammering the sidewalk. If it's at a park, find a spot that won't be overrun by a preschool outing or a polka band rehearsal or a protest march. A nearby Pilates or yoga class is fine. Moaning isn't that distracting.

If it's at a person's office, get there early so that you can get a sense of the vibe in the office. You'll overhear things, you'll see interactions, you'll be able to chat up the secretary or the intern. (Both could come in handy when you're wanting to follow up or get more information. Be *very* nice to them.) All of this will contribute to your comfort level and your source's. Besides, if you're already there, you might get a few extra minutes of interview time.

If I am going to interview someone at his or her downtown office, I will occasionally do a practice run the night before, just so I can get a sense of where it is, where to park, how long it will take to get there.

If you're late to an interview, well, you have created a big problem to overcome. You want the person comfortable and confident when talking to you. It's hard to build rapport when your source thinks you are a moron. It's inexcusable.

Notice the Details

Pay attention to the specifics of your surroundings. When your interview begins you can use some of those details to build rapport, but be brief about it.

How you spend the first few moments (yes, moments, not even minutes) before the formal part of the interview begins will usually have an impact on the quality of your discourse. Even if you have a short time for the interview, you will want to come across professionally and make your source comfortable. Dust off your best social skills, and be authentically human so that it won't feel like you and your source are in these stilted roles of "interviewer" and "interviewee." You want to make it less awkward.

I usually comment on what is on walls—a bowling trophy, a picture of the source holding a big fish, drawings by children. You can comment on these (and make sure you take note of them as details for your story's description) in an attempt to find some shared humanity. When I saw a Bible on Lou Holtz's desk I asked him if there was a particular translation he liked, and what his favorite Bible verse was. The questions had nothing to do with my story, and I don't remember what his answers were, but it helped establish some common ground.

Record? Take Notes? Both.

How will you keep track of what your source says? Are you going to record the interview? Take notes? There are certain interviews that you should definitely record. I'll go into more detail about that in Chapter 9, but there are some ground rules you should start thinking about now. It's pretty simple, really: 1) You must take notes. 2) You must take notes. 3) You must take notes. Remember the movie *Almost Famous,* in which William is constantly battling his old-school tape recorder. The cord is never long enough and it craps out occasionally. He resorts to having little scraps of paper, which doesn't help his cause when the band denies the accuracy of the story.

If you are going to record an interview, you absolutely

must have an adequate recording device. You must also have a pen that works. Actually, have more than one. If one runs out during your note-taking, think about how awkward it will be to say to your source, who is spilling her guts to you, "Uhh, do you have a pen I can borrow?" Better still, have a sharpened pencil or two ready. Why a pencil? Who even uses pencils anymore? If you are outside, talking to someone, taking notes, and there is rain, snow, a drizzle, or a mist, your pen won't work on wet paper. But a pencil will. Being ready is part of the process of interviewing.

Again, even if you record an interview, you still *must* take notes.

I have seen too many "recorded" interviews that never got recorded, or got accidentally erased, or had batteries die, to depend entirely on a tape, a voice recorder, or another mobile device. A recording doesn't note body language, facial expressions, demeanor. You still have to get those elements in your notes.

But note-taking must be done in such a way that it can't disrupt the conversational vibe of the interview. Writing notes while only briefly looking down at your notebook is an acquired skill. It's a dance of looking down, looking up to regain eye contact, looking down to write, looking up again, nodding, and so on.

This is something you can practice. I have students pair off and interview each other just so they can get some experience writing without breaking eye contact with their source. An occasional glance down at a notepad is not that distracting to a source, but a long, protracted look at the top of a person's head is. When you're taking notes, you don't care if your words are staying between the lines on the paper. You're just writing as quickly and accurately as you can. Penmanship doesn't matter. The only person who has to be able to read it later is you.

When I am interviewed, I am always suspicious of the writer who doesn't take enough notes, and I am bored with the writer who forgets we're in a conversation and is locked into writing down every word.

Richard Ben Cramer viewed it similarly.

"I've been interviewed a lot during book tours, and I see how newspaper people, in particular, do it," he said. "They'll ask you a question. And as you start to talk they bend their heads to their notebooks and try to get down every word. They barely look at you again for forty-five minutes. Now that's *entirely* the wrong way to get any sense of anybody!"[4]

The writer Lawrence Weschler doesn't record his interviews at all.

"The tape recorder *falsifies* the situation in two ways," he said. "First . . . as any writer knows, the moment you turn the tape recorder off you get all the *really good* stuff. The second way . . . is that the transcript is an entirely false record of what has taken place between a subject and a journalist. For what is actually taking place is a *series* of communication events. . . . These include your expression, my response to your expression (seeing you are bored, interested, excited), my voice going

---

[4] Boynton, 39.

up, my voice going down. . . . *None* of that is conveyed in the flat transcript."[5]

Weschler makes a good point. You might get exactly what is said, but the interview is much more than that. And his point about what happens after the recorder is turned off? Is the information still usable once you put your recorder and notebook away? Yes. You're still there. You're still a writer and she is still a source. It's fair game, unless you're told it's not.[6]

For the story I did on the district attorney race, I was in the DA's office for my interview with him. When we were done I thanked him, turned my recorder off, and put my notebook away. Then he became a different person and began disparaging someone I had asked him about previously. He worked himself into a rage as he described her. I slowly pulled my notebook back out and when he saw it he shouted, "Put that away!"

Since what he said was so provocative and mean, I thought I should use it in my story. But since he wouldn't let me write it down or record it, I knew he'd be able to deny that he said it. And who will the courts believe? Me or the highest-ranking law enforcement person in town? So when I got to my car, I summarized what he said, and focused more on his Jekyll/Hyde routine—how he went from choirboy when speaking about this person on the record to this madman when he thought the interview was over.

---

[5] Boynton, 422.
[6] We'll talk more about this in Chapter 9.

Alex Kotlowitz is also against recording interviews, claiming that it makes him a "lazy interviewer." As he puts it, "When you're taking notes, it forces you to concentrate on what you're hearing, to think of the next question. On a more practical level, transcribing tapes takes forever."[7]

All of that said, if you *do* decide to use a recording device, make sure you:

- Have new batteries installed (and bring some extras) or have recently charged the device.

- Have the charging cord handy and try to sit where you can keep it plugged in.

- Have tested, retested, and tested again how to use it. I have seen too many reporters show up to interviews with borrowed devices and then waste an extraordinary amount of time trying to figure out how to use them.

- Know how to retrieve the information without deleting it. Just saying.

Dress Appropriately

By this point you have considered the inanimate dimensions of interviewing, such as locations and devices. But before you

---

[7] Boynton, 147.

barge out the door ready for that long-awaited conversation, take stock of a couple more things.

How should you dress for an interview? The answer to that question will come from this question: What will make my source take me seriously?

If you dress too casually, you communicate that you don't take the interview seriously. If you dress too formally, you communicate that you've never done this before or that you don't pick up on social cues. Business casual is almost always the best call, even if you're interviewing the checkout boy in a surf shop. You want to be seen as a professional.

I gave this advice to my students who were being interviewed by the great broadcaster Dick Enberg as potential interns in the booth with him during San Diego Padres baseball games. He always interviewed them at a coffee shop just a few blocks from his house. I warned them that he would be in a warm-up suit because he'd be coming into the shop from his morning walk. But that didn't mean they could match his casual attire. He told me later that he was always impressed with how professional the students looked.

If you are going to interview a dignitary or government official, you'll want to step it up from business casual. Show some respect. Look like you belong there. Maybe even do some surveillance in advance to see how people dress around this person's office, and match that.

I miscalculated on this one when I arranged a breakfast interview with a local dignitary in San Diego. I knew he was a big deal, and we were meeting in a breakfast place full of judges, lawyers, CEOs, and other big deals. But I also knew that he was passionate about baseball. So for our meeting I wore my very old pinstriped Minnesota Twins jacket, thinking this would be an instant rapport builder.

When I walked up to the booth where he was sitting, he looked me up and down with what I am sure was a sneer, and he said, "Not really what I expected the head of a university journalism program to wear."

My bad.

Empty Your Bladder

This may sound bizarre, but hear me out. I try to make sure I have gone to the bathroom just before I arrive. On big interview days I usually drink a lot of coffee and get amped up for what I know could be inspiring, combative, adversarial, ugly, beautiful—no matter how it goes, a good interview can be intense. I know I need to be hyperaware and quick on my feet. I want to have the mental reflexes of a goaltender in a shootout. But when you have just twenty minutes, you don't want to have to interrupt the interview to visit the bathroom. Besides, it's tacky. And no one will want to shake your hand.

Always, always go to the bathroom before your interview. Here's my proof: Not long ago I was just finishing an interview with a person whose name many of you would recognize, when, with about five minutes left in our appointed time, my bladder let me know that all of that coffee and water from the previous hour needed an outlet. It was giving me a six-minute warning. I tried to concentrate on the interview the rest of the way, bouncing my knees, breathing Lamaze (oooh oooh, eeeh eeeeh), trying to resist the urge to grab my crotch like a little kid not wanting to leave his birthday party before he has an accident.

The source kept talking. He was animated and excited about what he was saying—I had really struck a nerve with him. Good for me! But I had trouble concentrating on his words and my notes. My blood was pooling in my kidneys, not my brain.

When I stood to thank my source, and he stood, and we shook hands, I lost control and peed myself all the way to my shoes. I was wearing dark pants, thankfully, and carefully made my way out of his office, hoping I wasn't leaving wet footprints. I carefully walked down the stairs to the parking lot, and berated myself all the way home. I have no idea if the source knew. I have been with him a few times since, and he has never mentioned it. But, then, exactly how would one bring that up in a conversation?

When It's Not Face-to-Face

So far, this chapter has focused on all of the things to consider for a face-to-face interview. But what if the interview isn't in person?

It is still possible to conduct good interviews when you're

not physically in the same room. Skype, FaceTime, and other video calling services can still capture facial expressions and body language to a certain degree. It's more difficult to feel like you're personally interacting, but it's worth doing, considering the alternatives.

What about phone interviews? Again, they're better than no interview, but they have their limitations. It's harder to follow up, to stop the person from going off on a rabbit trail, to keep the person from multitasking while talking to you. It's pretty annoying to talk to someone on the phone while you can hear that person typing in the background. And at the risk of belaboring the topic of urinating, I am quite certain I heard a person I was interviewing flush a toilet.

Either way, he or she is not focusing much on an answer to your question. If the person is on speakerphone with you, ask who else is in the room while you are talking. I once interviewed someone who was driving and put me on speakerphone, and it turned out his whole family was in the car listening in. That felt a little weird.

Email interviews, too, have advantages and disadvantages. The advantages are that you can have a specific quote from your source, and that it will be just as the person wanted to say it. No one will be able to accuse you of misquoting if you have the quote right there on your screen.

The disadvantage is that people rarely speak the way they write, so you sacrifice some of the humanity of the person's response. It sounds more stilted, more formal. For some interviews, that's fine. But for others, it loses the chemistry of the interaction. You don't get the same immediate follow-up of saying, "Wait—what? You really let the air out of a police car's tires when the officer wasn't looking? Did you think that one through?" I don't know why I just used that as an example, although I did that very thing when a cop came to the campus when I was in college. See? You don't get to ask a follow-up.

Another disadvantage is that the best quotes are usually the most spontaneous ones. In email there is more careful thought given to a response. Again, it may be more technically accurate, but all of the emotion is gone, and it's the emotion that makes your stories more interesting.

And finally, you don't really know who is answering that email. Is it the person's PR representative? Her administrative assistant? Edward Snowden? Any number of people could be answering your questions. If you conduct an interview via email for a news organization, virtually all outlets require that you include a phrase in the story such as "said Smith, in an email interview." That kind of transparency lets the reader know why the response seems to sound more carefully crafted.

I still wonder about an interview I did back in the 1990s when I had a standing feature in *Boys' Life* magazine, the official magazine of the Boy Scouts of America. My column was about people with interesting careers (baseball umpire, astronaut, etc.), and one month my editor, Doug, told me to profile a country music singer. I lined up an interview with Garth Brooks. Sort of.

His agency said that he wasn't available by phone because he was on tour in Canada with spotty reception, but I could send my questions via fax to the tour bus and he would fax back his answers. Remember, this was the nineties, and yes, it felt as weird to do it as it does to even write about it now. It felt like the scene in the movie *The Insider* where Al Pacino and Russell Crowe are faxing back and forth. It was time-consuming and bizarre, but the answers seemed legitimate. I have this gnawing doubt, though, about whether I was really getting answers from Garth Brooks. How do I know that I wasn't faxing his PR person on his fourth mimosa lounging at a pool in Nashville? In short, I don't.

So, Doug, if you're still alive and reading this, I cannot say for sure that my interview with Garth Brooks was really with Garth Brooks. Sorry. And I already cashed the check.

CONDUCTING GOOD INTERVIEWS TAKES MORE than just showing up and talking. Whatever your profession, the location of the conversation *is* part of the conversation. It can help or hurt. Wherever the interview takes place, though, makes a statement.

Think through the location so you'll put the person the most at ease. Get there in plenty of time. Know how you're going to begin. Know how you're going to keep track of what the person said. These simple elements may be the difference between something good and something great.

CHAPTER 6
Okay, Go!

Starting the Conversation and
Keeping It Rolling

It may seem obvious, but the best questions are the open-ended ones, where the source has a chance to explain something, and even provide an anecdote to illustrate it. If you prepared properly, you won't need to ask a closed-ended question like "Where did you serve in World War II?" or "What is voodoo?" On the other hand, you don't want to ask questions that are *so* open-ended that they paralyze the interviewer into giving meaningless answers. You may be headed in a direction, but you want to have a clearer sense than just knowing whether you are north or south of the equator.

The quality of your questions will have a direct impact on the quality of your interview.

I mentioned in Chapter 2 that my father spent a year in a weather station on the Arctic Circle during World War II. If you

want to see him hem and haw and clear phlegm awkwardly
and furrow his eyebrows and look out the window, ask him,
"What was it like being on the Arctic Circle for a year?" That
kind of a vague question won't get much of a response other
than something equally vague, like "Cold." Why? Because *nothing* is like being on the Arctic Circle for a year. To get the kind
of answer you're hoping for, you have to ask this question differently. Something like, "What did you do for food up there?" Or,
"What was the most difficult part about being there?" Or, "What
was the most fun part about being there?" "Did you date any of
the indigenous women while you were there?" I really did ask
him that last one. He gave me a politically incorrect response that
I can't really share here, but the short answer is "No." Those kinds
of questions will get you into topics such as loneliness, seeing
polar bears, trading cigarettes for ivory carvings—something that
will provide insight, not just an obvious fact.

This presumes, of course, that you have done enough
preparation that you will have the kind of questions that will
lead your source into saying something interesting. If you
were going to interview my father, for instance, then you
would probably already have found out where he was during
the war, which means you would have done some reading
about what the conditions were like up there, what the hard-
ships were, who the inhabitants of that region are. If you know
those things going in, then you'll be more prepared to ask him
to give you some insight, some understanding, some anecdotes.

Leaning forward, keeping eye contact even when taking
notes, giving nonverbal cues to keep talking, looking quizzical

if something doesn't make sense—all are part of conducting an interview. Effective interviewers know how to keep the conversation going. And that's what an ideal interview really is—a conversation.

The Tao of How

If you want to conduct a good interview, you simply must know a great deal about the topic before you start. Then when the interview does start, you can lead it more intentionally and get something useful, rather than a vague platitude.

Interviews after Olympic events are prime examples. A runner or a skier or a skater or a gymnast has just completed something that only a freak of nature could complete—something the athletes have been obsessing about for the last four *years* of their lives, and the interviewer asks, "What was it like to be out here?"

I rarely shout at my television, but I almost get hoarse during the Olympics. Note to reporters who interview Olympic athletes: *Nothing* is like being there. Ask a better question. Ask "How you were able to focus after that false start?" Ask how this victory or loss ranks with other wins and losses in that athlete's career. Ask about the impact of having a child during training two years ago and whether it made them a different kind of competitor. Lead the conversation with specifics. The vaguer your question, the more pointless the answer.

Doing your homework allows you to ask questions that

begin with "Why" or "How," which are guaranteed to get you further than "When" or "What" or "Who" or "Where."

Still at a loss? Here are some other tried and true paths of inquiry that are sure to get your source talking:

Juxtaposition

The line "Would you rather . . ." is the first line of a fun conversation-starting game, where you come up with strange and unrelated topics, just so the person will explain how he or she feels about something. But it's also a good interview question.

Ira Glass was asked on a podcast what he does when he doesn't get a satisfactory answer from a source, and one method he uses is to give people something to riff on: He'll propose a theory to the source just to get the person thinking and responding. "I find myself in a lot of interviews saying, 'Well is it more like this or is it like this? I can imagine it would be this way or this way. What is it?' . . . They're forced to go somewhere—to bat away one of your theories and to run at one of the others," he said.[1]

I asked a tangent to this question to a former NFL player who is now the pastor of a megachurch. "Which is harder," I asked him—"playing professional football or being a pastor?" He gave me a strange look when I asked him, because those two things aren't even close to being related. Finally he said,

---

[1] Ira Glass, "Q&A: Ira Glass on structuring stories, asking hard questions," interview by Jesse Thorn, *Columbia Journalism Review*, June 22, 2017, https://www.cjr.org/special_report/qa-ira-glass-turnaround-npr-jesse-thorn-tal.php.

"That's a serious question?" I nodded. He thought for a few seconds and gave me a great answer about the similarities and differences of a profession where people are trying to crush you, and playing professional football. Kidding. He really did give me a thoughtful response, and it was because of the juxtaposition of the two elements. Then I followed it up with "How are they similar and how are they different?" which was just a way to get him to amplify what he previously said.

The Noah Adams

Ira Glass once said in an interview that if he's ever feeling stuck, he thinks of public radio journalist Noah Adams and remembers that there is one question that you can always, always count on: "How did you think it was going to work out before it happened? And then how did it really work out?" The question works so well, Glass said, because it always yields two stories in response. "You get 'Here's how I thought it would go,' which is one story. And then 'Here's how the reality is different than the dream of that.' The jump between the two is just kind of interesting."[2]

"What first got you interested in . . ."

I asked this of Deepak Chopra regarding his early interest in medicine. Since I knew the answer already—the novel *Arrowsmith* was a big influence—it gave us a chance to discuss the power of reading, of literature, and of identifying with a char-

---

[2] Glass, *Columbia Journalism Review*.

acter. I'm pretty sure that the band Aerosmith had little to no influence on him.

Legacy

Asking sources how they want to be remembered is a chance for them to tell you what is really important. It goes right to their values and helps them formulate what they consider their greatest contributions.

"What do you make of . . ."

This gives you a chance to bring up an issue that your source can expound on. But it can't be so narrow that it's paralyzing. A good question would be, "What do you make of the people who say that climate change is a hoax?" I asked that of the environmental writer and activist Bill McKibben, and it launched him into a deep, articulate response. If I would have asked him, "What do you make of climate change?" he would have looked at me like my dad looked at people when they asked what it was like being in the Arctic for a year.

"What would you take if you . . ."

There are many varieties to this question. It could be the cliché "What would you want with you if you were stranded on a desert island?" or "What would you grab if you had to evacuate your home quickly?" We have had to face that question twice because of wildfires in our neighborhood, and we had little time to get out. It's very revealing. A different riff on this was when I auditioned for a reality television show that was going to be recorded and broadcast in Sweden. That's right, it was a Swedish reality show, and I wanted in! I made it to the second stage of auditions, thanks to a video testimonial that my son recorded of me making the case. When it came time for the Skype interview with the Swedish producer, we had a delightful conversation, but I could tell that she lost interest when she asked me, "If you come to Sweden to be part of this show, what would we find in your suitcase?" It's a fair question. A good one. Because it reveals something about my personality. And that's where I blew it. I said I would have lots of books and a journal. In retrospect, I know that answer put a big label on me that said "BORING!!!" (more accurately, the word in Swedish is "*tråkigt*"), which meant I would be a horrible reality show candidate. What *should* I have said? IKEA gift cards?

The *Jeopardy!* question

I have used this question several times, and have seen it used in job interviews. It's "If you were a contestant on *Jeopardy!*, in what category would you excel?" It's a great way to get a person talking about his or her interests, expertise, and passion.

"Help me understand . . ."

This puts your source in the role of expert, which is usually useful. If there is a difficult topic, saying something along the lines of "Help me understand how virtual currencies work" will get you further than "What is Bitcoin?"

"Excuse me?"

Use this when you really don't understand what the person said, or if the person said something outrageous and you want to give her the opportunity to explain. It's a great follow-up to something complicated, offensive, puzzling—it's an invitation for the person to keep going.

"How would your life have been different . . . ?"

I love asking this question, because it makes the source consider alternatives to how his or her life turned out. It reveals a lot about the person's personality and interests. I asked, only jokingly, this question of Kareem Abdul-Jabbar when we discussed his love for writing. "Did you ever think about how your life would have been different if you would have pursued journalism instead of basketball?" I asked him. "You could have been somebody!" He clearly saw that I was kidding, and said, "Yeah, we'll never know."

"You have said . . ."

This takes preparation, because it means you have read what this person has written, or listened to comments. But bringing up something someone said in the past is a chance for the person to show that he still feels strongly about the topic, or (even better) that he has changed his perspective.

"What is your favorite unimportant thing to do?"

This gets your source evaluating a number of things at once, and it often creates something personal and revealing. The interviewer Jesse Thorn asked this of the documentary filmmaker Werner Herzog. Herzog said it was watching soccer, which then allowed Thorn to delve into what interested Herzog about the sport.

Your mom was right

But there's more to it than just asking good questions. *How you ask the questions* will affect the answers as well. Your mom was right—it's not just *what* you say; it's *how you say it.*

Remember, a good interview is a conversation, not an interrogation.

BODY LANGUAGE MATTERS

When you ask questions, you want to show your source that you are listening with your whole body. Eye contact matters. Try to keep looking at your source, while only occasionally looking down at your notes. This takes practice. When your source is speaking, lean forward a little. Let your facial expression show that you are agreeing or confused or challenging. The occasional "Mm-hmms" and "Uh-huhs" are encouragements for your source to keep going. Be *very* aware of whether you are cutting the person off. You will learn a lot about whether you interrupt, cut off, disrupt, or dominate the conversation if you listen to a few of your interviews. It's humbling and instructive. That's why you should do it.

Keeping eye contact while taking notes is an acquired skill. Like texting and driving. Wait. Bad example. Anyway, you aren't born with this ability. But if you work at it, you'll get better.

Those nonverbal "Uh-huhs" will keep the source going. When you relax, they relax. If the purpose of your interview is to get more than just a fact or two, then the kinds of questions you ask and the way you ask them will have a great impact on whether you hear anything useful.

That's true for any profession. If you're a human resources person conducting an interview with a job candidate, and you see on the person's resume that she rode a bicycle across the United States, or climbed Machu Picchu, or won a gold medal in cup stacking (it's a thing—I know a guy who does it), that's a better place to start than asking "What was your first job?" At the beginning of an annual physical, my doctor (who must have looked at my chart before coming into the exam room) said,

"So you're still teaching journalism, eh? Why? I thought journalism was dead!" He didn't say it in an aggressive or mocking manner. He said it as a means to get us open with each other.

You're in Charge (or, at Least, You Should Be)

In every interview, someone is going to control it. My advice is to decide before the interview starts that the person controlling the interview is you.

The word "control" is a strong one, so let me explain. I don't mean that you are a dictator. You're more of a tour guide—a guide who has a good idea of where you need to go, what sites you need to visit, and where you need to end up, even if you take a few detours and rest stops. You want to skillfully keep the source on track, gently pull her back to the topic you set out to discuss, insist that your questions not be ignored, and rise to a challenge of your ownership, all while staying calm and focused. This comes with practice and experience.

Controlling an interview means you are sensitive to what will encourage your source to be open, and firm enough to keep the person on track. When you ask open-ended questions like "Why" and "How," you're sending the interview in a direction, but you're not dictating every turn or lane change. That's the key.

Control is a dynamic involved in virtually every interview, and you must be aware of who has it at all times.

A good tour guide isn't going to hand the steering wheel

of the bus over to the brashest tourists. She knows where she is going, and there are several ways to remind the tourists of who is driving.

Here's another way to look at it. Interviews can be like fencing. And by fencing, I don't mean building fences. I mean the fencing that is the weak sibling of sword fighting. I have seen plenty of interviews that seemed like sword fights, and I don't find them very useful. Fencing is a more artistic form of swordplay. It involves parry, riposte, touch, step back, advance. And, as the interviewer, you're the one who must do the most advancing.

If you are interviewing someone who has been interviewed a lot and is what I call "media savvy," that person may try to wrest control away from you. Your job is to be aware of that tactic, and keep it from happening. It can also happen with people who simply have strong personalities—people who are used to being in charge. Your job, if this happens, is to keep your cool, don't respond with aggression, but rein it back in. This is your interview.

You can only do this if you are actively listening, if you know what your purpose is for the interview, and if you have decided that there is going to be only one steering wheel.

There's a great interview (not online, unfortunately. I have it on an old VHS tape. Some of you readers have no idea what I just said) that Barbara Walters did with Mike Wallace in the 1980s just before Wallace was to take the witness stand in a libel case brought against him and CBS News by William Westmoreland, the general in charge of U.S. troops in Vietnam.

I mentioned it earlier when I referred to her asking about whether he dyed his hair.

In the middle of the interview, Walters asked Wallace a tough question about his character, and Wallace replied, "Do you think so?"

Right there it was obvious what Wallace was doing. Instead of answering her question, he snatched the role of interviewer away from her and made himself the one asking the questions. But she was wise to his method and she quickly responded, "What do *you* think, Mike?" Then he answered it, and the roles were restored.

Here is another exchange during that interview:

WALTERS: You have been accused of being—
WALLACE: *(interrupts)* A self-hating Jew. Right?
WALTERS: Right.
WALLACE: Yeah. So?
WALTERS: So?

A number of things happened in that brief exchange. Wallace, by sheer instinct because he's used to being the one asking the questions, tried to hijack the interview by finishing Walters's question and following it up with "So?" Now he's the one asking the questions. She recognizes it immediately and takes back the control with a quick comeback of "So?" It's like he grabbed the talking stick out of her hand, and she grabbed it back.

By taking the approach she took, she was able to communicate to him that, despite his efforts to control this interview, she had it locked down.

If you do not take charge of the interview, your subject can go off topic and may even try to run out the clock by not stopping talking. You have to gently pull the person back into the question. That takes active listening on your part, and the confidence to communicate to your source that this is your interview, not his.

If you see that they are losing their train of thought, or they don't understand your question, or are extremely nervous, it is your responsibility to calm them down and get them back on topic.

How do you get your source back on track? There are several methods.

Use your hands

Reach forward. I saw a journalist do this in a very effective manner. She was interviewing a CEO and asked him a question about his company. It was as if his mind shut down and he started playing a tape of his company's PR shtick. She let him ramble for a moment, and then in a nonoffensive and nonsexual way, she reached over and barely touched his arm to interrupt him.

"I know what your corporate website says," she told him gently. "I want to know what *you* think."

Reaching across to touch your source on the arm is a perfectly acceptable way to bring the interview back under your direction. Then follow up that nonaggressive act with the question he was avoiding.

Reach up. If you don't understand what is being said, or if you think the source has gone on way too long, put your hand in the air. Not high in the air, like you're in class and want to ask a question, and not in front of you as if you're trying to stop traffic. Shoulder level, hand up, and a nonthreatening "Hold on—I'm not sure that's what I was asking about. I thought we were talking about baseball. That's what I was here to talk with you about, and I know we have limited time. Let's get back to that if we could, and then if there is time, I would love to hear more about your trip to Disneyland." That kind of approach will get it back to you most of the time.

Use your head

Nod to keep the person going. Look quizzical if you don't understand or don't believe what you're hearing. Raise your eyebrows if you are surprised or incredulous. Shake your head if you're just not buying it, or you're amazed.

Use your body

Lean forward when you're trying to emphasize something or challenge your source, lean backward when you're taking in what she's saying. Don't slouch (there's your mom's voice again).

In the movie *Frost/Nixon,* you see this exact issue play out. David Frost (Michael Sheen) and his team know they have great questions for the series of interviews with Richard Nixon (Frank Langella) over several days. Nixon and his team believe that Frost is a lightweight and will be easy to manipulate.

When the interview begins, Frost seems starstruck. He lets

Nixon ramble, pontificate, and revise recent history into what sounds like a flawless presidency. Frost sits back in his chair, eyes wide, fake smile plastered on his face, and lets Nixon dominate. Watching the movie, I kept thinking, "Dude! Jump in there! Cut him off! Don't you see what he's doing? You gotta get control of this interview!" His team, watching from another room, has the same concerns. By the last day, though, Frost gets forward in his chair, leans in, challenges Nixon when he is lying, and has a spirited give-and-take. The filmmakers gave it the feeling of a heavyweight boxing match—punch, counterpunch, head fake, jab, knockout.

Toward the end of the Frost/Nixon interview, when Nixon is clearly trying to not indict himself any further, the Frost character skillfully uses another crucial interview technique. He lets silence hang there, between question and answer. He doesn't jump in and fill the quiet. The silence becomes part of the interview. There is no question who is in charge at that point.

Shhhh

Silence is part of the grammar of an interview. It sounds counterintuitive, but silence is one of the ways to retain control. Reflexively we are uncomfortable with it, but with practice, it can become a crucial part of your interaction. Hold off on your instinct to rush in. Your source might be thinking. She might be hoping you'll jump in and change the subject. It might feel awkward.

Leave it for a while. Count to ten. Count to twenty.

Eventually you will learn to trust it.

In 1973 Mike Wallace interviewed John Ehrlichman soon after Nixon fired Ehrlichman from the White House staff for his involvement in the Watergate scandal and other nefarious deeds. In the interview, Wallace read a list of offenses Ehrlichman was accused of:

"Plans to audit tax returns for political retaliation. Theft of psychiatric records. Spying by undercover agents. Bogus opinion polls. Plans to firebomb a building. Conspiracy to obstruct justice. All of this by the law-and-order administration of Richard Nixon."

Then Wallace just looked at Ehrlichman. It was a standoff for eight long seconds. Then Ehrlichman smirked and said:

"Is there a question in there somewhere?"

It was a golden moment in interviewing. It revealed so, so much, and silence played a big part of it.

Bill Zehme of *Rolling Stone* magazine showed great skill in his 1990 interview with Warren Beatty. The actor, who is known for being cagey and evasive in his responses to questions, was the same way with Zehme. The magazine published the interview as a Q&A, with a question from *Rolling Stone,* and the answer from Beatty, along with how long it took Beatty before he answered the question: "[Pauses 27 seconds]." In the middle of another answer, *Rolling Stone* wrote "[Ponders, 57-second pause]." This goes on throughout the interview. It was an effective way of showing that Beatty and Zehme sat in silence for a long time on many questions, and it showed the dynamic of the interview.

Using silence means you are telling your source that you can wait him out. It tells him that silence isn't an answer, and he's not going to get out of answering—you'll just sit there until the source begins talking again. This doesn't work very well for television (at least not for more than a few seconds), but it is useful in other settings.

During one of the wars the United States was engaged in concerning the Middle East, I was approached by a military investigator with a story idea he thought the public should know about. His military branch wasn't moving quickly enough on an issue that could potentially harm our soldiers, in his opinion, and he thought a story in the news media would speed things up. He told me that he had evidence a weapons contractor had falsified the company's test results in order to get the contract with the U.S. Department of Defense, and that the weapons were being used in the Middle East. The problem was that the weapons were routinely failing. This put U.S. military personnel in harm's way, he said, and it ripped off taxpayers who were pouring millions into this company.

I knew this was a big story, but I also knew it would take a person who had contacts in the Pentagon to do it well. So I called a friend from a large news organization, told him about it, and suggested the three of us meet. I arranged for us to meet at a public library, in a study room. When we all arrived, I introduced the reporter to the investigator and anticipated a spirited exchange between the two. Here's what happened instead:

The reporter and investigator sat on opposite sides of the table. The reporter got out his notebook and pen, leaned his chin into his hand, and just looked at the investigator. The investigator was also clearly waiting for a question, so he waited, too, nervously looking from the reporter to me and back. The reporter just waited. I heard him exhale through his nose.

Finally, the investigator reached into his briefcase and pulled out a notepad and pen and began drawing the weapon.

"This is how this weapon is supposed to work," he explained. "And this is how it is working in the field."

About thirty minutes of this monologue occurred without the reporter making a sound. Eventually he asked a few questions, and then it became more of a dialogue.

When it was all over and the investigator left, I asked my reporter friend about his method. I'd never seen him do this before.

"I judged right away that he was nervous," my friend said of the investigator. "I didn't want to spook him, so I figured he would talk when he was ready."

For people who have very little experience in being interviewed, as was the case with this investigator, you have to be sensitive to what will encourage them to be open.

There are exceptions to this matter of retaining control, of course. When I interviewed Ray Bradbury, every question was an adventure because I didn't know if he would come anywhere near answering it. He just went off on rants. The thing about Bradbury, though, was that it didn't matter. He was this combination of Mel Brooks and Albert Einstein, so I didn't care if he answered my question specifically. I just wanted to get him talking. He was entertaining and deep regardless of what he said. Often, after finishing a rant, he would look at me out of the corner of his eye and say, "Now what the hell was the question?" It didn't matter. It was Ray Bradbury. People had come to hear him talk about anything, not to hear me insist that he answer my questions.

The author Richard Preston intentionally does not employ any of the tactics above. He purposely lets his sources take charge. He was asked if it wouldn't be more efficient if he took control of the interviews he conducts. "Perhaps, but then I'd probably learn less about the person," he said. "If they're *really* interested in something, there is a reason for it. So then *I* become interested in it, and want to know *why* they are interested in it. That's generally how my interviews work."[3]

Pay attention

In Chapter 4 I mentioned that there is an element of improvisation in any good interview, and here is where it really applies: On the one hand, you have questions you want to ask, or at least topics you want your source to address. On the other, you don't want to be so tied to those questions that you stop paying attention to what the source is saying. Your source might say something that will just beg for a follow-up from you, such as "What do you mean?" "Like what?" "I'm not sure I understand." You get to ask those questions when you're actively listening to what is said. You're alert enough

---

[3] Robert S. Boynton, T*he New New Journalism* (New York: Vintage Books, 2005), 308.

to explore those detours, but you're in control enough to be ready to come back to the main road.

The social worker I mentioned earlier wasn't expecting the new mother whose baby was in the NICU to say that the baby's illness was punishment from God for something the mother had done when she was a teenager. But since the social worker was actively listening, she could address that issue further and know that this deep-rooted religious belief was part of the family's environment. That knowledge was very useful in how the social worker could proceed.

One of the religious magazines I used to write for put together a package of assignments for me. They didn't want to pay to send me to the East Coast three separate times, which made sense, so they bundled them and sent me out there for a few days. One was to cover a convention in Washington, D.C., where a number of distinct religious groups were gathering, and the keynote speaker at the end of the convention was Tony Campolo, a fiery, provocative, controversial, funny, deep writer and speaker. His face was on all of the publicity for this convention—posters, media ads—everything. He was one of the big draws for people to attend.

I went to the convention, covered the main events, and looked forward to hearing Campolo blister the audience in the final gathering. But instead of Campolo, someone else spoke. There was no explanation for why Campolo wasn't there. The organizers acted as if everything was normal, and when I asked them, they all said they didn't know what had happened for the switch to occur. Everyone played dumb.

As it would any good journalist, this made me curious, and I decided to follow up on it later—maybe when I got back from doing this package of stories.

My next assignment was, conveniently, to do a story about Tony Campolo. He was on the faculty of Eastern University in Pennsylvania and involved in humanitarian efforts for the people of Haiti. The newest effort was for people in the United States to donate their used eyeglasses so that his ministry group could distribute them in that very poor nation. My magazine wanted a story on this new glasses venture.

I took the train from Washington to St. Davids, Pennsylvania, and walked from the train station to the campus. I followed my own advice by arriving at his office earlier than my appointment time and looked around. Then I sat down and concentrated on my questions about glasses and Haiti.

At the appointed time he came out of his office and invited me in and shut the door behind me. Before I had a chance to small-talk, to build rapport, to convince him I was just a regular guy and not "the enemy," he said, "I'll bet you're here to find out from me why I got disinvited from that big convention in Washington, D.C."

Wait. What?

"Am I right?" he said. I could tell he was charged up.

"I'm here for two reasons," I said, my mind going at warp speed. "Yes, I want to know what happened in Washington . . ."

Let me stop right there for a Frank Underwood moment where he looks at the camera and explains what's going on in his head. This is what I mean by improvising: I was curious, but that wasn't what I had gone there to learn, and I had no real idea what Campolo was talking about. But he clearly wanted to talk about it, and as my mind connected dots to his not being the keynote speaker at the convention I just left and his stating just now that he was disinvited, my instincts told me that there was a big secret waiting to be exposed, and I was maybe the only person in the entire world who had this kind of access to Campolo. This was conflict and prominence in the religious world. It smelled terrific. However, I also had a very specific assignment that my magazine sent me to do, and my editor would not be interested in the scandal—only the glasses and Haiti. Here's what I did:

Back to live action, roll camera.

"I do want to talk to you about Washington," I said. "I can't believe they did that! But I have to first satisfy my editor and talk to you about the glasses program for Haiti, so let's get that out of the way in the first few minutes and then get back to that crazy set of events. Okay?"

"Fine," he said.

The appointment was for an hour (in this case, an hour seemed appropriate, but you won't always get that much time), so we spent about fifteen minutes talking about Haiti, but I couldn't concentrate on it. This was a case where I was way too dependent on the recording of the interview. I hoped it was capturing the Haiti stuff and I would get back to it when I got home. Instead, I kept writing other questions in my notebook about what must have happened in Washington.

Finally I said, "Okay, I think I have enough there. Now, what happened in Washington?"

He explained how the organizers of the convention got complaints about his being the keynote speaker, because many of their constituents thought Campolo was too liberal. They didn't want a left-leaning speaker polluting the minds of the young people. His message was love, mercy, and forgiveness, and the organizers wanted outrage, judgment, and exclusivity. Some of the big-dollar funders were threatening to pull their money out of both the convention and the groups they were supporting if Campolo was given the microphone.

The convention organizers were forced to decide whether they wanted Campolo to challenge the audience and risk losing donors, or to keep the money and get a "safer" speaker who would perpetuate the donors' beliefs. Obviously they chose the money. They asked Campolo to back out, and when he wouldn't, they booted him and called him a heretic (how's that for a distraction from the real issue?). This happened just days before the convention. That's why all of the publicity still had his face on it.

I had a million questions about this, but I also knew that my appointment was for one hour. When the time was up I said, "We've used the hour I asked for. But is there any way we can keep talking about this?" (As I said in Chapter 2, make sure you define how much time you need when you ask for the interview. In this case I asked for an hour and got it!) He made a couple of calls and cleared his calendar. We talked for another hour in his office, then went to the dining hall for lunch, then walked around campus while he vented. He clearly wanted to keep talking about this.

Fulfilling my magazine's assignment, I did the story about the convention and mentioned the controversy only briefly, and I did the glasses story. I did the Campolo disinvitation story for a different magazine.

I mentioned that the magazine I was working for gave me three assignments to cover while I was back east. The other was to do a story on the former NBA star Julius Erving, "Dr. J," and his new television show on ESPN. So after I was done with Campolo at the end of the day (remember, I had asked for just an hour in the morning, and ended up getting the whole day), I took the train to Philadelphia. The next morning I was in a TV studio with one of the greatest basketball players ever. When we were done with the interview I noticed that there was a basketball hoop in the corner of the studio.

"A little one-on-one?" I asked him, nodding toward the hoop.

He laughed. Then stopped when he saw me looking at him.

"Are you serious?" he said.

"Are you afraid of me?" We were both in jackets and ties, and I took off my jacket.

He shook his head as we walked to the hoop.

Have you ever seen the *Saturday Night Live* sketch where the singer Paul Simon plays against the NBA great Connie Hawkins? Simon is five foot three and Hawkins is six foot eight. They played while the song "Me and Julio Down by the Schoolyard" was in the background.

Our game was nothing like that.

In both the Campolo and Erving interviews, improvisation made them work. With Campolo, he brought up something he felt strongly about and I went with it, encouraging him to tell me more. I was going on pure instinct, hoping there was something usable to go along with all of his passion. Turned out that there was.

With Erving, I noticed the incongruity of a basketball hoop in a studio that had millions of dollars of lights, cameras, and other equipment. You can't just pretend you don't see a basketball hoop when you're talking to an NBA star. And that's the point. Paying attention to surroundings, showing some curiosity, following up on the incongruity, risking humiliation, can get you into some great conversation you weren't anticipating. You can get deep while playing H-O-R-S-E.

For some reason, I simply can't remember who won the game.

Neutrality and intimacy

Occasionally in an interview, there is only one thing to talk about, and you can just introduce the topic and see where the conversation goes. For one of the most significant interviews I have ever done, I had no questions prepared. Just a statement. And I hoped I would be able to improvise from there.

I was in Kosovo working on a book chapter involving Merita Shabiu, an eleven-year-old Albanian girl who was raped, murdered, and dumped in a snowbank by a U.S. soldier during the NATO action in that country. The soldier is now serving a life sentence in a federal prison. I wasn't there to write about the crime (plenty had been written about that) as much as about what happened after she was killed. A U.S. military doctor visited with the family to provide medical care for them. The doctor even designed what the family wanted on Merita's tombstone. The soldiers at the NATO base collected money for the family so that their daughter could have a dignified burial. There was enough money left over to give the family two cows.

The family lived in the mountains, so I accompanied the military doctor for another visit, more than an hour up the mountain to the village where the Shabiu family lives. They were overjoyed to see the doctor, and he introduced them to me. They showed great hospitality despite their poverty—scrounging up some biscuits and hand-rolled cigarettes. Their house was simple and spare. Merita's backpack still hung on the wall, as if they were expecting her to pick it up and head off to school, the way she did on that day she never came back.

We gathered in the main room of their house—Merita's mother and father, the doctor, an Albanian interpreter, and me.

All I said was, "Tell me about Merita."

It was beautiful, awful, heartbreaking, and life affirming all at the same time. They told me about her—showed me pictures, shared her dreams of being a doctor, described how she would go to a hillside outside their village and wave as the

NATO jets screamed by to stop the slaughter from the Serbs. They told about the day she disappeared, about how they had to identify her body, about the bullet hole in her forehead, about how they buried her in a local cemetery, about the doctor's visit, about the donations from the other soldiers, about the cows, about the proper burial that eventually occurred.

We were there more than four hours. All I did was make that one request, and then follow up with questions about what they told me. As we were wrapping up our very emotional conversation, the doctor said he had a question for them. He asked them about Merita's killer.

"Do you have a message you would like me to take to him when I return to the United States?" he asked.

The parents discussed this at great length with the interpreter, and finally said that it was too soon to ask that question. The doctor asked one more.

"Do you think he should be killed for what he did to your daughter?"

There was more discussion that we couldn't understand. Finally, Merita's father said, "He is already paying the price for his actions. We don't see the purpose of two mothers weeping. One is enough."

When we were leaving I asked if I could see where she was buried. We stopped by the cemetery on our way out of town, and there were several plots of Albanian citizens who had been killed in the recent war. Off in the corner, standing like a sunflower overlooking a field, was Merita's tombstone. Her face was etched into the granite. Her name and the dates of her short life were below the picture. And underneath that were these words:

"She taught us to love one another."

There is no way to be neutral in an interview like that. I felt rage at the soldier who did this. I felt sorrow for the Shabiu family. I felt moved by the kindness and generosity of the soldiers who contributed to the family, and the doctor who served them.

But it was personal for me. My daughter at the time was also eleven. It felt too close to home. And maybe that's why the conversation with the Shabiu family seemed so deep and intimate.

Several times since that interview I have wondered whether I was *too* close to that situation. I couldn't stop thinking about how I would feel if that were my daughter. Should I have declined that assignment because of my own personal conflict of interest?

No.

It was precisely *because* of my own emotional attachment that I was able to ask better questions, parent to parent. I knew what direction to take the interview because I knew what I would want to consider had it been my own child. And I simply wanted to grieve along with this inconsolable couple. The point of my book chapter wasn't to find balance among all of the voices involved or to create a false equivalence of the killer's perspective juxtaposed with Merita's. It was to find common ground with readers, and that common ground had to do with loss and grace and forgiveness.

Podcast host Jesse Thorn asked Ira Glass about this kind

of intimacy in interviews, and I think he captured what has happened with me on occasion. It especially happened in this interview with the Shabiu family. Here is a slightly edited version of what Glass said:

> If it's going well, and the person is really talking from the heart about a thing that means something to them, and I'm talking back to them, and we're understanding each other, I start to feel really close to them. They really share their emotions, and then I react with my real feelings about what happened to them. And we're talking back and forth and back and forth, and we feel like we're understanding each other, and we're sharing a thing that's real. . . .
>
> When you're having a great conversation with somebody, man, woman, child, any age, any sex—it doesn't matter who they are at all—I really start to love them. It's the actual accurate word for what's happening. . . . It doesn't happen every day. The goal is to have a moment that's special.[4]

Remember, it's a conversation. You're not filling out a questionnaire. Listen, listen, listen. Ask open-ended questions, be ready to take some detours, embrace the silence, don't dominate—but make sure you're in control, and be ready to be surprised with the result.

---

[4] Glass, *Columbia Journalism Review.*

An Interview That Started Out Well, Went off the Rails, and Got Better Again

Chris Wallace of FOX News Interviews Former President Bill Clinton

Broadcast on September 24, 2006

I KNOW THAT NOT EVERYTHING in life is like a hockey game, but lucky for me (and maybe you, depending on how you feel about hockey), a good number of things are. I go to hockey games because I love to watch the players achieve something that seems so difficult. They are operating at breakneck speeds, balancing their bodies on the equivalent of knife edges. They collide, pivot, go backward and forward, and there are so many moving parts operating uninterrupted for so long, that it's a pleasure to watch it when it is done well. I think it's like watching a ballet production that has several people dancing at the same time. They're all moving independently, but with a singular purpose. It looks synchronized, improvisational, and haphazard all at once. One person's action affects every other person's actions every second.

Some people, though, watch hockey because they like to watch the players fight. They find it entertaining. I suppose it's similar to people who watch NASCAR just to see the crashes. Personally, I don't see how fighting elevates anyone's soul the way a skillfully played game can, but that's just me.

I feel the same way about interviews: Some people love it when the source and the interviewer get riled up, the way Bill Clinton and Chris Wallace do here. It's entertaining. They think it's a great interview because Clinton wagged his finger in Wallace's face.

This interview is so much more than the conflict, though. I like this interview for the structure of it, and for the intellectual exchange. I love the way Wallace asks open-ended questions, drawing Clinton into giving something beyond standard cliché answers. In this case Wallace's questions give Clinton the chance to give historical insight and articulate personal achievement and failure.

There are many interviewing techniques evident in this conversation, and so many layers to it. The mere idea of the interview was interesting because it was on FOX News, which had been relentless in its criticism of Bill and Hillary Clinton over the years. As you'll see in the introduction, it was also interesting because they made it clear that they invited Clinton to talk about the humanitarian efforts he had been involved in since he had been president, as long as they could also ask him about anything else. So right off the bat you know this was a calculated risk by both sides. It was a risk to Clinton, because he would undoubtedly have to defend himself about any number of things that happened while he was president, but he also knew he would get to promote the work being done by the Clinton Global Initiative (CGI) to reduce poverty and disease. It was a risk to FOX News, because there was a good chance that viewers would see Clinton as a sympathetic character, yet it was worth the risk so that they could ask him point-blank about what they felt were his failures as a president.

Again, I encourage you to read or watch this interview in full.[1] I took out some of the longer rants, but left the structure intact. And you'll see that there is a clear structure. Wallace starts out complimentary and even philosophical. Then it gets more pointed, and even aggressive; there is an attempt to re-cover a sense of equilibrium, which at first back-fires, then it settles down. It is shaped just like a story, with rising action and falling action, a climactic point, and then movement toward a resolution.

There is a clear "why" to the interview—Clinton had just hosted a forum for the CGI. Wallace, the interviewer, is clearly prepared, but readily shifts gears when the response warrants it.

---

[1] You can find a transcript here: William Jefferson Clinton on *FOX News Sunday*, interview by Chris Wallace, September 24, 2006, transcript by FOXNews.com, September 26, 2006, http://www.foxnews.com/story/2006/09/26/transcript-william-jefferson-clinton-on-fox-news-sunday.html.

There is an order to the questions, yet it feels like a conversation. There is a struggle off and on for control of the interview. There is the tough question. In the end, what viewers got was so much more than just information. The interview revealed complexity, humanity, a collision of competing ideas, and insight. It also had some skirmishing, which can be somewhat entertaining. So it was like a hockey game—a combination of finesse and fisticuffs.

FOX NEWS SUNDAY'S CHRIS WALLACE: This week President William Jefferson Clinton hosted his second annual Global Initiative forum in New York. More than $7 billion was pledged to tackle some of the worst problems in developing countries, such as poverty, disease, and climate change.

As part of the conference, Mr. Clinton agreed to his first one-on-one interview ever on *FOX News Sunday*. The ground rules were simple: fifteen minutes for our sit-down, split evenly between the Global Initiative and anything else we wanted to ask. But as you'll see now in the full, unedited interview, that's not how it turned out.

This is a good introduction. It states what Clinton had been doing recently that was noteworthy and established a context for the interview. Stating the ground rules is important because it would be safe to assume that these two were adversaries, and this is FOX News' way of being transparent about what they agreed to. It's also important that they said the interview was unedited, because then no one can

*wonder if FOX left something out to make Clinton look worse or to
make them look better. Editing is a form of manipulation, which isn't
necessarily bad. But editing can frame a response, shift around the
order of the questions, and otherwise present a vibe that is different
from the one that actually happened. In this case it is a way to be
honest with the audience.*

> **WALLACE:** Mr. President . . . In a recent issue of the
> *New Yorker* you say, quote, "I'm sixty years old and I
> damn near died, and I'm worried about how many
> lives I can save before I do die." Is that what drives you
> in your effort to help in these developing countries?

*This is a great opening question. Wallace starts with a "legacy"
question, asking Clinton to talk more about what is motivating him
in his charitable work. Wallace brings up Clinton's recent health issue,
which is a good piece of information for viewers, and he quotes from
the* New Yorker, *showing that he is prepared for this interview. Legacy questions are usually wonderful ways to get started. The person
can talk about himself a little and let down his guard. Anyone who
has been interviewed before, though, knows that a legacy question is a
type of setup for a more difficult question later.*

*Clinton, as he is known to do, then gives a lengthy and informa-
tive answer.*

> **WALLACE:** How do you rate, compare the powers of
> being in office as president and what you can do out
> of office as a former president?

I love this. It's sort of a "would you rather" kind of question. It allows Clinton to go further into explaining what being president is like, and what it's like to trade that position in and use it for humanitarian purposes. It's a question designed to draw out Clinton's thinking and passion.

CLINTON: Well, when you are president, you can operate on a much broader scope. So, for example, you can simultaneously be trying to stop a genocide in Kosovo and, you know, make peace in the Middle East, pass a budget that gives millions of kids a chance to have after-school programs and has a huge increase in college aid at home. In other words, you've got a lot of different moving parts, and you can move them all at once. But you're also more at the mercy of events.

WALLACE: So what is it that you can do as a former president?

Great follow-up. He didn't let Clinton go on too long (as Clinton is known to do), but moved him along to the second part of the question, skillfully prompting him to focus on the CGI.

CLINTON: So what you can do as a former president is—you don't have the wide range of power, so you have to concentrate on fewer things. But you are less at the mercy of unfolding events.

So if I say, look, we're going to work on the economic empowerment of poor people, on fighting AIDS and

other diseases, on trying to bridge the religious and
political differences between people, and on trying to,
you know, avoid the worst calamities of climate change
and help to revitalize the economy in the process, I can
actually do that.

I mean, because tomorrow when I get up, if there's
a bad headline in the paper, it's President Bush's
responsibility, not mine. That's the joy of being a
former president. And it is true that if you live long
enough and you really have great discipline in the
way you do this, like this CGI, you might be able to
affect as many lives, or more, for the good as you did as
president.

*This is a good, thoughtful response. Clinton is at ease, Wallace is
in control, and the information so far is heartfelt and interesting.*

WALLACE: When we announced that you were going
to be on *FOX News Sunday*, I got a lot of email from
viewers. And I've got to say, I was surprised. Most of
them wanted me to ask you this question: Why didn't
you do more to put bin Laden and Al Qaeda out of
business when you were president?

There's a new book out, I suspect you've already read,
called *The Looming Tower*. And it talks about how the
fact that when you pulled troops out of Somalia in
1993, bin Laden said, "I have seen the frailty and the
weakness and the cowardice of U.S. troops." Then there

was the bombing of the embassies in Africa and the attack on the *Cole*.[2]

I understand what Wallace is doing here. Rather than look like he is directly asking Clinton why he didn't do more, he backs into it by saying most of his viewers wanted to know. A lot of interviewers do this so that it doesn't look like a direct personal challenge. I have taken this approach myself on occasion, just so it won't look too aggressive. In addition, this kind of crowdsourcing is a way to find out what is on the audience's mind. If there are some specific issues that many of them want addressed, then it's a good idea to bring it up.

CLINTON: Okay, let's just go through that.
WALLACE: Let me—let me—may I just finish the question, sir? And after the attack, the book says that bin Laden separated his leaders, spread them around, because he expected an attack, and there was no response. I understand that hindsight is always twenty-twenty. . . .

Wallace is being polite, but firm. He's in charge of the interview. And even though he is interviewing a former president, he is trying to ask his tough question in a respectful manner before Clinton can butt in. You can see that Clinton is gearing up for it. It may seem too early to ask this kind of question, but remember, the ground rules were that

---

[2] Terrorists bombed the USS *Cole* on October 12, 2000, killing seventeen American sailors.

half of the interview had to be about the Clinton Global Initiative,
which means Wallace had seven and one-half minutes to ask about
these other issues. He's already asked the rapport-building question,
so he is turning up the heat before he runs out of time. As I have said
elsewhere in the book, your source is expecting you to ask the tough
question. Clinton was clearly expecting this.

CLINTON: No, let's talk about it.

WALLACE: . . . but the question is, why didn't you do
more, connect the dots and put them out of business?

Clinton begins his answer, going back in history to provide con-
text. After a few minutes, Wallace interrupts him.

WALLACE: I understand, and I . . .

Wallace is trying to keep this from being a speech. I would have
tried to interject and get back to the question also.

CLINTON: No, wait. No, wait. Don't tell me this—you
asked me why didn't I do more to bin Laden. There
was not a living soul. All the people who now criticize
me wanted to leave the next day.
You brought this up, so you'll get an answer, but you
can't . . .

WALLACE: . . . bin Laden says that it showed the
weakness of the United States.

Wallace gets to finish his point, and he is trying to narrow Clinton's response rather than get all of the history and context. But Clinton starts down a different historical trail. I'm sure the context was useful from his perspective, but I can see a viewer losing interest. And the history wasn't the point of the interview. So Wallace interrupts again.

> **WALLACE:** . . . with respect, if I may, instead of going through '93 and . . .
> *Wallace is trying to get Clinton to focus on the question.*
> **CLINTON:** No, no. You asked it. You brought it up. You brought it up.
> **WALLACE:** May I ask a general question and then you can answer?
> **CLINTON:** Yes.
> **WALLACE:** The 9/11 Commission, which you've talked about—and this is what they did say, not what ABC pretended they said . . .
> **CLINTON:** Yes, what did they say?
> **WALLACE:** . . . they said about you and President Bush, and I quote, "The U.S. government took the threat seriously, but not in the sense of mustering anything like the kind of effort that would be gathered to confront an enemy of the first, second, or even third rank."
> **CLINTON:** First of all, that's not true with us and bin Laden.

WALLACE: Well, I'm telling you that's what the 9/11 Commission says.

This is a good response. Wallace is making it clear that this is not Wallace challenging what Clinton did or did not do. He is quoting from an official document.

CLINTON: All right. Let's look at what Richard Clarke said. Do you think Richard Clarke has a vigorous attitude about bin Laden?

This is an interesting pivot by Clinton. He is ignoring what the 9/11 Commission just said about him, and is introducing a different credible source.

WALLACE: Yes, I do.

Clinton then goes into great detail about the merits of Clark, his national coordinator of counterterrorism.

WALLACE: But . . .
CLINTON: No, wait a minute.

(Cross talk)
Wallace challenges how serious the Clinton administration's response was in Somalia by questioning whether launching some cruise missiles was effective. It shows he knows the issues well. This sets

Clinton off on more detail of what he attempted to do as president in trying to get Osama bin Laden.

WALLACE: Do you think you did enough, sir?

This is a great question. It gives Clinton a chance to give a declarative sentence that evaluates what he did.

CLINTON: No, because I didn't get him.
WALLACE: Right.

Even though it's just one word, I think Wallace saying "Right" is gratuitous, and makes him more of an adversary, as if he's saying, "Yup, you didn't do enough." I don't think it's helpful to appear to side with the critics. It sounded a little self-congratulatory. Smug, even.

CLINTON: But at least I tried. That's the difference in me and some, including all the right-wingers who are attacking me now. They ridiculed me for trying. They had eight months to try. They did not try. I tried. So I tried and failed. When I failed, I left a comprehensive anti-terror strategy and the best guy in the country, Dick Clarke, who got demoted. So you did FOX's bidding on this show. You did your nice little conservative hit job on me. What I want to know is . . .
WALLACE: Well, wait a minute, sir.

I thought Clinton's last response was honest and refreshing. He admitted failure. But then he made it personal. It may be true that FOX News was hoping to get him to say he had failed in his effort to get Osama bin Laden and use that admission as a way to embarrass him, but so far it seemed like a legitimate exchange. Clinton, on the other hand, felt like he had been set up.

CLINTON: No, wait. No, no . . .

WALLACE: I want to ask a question. You don't think that's a legitimate question?

Wallace is defending himself without getting too aggressive.

CLINTON: It was a perfectly legitimate question, but I want to know how many people in the Bush administration you asked this question of. I want to know how many people in the Bush administration you asked, "Why didn't you do anything about the Cole?" I want to know how many you asked, "Why did you fire Dick Clarke?" I want to know how many people you asked . . .

Clinton has wrested control over this interview.

WALLACE: We asked—we asked . . .

CLINTON: I don't . . .

WALLACE: Do you ever watch *FOX News Sunday*, sir?

This struck me as unnecessary, but in the heat of the moment (and there was plenty of heat in this moment!) I might have done the same. Still, I felt that Wallace dropped his professionalism with his question.

CLINTON: I don't believe you asked them that.

WALLACE: We ask plenty of questions of . . .

CLINTON: You didn't ask that, did you? Tell the truth, Chris.

WALLACE: About the USS *Cole*?

CLINTON: Tell the truth, Chris.

WALLACE: With Iraq and Afghanistan, there's plenty of stuff to ask.

Wallace could have looked a little less flummoxed if he would have said something like, "We'll have our researchers get an answer to your question as soon as possible." The interview is going off the rails here, and Wallace let Clinton become the one asking the questions.

CLINTON: Did you ever ask that? You set this meeting up because you were going to get a lot of criticism from your viewers because Rupert Murdoch's supporting my work on climate change.

This shows that Clinton had also done his homework before the interview. He knew that some FOX News viewers hated the idea of Murdoch and Clinton collaborating on anything.

And you came here under false pretenses and said that you'd spend half the time talking about—you said you'd spend half the time talking about what we did out there to raise $7-billion-plus in three days from two hundred fifteen different commitments. And you don't care.

WALLACE: But, President Clinton, if you look at the questions here, you'll see half the questions are about that. I didn't think this was going to set you off on such a tear.

Wallace is keeping his cool. Good for him.

CLINTON: You launched it—it set me off on a tear because you didn't formulate it in an honest way and because you people ask me questions you don't ask the other side.

WALLACE: That's not true. Sir, that is not true.

CLINTON: And Richard Clarke made it clear in his testimony . . .

WALLACE: Would you like to talk about the Clinton Global Initiative?

Even though this isn't a smooth segue, Wallace is trying to change the subject to get to the other part of the interview. I agree with his approach. It probably had to be this abrupt to keep things from getting more personal and agitated. He is wise to do so, but in this case Clinton ploughed ahead. Wallace did an admirable job in their subsequent back and forth, allowed Clinton to say his piece, professionally deflecting Clinton's criticism of FOX, and eventually guiding their conversation back to the CGI.

WALLACE: . . . One of the main parts of the Global Initiative this year is religion and reconciliation. President Bush says that the fight against Islamic extremism is the central conflict of this century. And his answer is promoting democracy and reform. Do you think he has that right?

Wallace has finally regained control of the interview, and it seems that both of them are reluctantly going on to discuss the Clinton Global Initiative.

CLINTON: Sure. To advance—to advocate democracy and reform in the Muslim world? Absolutely. I think the question is, what's the best way to do it? I think also the question is, how do you educate people about democracy? Democracy is about way more than majority rule. Democracy is about minority rights, individual rights, restraints on power. And there's more than one way to advance democracy.
WALLACE: Last year at this conference, you got $2.5 billion in commitments, pledges. How'd you do this year?

This is a great way to get Clinton to continue.

CLINTON: Well, this year we had—we had $7.3 billion, as of this morning.

WALLACE: Excuse me?

Another good tactic, and a shorthand means to ask for more details.

CLINTON: $7.3 billion, as of this morning. But $3 billion of that is—now, this is over multi years. These are up to ten-year commitments. But $3 billion of that came from Richard Branson's commitment to give all of his transportation profits for a decade to clean energy investments. But still, that's—the rest is over $4 billion.

And we will have another hundred commitments come in, maybe more, and we'll probably raise another, I would say, at least another billion dollars, probably, before it's over. We've got a lot of commitments still in process.

WALLACE: When you look at the $3 billion from Branson, plus the billions that Bill Gates is giving in his own program, and now Warren Buffett, what do you make of this new age of philanthropy?

This is an effective way to get a source to give a personal insight into a big idea. I'm an advocate of questions that begin with "What do you make of . . ." They're open-ended enough to get the person thinking.

CLINTON: I think that, for one thing, really rich people have always given money away. I mean, you know, they've endowed libraries and things like that. The unique thing about this age is, first of all, you have a lot of people like Bill Gates and Warren Buffett who are interested in issues at home and around the world that grow out of the nature of the twenty-first century and its inequalities—the income inequalities, the health-care inequalities, the education inequalities. And you get a guy like Gates, who built Microsoft, who actually believes that he can help overcome a lot of the health disparities in the world. And that's the first thing.

The second thing that ought to be credited is that there are a lot of people with average incomes who are joining them because of the internet. Like in the tsunami, for example, we had $1.2 billion given by Americans; thirty percent of our households gave money, over half of them over the internet.

And then the third thing is you've got all these—in poor countries, you've got all these nongovernmental groups that you can—that a guy like Gates can partner with, along with the governments.

So all these things together mean that people with real money want to give it away in ways that help people that before would've been seen only as the object of government grants or loans.

WALLACE: Let's talk some politics. In that same *New Yorker* article, you say that you are tired of Karl Rove's BS, although I'm cleaning up what you said.

It doesn't seem that half of the interview went to the Clinton Global Initiative. I question this topic because Karl Rove is popular among FOX News viewers, and it seems like a "red meat" question to have Bill Clinton—a person the right wing loathes—criticize Karl Rove—a person the right wing loves. We're not going for insight here.

CLINTON: But I do like the—but I also say I'm not tired of Karl Rove. I don't blame Karl Rove. If you've got a deal that works, you just keep on doing it.

WALLACE: So what is the BS?

CLINTON: Well, every even-numbered year, right before an election, they come up with some security issue. In 2002, our party supported them in undertaking weapons inspections in Iraq and was one hundred percent for what happened in Afghanistan, and they didn't have any way to make us look like we didn't care about terror. And so, they decided they would be for the homeland security bill that they had opposed. And they put a poison pill in it that we wouldn't pass, like taking the job rights away from a hundred seventy thousand people, and then say that we were weak on terror if we weren't for it. They just ran that out. The Democrats—as long as the American people believe that we take this seriously and we have our

own approaches—and we may have differences over
Iraq—I think we'll do fine in this election.

But even if they agree with us about the Iraq War, we
could be hurt by Karl Rove's new foray if we just don't
make it clear that we, too, care about the security of the
country. But Rove is good. And I honor him. I mean, I
will say that. I've always been amused about how good
he is, in a way.

But on the other hand, this is perfectly predictable:
We're going to win a lot of seats if the American
people aren't afraid. If they're afraid and we get divided
again, then we may only win a few seats.

WALLACE: And the White House, the Republicans
want to make the American people afraid?

*This is another good follow-up question. Wallace knows his au-
dience, which is largely Republican, and Clinton has just made a
generalization about how Republicans operate. Instead of saying,
"Oh, come on!" Wallace is a little more gentle in challenging the
assumption. Nonetheless, it's a challenge.*

CLINTON: Of course they do . . . they want another
homeland security deal. And they want to make it
about—not about Iraq but about some other security
issue, where, if we disagree with them, we are, by
definition, imperiling the security of the country.
And it's a big load of hooey . . . . We've got a huge
military presence here in this campaign. And we just

can't let them have some rhetorical device that puts us
in a box we don't belong in.

That's their job. Their job is to beat us. I like that about
Rove. But our job is not to let them get away with it.
And if they don't, then we'll do fine.

WALLACE: Mr. President, thank you for one of the
more unusual interviews.

CLINTON: Thanks.

This was, at times, like watching a couple of heavyweight
boxers battling it out, sometimes even after the bell had rung.
Wallace knew where the interview needed to go, and he
guided it there. Clinton tried to hijack it at times and call out
what he considered were unfair tactics. Wallace is a seasoned
interviewer, and Clinton is a seasoned interviewee. It was a
pleasure to watch both of them do their jobs well.

CHAPTER 7
Don't Avoid the Hard Part

What's Most Uncomfortable Might Also Be the Most Important

SOMETIMES YOU HAVE TO ASK tough questions. Questions that might be delicate, uncomfortable, probing, personal, thought-provoking, revealing, sensitive. Human resources professionals have to ask them. Educators have to ask them. Nurses, doctors, lawyers, social workers, parents, and pastors have to ask them. If you ask only easy, stock questions that everyone else has asked, then why are you even doing this interview?

Tough questions don't have to be mean, embarrassing, inappropriate, or invade anyone's privacy—in fact, most of the time they *shouldn't* be. The goal isn't to have a "gotcha" moment. The goal is to get your subject to think about their answer and say something new, rather than popping out the same ol' rote response she or he has given many times already. You want something fresh, some insight, some new understanding—regardless of your profession.

If you're a writer, chances are that the person you are interviewing has been interviewed before. Remember what we talked about before. If you're just going to go over the same material as the others, then don't bother. Readers and viewers can just look at previous interviews with this person. They don't need you to repeat what is already widely known and addressed. "If the reporter isn't going to try to make it interesting, then neither am I," a pro hockey player told me when we talked about interviewing.

When you ask tough questions in an interview, you want to do it so that:

- You can reveal a new perspective or at least give your source a chance to explain or refute what has already been reported.

- You can challenge your source and provoke a deeper reflection than what has been previously provided. This helps you avoid getting a boring recitation of the same tired answers.

- You can hold someone accountable for something he did or said.

Asking those questions may be uncomfortable for both of you. But shining that bright spotlight of scrutiny on an issue is sometimes the most important part of your exchange.

If you have prepared properly, you should already know

the answers to these tough questions, but remember, the reason you are doing the interview is to get the person's perspective and capture some unique emotion or drama, not just the facts.

Let's take these reasons for asking tough questions one at a time.

New Perspective

In the movie *Spotlight,* where investigative reporters from the *Boston Globe* look into the abuse committed by priests and the subsequent cover-up of the Catholic Church, there is a scene where the reporter Sacha Pfeiffer, played by Rachel McAdams, tracks down a retired priest and knocks on a door. An elderly man comes to the door, and she introduces herself. The reporter's instincts were superb, because she assumed she would have limited time, and she is quick on her feet once she asks her first question.

SACHA: Hi, I'm looking for Ronald Paquin.

FATHER PAQUIN: Yes?

SACHA: You're . . . Father Paquin?

FATHER PAQUIN: Yes, that's right.

SACHA: My name is Sacha Pfeiffer, I, I'm a reporter with the *Boston Globe.*

FATHER PAQUIN: Okay.

SACHA: Could I ask you a few questions?

FATHER PAQUIN: Go ahead, dear.

SACHA: We've talked to several men who knew you when they were boys at St. John the Baptist in Haverhill? They told us you molested them? Is that true?

FATHER PAQUIN: Sure. I fooled around. But I never felt gratified myself.

SACHA: Right, uh, but you admit that you molested boys at St. John the Baptist?

FATHER PAQUIN: Yes, yes, but as I said, I never got any pleasure from it. That's important to understand.

SACHA: Right. Can you tell me where and how you, uh, fooled around with these boys?

FATHER PAQUIN: I want to be clear, I never raped anyone. There's a difference. I should know.

SACHA: How would you know?

FATHER PAQUIN: I was raped.

SACHA: I'm sorry . . . who raped you?[1]

Father Paquin's sister then appears and ends the interview. In a situation like that there is no time to build rapport or establish shared humanity. In this case one must realize that she might not get another chance to ask him, so Sacha went immediately for the uncomfortable—but very necessary—

---

[1] Tom McCarthy, and Josh Singer, *Spotlight*, screenplay script, 89–90, https://s3.amazonaws.com/thescriptlab/screenplays/2015/Spotlight -Final-Script.pdf.

question. The reporters had reason to believe Father Paquin was a molester, but they needed to give him the chance to respond to the accusation and maybe even explain his actions. If he denied it, that needed to be part of the story. If he admitted it, that was part of the story, too.

No matter how unsavory, a question like that must be asked.

On a much tamer level, when I was preparing for my interview with Tracy Kidder I could see from his books that he depended a lot on people's memories. Some of his material was verifiable through fact-checking and corroboration with others, but several times I could tell he was relying on a person's memory. How trustworthy are people's memories?

So much of his work depends on people telling him the truth and recalling incidents and personal histories—how does he know these things are accurately recalled? When I asked him about it, he was very forthcoming about how he sometimes simply has to trust his sources. I could tell that he wasn't bothered by the question. Nor should he have been—I wasn't calling his work a fabrication; he knew I wasn't accusing him of anything. I just wanted to know his process of verification and trust. He was expecting the question.

Challenge

If you don't try to get past the surface, the PR, the lies, the propaganda, the dominant narrative, the built-in assumptions, then you aren't contributing anything new to the discussion.

Whatever your profession, sometimes you just have to show some courage and address what needs addressing.

But while every interview isn't necessarily going to have a "gotcha" question, most interviews will have some opportunity for deeper exploration. Human resources professionals aren't setting traps for their potential employees. Nurses aren't looking for ways to embarrass patients. But the difficult questions are the ones where you are getting to the heart of the matter, whether it's a person's employment history, a financial statement that doesn't make sense, or a contradiction that bears explaining.

As the head of a journalism program, I often get asked to evaluate other journalism programs. For one particular university, a simple Google search showed me that there were a lot of accusations by former students that the school was not delivering on promises, and the students were dropping out under the weight of a lot of debt. Also, the school was being investigated by the Department of Education. And their graduation rates were extremely low.

For two days, an assessor from another university and I met with the staff of the school, some faculty, and some handpicked students. The reports were meticulous and professional. The presentations were superb. If I didn't already have material that contradicted what I was hearing from the staff and administrators, I would have given them a glowing assessment for their accreditation. But the other assessor had the same misgivings I did, so we invited the dean of the school to join us for coffee off campus. We asked her if she could explain how the numbers we were seeing from the Department of Education were so different from the ones her staff had presented us. And I asked about that one professor whose only professional writing experience was that he had written some country music lyrics. It wasn't an attack—and I have to believe she knew it was coming—but even so, her explanations were, well, frankly lame. When she was done, she looked at us with the kind of fake, pained expression that meant, "Of course you guys know what's really going on here, but there's no way I'm going to come out and say it. I'm just going to nod and laugh awkwardly. More coffee, anyone?"

What you're trying to do in situations where tough questions are called for is to get to the heart of what is going on. If you're doing it just to score points with some bloodthirsty audience, well, then, you should take up boxing. But if you're doing it because you want to understand something more clearly, then there is an obligation to burrow in, as long as it's done in a humane way. Remember, an interview is a conversation, not an interrogation. It's not about winning. It's about gaining understanding. It's about seeking truth.

I interviewed a prominent writer and speaker in the religious world in front of an audience, and as I searched for themes in his writings, I noticed something about his lifestyle. He writes prolifically about the deeper, mystical dimensions of the Christian faith, and about how contemplation, prayer, silence, and retreats must be part of any leader's spiritual practice. I also saw that this guy keeps an incredible travel, speaking, and writing schedule, and was a million-mile member of an airline because he teaches at two universities, one on each coast, *each week*. And to top it off, I saw that all of his mentors and heroes of the faith had died at relatively young ages, from heart disease and stress-related illnesses.

You can see where I'm going with this.

About two-thirds of the way into a very delightful interview, I brought up the topic I described above.

"What safeguards do you have in your own life so that you won't end up like your heroes and mentors?" I asked.

I sensed a collective gasp from the audience, and then they went completely quiet.

The person I was interviewing looked at me quizzically for just a moment, and then slowly smiled. He was clearly trying to think of a response.

"You just warmed the water before drowning the cat," he said.

Everyone laughed. It broke the tension. We just sat there for a few more moments. And then he tried to answer the question. He talked about his struggle to practice what he preached (and wrote). It was a great moment of honesty and humanity.

I wasn't trying to embarrass him. I just wanted to explore this topic of how busy people can protect themselves. Members of the audience had to be wondering about the same thing.

Picking up on contradictions (or at least on paradoxes) is a very effective way of getting at a tough question. These questions don't have to come across as accusations. They can be gently introduced with a phrase like "Help me understand something." Or "So-and-so said it happened this way, but you say it happened that way. Can you see how this is confusing?"

I tried to develop an apparent contradiction into something interesting for a magazine profile on John Polkinghorne, after watching a video of Polkinghorne debating his longtime friend Steven Weinberg, a Nobel Prize–winning physicist. The debate was at the Smithsonian, on the topic of faith and science. As I mentioned before, Polkinghorne became a priest in the Anglican Church when he was in his forties after a world-famous career as a physicist at Cambridge University. Weinberg is an atheist who has also had a world-class career in physics. Polkinghorne and Weinberg have a long and deep friendship. In the video they were discussing quarks, the smallest known particles at the time.

In the debate, Weinberg said, "We don't believe in quarks because anyone has seen one. We believe in quarks because the theories that include them work."

That struck me as an odd thing to say, because many people who are part of religious traditions would say something similar about why they believe what they believe. They've never seen God, but when they include God in their lives, they say their lives mean more.

I interviewed Weinberg on the phone for my magazine piece about Polkinghorne, and I tried to draw this parallel between what he said about quarks and why people have a faith.

"Aren't they both unseen realities?" I asked.

"Not at all," he replied. And then he explained why they were different.

What I perceived as a contradiction wasn't a contradiction to him at all. It wasn't a threat, or an accusation or a gotcha. It was a way to delve deeper into the subject. It was a tough question because it challenged him to square his approach to physics with his approach to a belief in God.

You remember Madame Brigitte, the voodoo priestess in Haiti? Well, when I interviewed her I knew that my readers had a stereotype about voodoo. So did I, until I read a lot about it and talked to knowledgeable people about it. And even though it looks like an indelicate question in isolation, keep in mind that our conversation had already gone more than an hour, and I had credibility with her because she knew I had done a lot of preparation on the topic.

"I apologize if this next question will sound offensive to you," I began. When this was translated into Creole for her, she smiled broadly. That smile told me she knew what was coming. "But in the United States, it seems like the only time voodoo is referred to is through horror movies or comic books or missionaries, where there are dolls with pins and people curse others by sticking pins in the dolls."

I waited until that was translated. She smiled even more.

"Why are some people so afraid of what you do?"

She gave a beautiful response, full of history and commentary about human nature and how we fear what we don't understand. She was ready for the question.

That Pesky Thing Called Accountability

The Border Patrol supervisor I mentioned earlier was also expecting a difficult question, even though he still snapped on me. Remember, this was after an officer on the U.S. side of the border shot an eleven-year-old boy on the Mexico side and nearly killed him. I asked about the training and danger and preparation involved in being a Border Patrol officer. I did a ride-along to experience in a small way what a shift on the border was like. I asked the supervisor about harassment from people on the other side of the border. I asked about being pelted with rocks. And then I asked this:

"Don't you think it's an overreaction, though, to get hit by a rock by a little kid and respond by shooting him?"

The second that question was out of my mouth the supervisor grabbed a glass ashtray and leaped across his desk, kicking over his chair behind him. In a flash he grabbed my shirt and swung the ashtray at me, stopping when it was a centimeter from my face. Purple-faced and screaming, he said, "Now, don't you think you'd hit back?"

I said, "Well, I sure wouldn't shoot you."

I wondered in that moment whether I would get my face bashed in.

He shoved me back in my chair, picked up his own chair off the floor, and threw my photographer, Eugene, and me out of his office. No cooldown time that day. I really don't think I surprised him with that question. He was trying to make a point. So was I.

In retrospect I think I had a few other thoughts in that moment. One was: "I am a dead man." Another was about the photographer: "Take lots of pictures, Eugene. You'll need these for the autopsy." The third was the punch line of a joke my kids and I loved to tell: "Cabin boy, bring me my brown pants." I can tell you the whole joke sometime in person. But I think you get the gist with the punch line.

When Eugene and I walked out of the supervisor's office, a number of officers were standing nearby—they could hear everything—and they all had pretty good smirks on their faces. Big Poppa had just schooled an enemy of the people. I nodded to them as I left, trying to act as if this kind of thing happened to me all the time. I was trying to portray that I was a tough hombre, too. Then I got to my car in the parking lot and realized I had locked my keys in it.

I had to swallow several gulps of pride before walking back into the office and sheepishly asking, "Would any of you gentlemen have a slim-jim so I could unlock my car?"

What's the word I'm looking for? Oh yeah. Humiliating.

Let me repeat myself: Ask the tough question. If you don't, the false narrative, the PR spin, the carefully cultivated persona, will dominate. That's how we buy dumb products, elect incompetent leaders, and get into pointless wars. Perpetuating myths doesn't serve your audience or the truth.

Here's an example of how asking the tough question can reveal the empty promises of a local entity. In the late 1990s the San Diego Unified School District hired a prominent local attorney as the superintendent of schools. It was a strange choice, since he had no experience in education other than having gone to law school, but the school district was a mess, and the feeling was that we needed someone who wasn't so entrenched in the system to clean it all up.

Soon after he took office, he hired a second-in-command and gave him the title "chancellor of instruction." The new hire came from the New York City public school system and was portrayed by our new superintendent as a kind of messiah who would save the schools. A news conference was called at a local high school auditorium to introduce this new oracle.

In those days I was freelancing for the *New York Times,* and they wanted me to go to the news conference to ask some specific questions—not about San Diego schools, but about the new chancellor's difficult time with the New York school system he was leaving. They sent me some documents as background.

So I went to the news conference and listened to the superintendent rave about the chancellor's achievements in New York and about the immediate difference he was going to make in San Diego. Other school board members did the same. Then the new chancellor gave some remarks about how much he was going to do for us and that he was going to do it very quickly. It was a lovefest. There weren't any facts in all of this—more of a "hype springs eternal" kind of affair.

The local media bought it, and asked questions that allowed the gushing to continue. They asked questions like "How soon will students' test scores go up now that you're here?" Seriously—they asked that.

I raised my hand.

"How much did your decision to come to San Diego have to do with the ethics probe back in New York, where you were accused of violating ethical standards and professional misconduct?" I asked.

You would have thought that I had just dropped my pants and crapped on his birthday cake, judging by the looks on the school officials' faces, and on the faces of the other members of the media.

"It had nothing to do with that," he said, with what I perceived as mock offense. "I'm here to make a difference in San Diego."

More reporters asked about how he was going to save us all, and then it was my turn again.

"When you were investigated for using school board employees to paint your home and babysit your children, did that help in your decision to come to San Diego?" I asked.

He and the superintendent acted surprised and hurt and insulted, but I have to believe that they knew someone would know that he was leaving New York under a cloud of suspicion. They had to know it was coming.

More important, those are the kinds of questions that readers and viewers *deserve* to have asked on their behalf. Shouldn't the parents and education community of San Diego—the people who are paying his salary and are entrusting their children to him—know if Wonder Boy was actually fleeing a bad situation that he had created at his last job?

When the news conference was over, I stayed in the auditorium for a while and wrote up my notes and called my quotes in to the editor in New York. When I left the building, the superintendent and the chancellor were outside waiting for me.

The superintendent spoke first.

"Who are you?" he said.

"I'm Dean Nelson, with the *New York Times,*" I said.

"Well of course," the superintendent said, rolling his eyes. "Of course the *New York Times* would presume that a person would leave New York for San Diego only if he was avoiding a scandal."

"Well, is he?" I asked.

"Of course not," the chancellor said. Then he repeated his promises of making the San Diego schools great again.

We shook hands and went our separate ways.

People in authority, especially those whose salaries are paid by taxpayers, deserve a level of accountability that they don't always appreciate. But the public appreciates it, and deserves it.

"Tough" vs. "Gotcha"

Every interview doesn't have to have a "gotcha" question. But if there is a question out there, and it still hasn't been resolved in the minds of the audience, then I believe it's not only appropriate but also necessary to ask it.

The source knows it's coming, and the readers and viewers hope it's coming. You have to ask it directly—not through insinuation or hints. It's unfair to raise questions about a person if you haven't raised the questions to the actual person. If there is something to say and inquire about, then you have an obligation to do it in as direct a manner as possible.

"Anything shitty we're going to say about somebody, we say it to their face," said Ira Glass.[2]

The importance of asking the difficult question isn't just in journalism. A therapist is going to probe until she gets to what she perceives is the root of an issue. A lawyer is going to ask you to explain your contradictory alibi. A nurse is going to ask why you have those burn marks on your wrists. If those tough questions aren't on the table, then we aren't going to get anything interesting, useful, or new.

What's the difference between a tough question and a gotcha question? A gotcha question is more on the sensational side, where you prove to your source and audience that you're brave enough to expose a contradiction or some hypocrisy. It's less about the answer, and more about you getting to ask it and put someone on the spot. Now, I'm all for exposing the truth—I am a journalist, after all—but if the exposure isn't heading the audience toward something, and the only purpose of it is to say that this person is a schmuck, or prove that you did your homework, then I have to wonder how useful it is.

As Mike Wallace used to say, there is a difference between asking a question that provides heat for heat's sake and one that provides heat for light's sake. If you're asking a question just so you can embarrass someone, then it has questionable

---

2   Ira Glass, "Q&A: Ira Glass on structuring stories, asking hard questions," interview by Jesse Thorn, *Columbia Journalism Review,* June 22, 2017, https://www.cjr.org/special_report/qa-ira-glass-turnaround-npr-jesse-thorn-tal.php.

value. If you're asking a question so that you can really get to the heart of something, then it's acceptable.

Remember, this isn't about you strutting your stuff or placating your ego or scoring points. This is about what the audience deserves and needs to know. This is about getting to the truth of a matter.

In the Barbara Walters/Mike Wallace interview I mentioned before, I said that she asked him a difficult question. Throughout the interview she actually asked him several difficult questions. I have an annotated transcript of the interview in an appendix following this chapter. But one of the difficult questions she asked was why so many of the questions in his interview with General William Westmoreland, the commander of all U.S. troops in Vietnam, were written by someone else. She asked about the accusation that Wallace was just a puppet in someone else's hand.

A number of fascinating things happened in that exchange, but a key one to keep in mind is the sportsmanlike heads-up she gives Wallace by saying, "I want to ask you about one specific thing about you, which is interesting, and which perhaps is painful to you, perhaps not." It's not a bad idea to warn the person that a difficult question is coming. That's why I preceded my question to the voodoo priestess about stereotypes by apologizing in case the question seemed offensive. Comments like this serve as a kind of foghorn that we're headed into some rocky waters.

Wallace knew those questions were coming; the audience undoubtedly expected those questions to be addressed. Not only would Wallace not have respected her without them, but the audience wouldn't have, either. She had to ask the tough question.

Exceptions

When I interviewed Dave Eggers for our Writer's Symposium, I did something I rarely agree to do. I promised to *not* ask him a particular question.

If the interview were part of a story I was writing about him, I never would have agreed to it. Typically, a source doesn't dictate what you can and can't talk about. There are some exceptions. For example, in the *Frost/Nixon* movie the Nixon camp demanded that no more than 25 percent of the interview would be about Watergate, and Frost agreed, but in most cases journalists don't want restrictions. They want to talk about whatever they think is in the public interest.

The Writer's Symposium, though, has a different purpose from standard journalism. Its purpose is to model, celebrate, inspire, and encourage great writing. So if the only way I can get a prominent writer like Dave Eggers to attend is to concede one question, that sounds fine to me. Plenty left to talk about.

The question had to do with one of his books, *Zeitoun*. The main character of the book, Abdulrahman Zeitoun, was a hero after Hurricane Katrina in New Orleans. It's a wonderful book. But after the book was a wild success, the main character was accused of domestic violence, and a question was raised about whether Eggers still stood behind the man he had written so glowingly about. So when Eggers agreed to participate in the Symposium, he did so on the condition I would not ask him about those accusations.

But during the audience Q&A, someone in the crowd asked about it. That made it a little awkward for him and me.

It was on the public's mind, and it hadn't been adequately addressed.

So is *everything* fair game?

Of course not.

Just because you have a microphone or a pad of paper doesn't mean you get to pry into a person's personal life just to satisfy your curiosity or an audience's demand for gossip. Discernment matters. Wisdom matters. Shared humanity matters. You're not just playing a role. You're trying to uncover significance and meaning. There is a difference between sensationalism and insight, between being a town crier and a town voyeur. Compassion and empathy are part of seeking the truth, too.

Timing Is Everything, Until It's Not

As I have already mentioned, if you have a tough question to ask, don't start your interview there. You have to ease into it. I generally place a tough question about two-thirds of the way into the interview. You must develop enough rapport for the person to trust you. Timing is everything.

Well, *usually* it's everything. If a person has a lot of experience in being interviewed, then some of these guidelines won't have the same effectiveness. Sometimes a source will want to get right to the controversy.

One year, a colleague and I conducted a high school sports journalism conference in Florida during Major League Baseball's spring training. We ran a competition throughout the country and selected one student from each state. The criteria were strict, and we had a committee peruse each application. We wanted the best high school student sportswriter each state had to offer. These kids were bright and motivated.

Since the Orlando area had many professional sports, we visited with not only the Los Angeles Dodgers where they used to train at Dodgertown in Vero Beach, but also the Orlando Magic of the NBA, the Tampa Bay Lightning of the NHL, the University of Florida, and the Tampa Bay Buccaneers of the NFL. It was the visit to the Buccaneers locker room that sticks out most in my memory.

Sam Wyche was the head coach at the time, and he had gotten into some trouble with the NFL because he didn't allow female reporters into the locker room. Male reporters were okay, but not women. Female reporters felt that being excluded from the locker room gave the male reporters an advantage for getting insights and quotes immediately after a game, and the NFL eventually agreed with them. But Wyche wouldn't budge. Every game he didn't allow women in the locker room, the NFL fined him. This did not seem to bother Wyche one bit.

About half of our young journalists were female, and so it

seemed to me that this would be an obvious question to raise during our time with Wyche and the Buccaneers. Speaking to the students over the loudspeaker on the bus headed toward the stadium, I cautioned them, though, not to start with that question. I explained the wisdom of easing into the tough questions, not starting with them.

When we arrived at the stadium we were ushered into the Buccaneers locker room, where some of the players had gathered after a workout for a mock press conference with our students. Wyche was there, too. A former NFL player with the Cincinnati Bengals, he was a big guy. So were the others.

We set the ground rules for the meeting. It was all on the record; if a student had a question he or she should raise a hand and, when called on, should stand, say his or her name and home state, and ask the question.

But before one question was even asked, Wyche made an opening comment about his stand on not having women in the locker room.

"I know that some bozo journalism teacher probably told you that you never start with the tough questions, but that's bullshit," he said. "I know that issue is on everyone's mind, so let's get started talking about it. Who wants to ask the first question?"

This was so abrupt that it startled the students. And I think they were intimidated by Wyche's size and gruff manner. Or maybe that was just me? Either way, these superstar students were struck mute.

"Come on!" he said. "You'll never get anywhere in journalism just sitting there looking dumb. Who wants to ask about women in the locker room?"

He seemed like he was getting a little agitated. We were wasting his time.

"Seriously? Somebody ask me about this!"

Now he was yelling.

Finally, the boy from Ohio stood up, introduced himself, and asked his question.

"So why are you opposed to women interviewing players in the locker room after a game?"

Wyche strode right up to the boy and towered over him.

"Drop your pants, son," Wyche said.

The boy looked perplexed, and slightly terrified.

"What?"

"I said drop your pants. Come on—I'll do it with you," Wyche said, and he began to unbuckle the belt of his own trousers.

I looked at the Buccaneer players. Most of them were smiling. I looked at the other students. Most of them looked horrified. Then Wyche ramped up the intensity.

"Son." His voice was much louder now, and he was getting red in the face. "I said drop your goddamn pants!" He had now completely unfastened his own pants.

The boy was frozen.

"Kid! Drop your fucking pants RIGHT NOW!"

I wondered what the headline might be in the next edition of the *Tampa Tribune*. "Wyche to Underage Boy in Locker Room: 'Drop Your Fucking Pants!'"

What's the word I'm searching for? Oh yeah. Nauseated.

The boy looked like he was about to cry, but he collected his wits enough to finally croak out, "Not in front of all of these strangers."

Wyche looked ecstatic.

"That's exactly my point!" he exclaimed. Then he strode back to the front of the locker room, fastened his pants, and said, "Now—who else has a question?"

Your sources are expecting you to ask the difficult question, and so is your audience. It may feel a little awkward, but make no mistake: They know it's coming.

Mike Wallace knew that Barbara Walters was going to ask him a gotcha.

Kidder was ready for my question about trusting people's memories.

The school district chancellor *should* have expected my question.

The Border Patrol supervisor knew what was coming.

Dave Eggers tried to avoid the question but couldn't.

Steven Weinberg challenged the question.

The religious writer engaged with the question.

The voodoo priestess was ready for the question. In fact, it amused her.

Sam Wyche would have been mad if we *didn't* ask the question.

YOU DON'T HAVE TO BE an extrovert, a showboat, or a jerk to ask a difficult question. You can be the shyest wallflower there is. But if there is a question that needs to be asked, you aren't advancing the cause by avoiding it. Your audience expects this from you, and so does your source. It won't always make your sources angry. They might even respect you.

Even more important, it's your obligation.

Still a Classic, and Better Than Frost/Nixon

Barbara Walters Interviews Mike Wallace

Broadcast in 1984[1]

THIS IS OBVIOUSLY A VERY old interview, but I love the structure of it. I used excerpts of it in previous chapters, but to appreciate how it is constructed, you really have to see it from beginning to end. It illustrates so many elements I mention in this book, such as how to structure an interview, how to keep control of it, how to follow up, how to show empathy, how to challenge, how to ask a tough question without attacking the person. Walters starts out in a pleasant manner with plenty of rapport building, it shows excellent preparation and research, it shifts a few times as to who is in control of the interview, it gets a little rocky, and then it has a nice recovery. It flows the

---

[1] Mike Wallace, interview by Barbara Walters, *20/20*, ABC, 1984.

way a good story flows. Walters can be predictable, especially when she ventures into emotional territory with her sources. She gets into the personal weeds with Wallace here, too, but in this case, I mostly admire it.

Some historical context before we dive in: Wallace had just released a memoir called *Close Encounters*, and he was about to go on the witness stand in a libel trial brought against Wallace and CBS News by General William Westmoreland. During the Vietnam War, Westmoreland was in charge of U.S. troops there. Wallace, in a special report by CBS, said that Westmoreland had misled the United States about how the war in Vietnam was going.

The interview begins with Walters and Wallace watching old videos of Wallace doing commercials for cigarettes and financial institutions.

It's a great start, and sets a comfortable tone. Wallace was about to be a witness in a big trial, and he knew that Walters was going to ask about it, but they start out watching something that made Wallace feel good. (Lightly edited for grammar.)

WALTERS: Look at that handsome fella. Thirty years ago is that?

WALLACE: Oh no, forty years at least.

WALTERS: Forty years ago.

WALLACE: At least forty years ago. Probably even longer ago than that. Chicago. I was the exclusive, if you will, announcer for the Household Finance Corporation out of Chicago. And that kind of thing put my children through private school and some of them into college. There was a whole succession of them back then. Forty years ago.

This is a nice, brief trip down memory lane for Wallace that reveals his evolution as a broadcaster. This is another "legacy" kind of beginning. Walters follows up with a flattering question about whether Wallace dyes his hair (answer: he doesn't) for a terrific softball beginning. She reminds him that people like him. That she's not out to get him. He's comfortable now. Sort of.

WALTERS: Well, let's look at something that you used to do, and you say that you no longer do now, or you no longer do now, and that is the ambush interview. We have an example.

This is a nice segue, and a signal not only that she has done her homework but also that the interview is going to get more pointed.

WALTERS: Now, you say you haven't done that kind of interview in what—five years?
WALLACE: Oh, at least. Yes.
WALTERS: At least.
WALLACE: Actually . . . Actually.
WALTERS: Where you just come up to somebody unsuspecting on the street [and] so on . . .
WALLACE: We, we, I confess to you, Barbara, that there's going to be one at the beginning of the new *60 Minutes* season which is that kind of . . .

WALTERS: Well, you had said that you'd stopped, and that you didn't think it was a good idea.

This is a great follow-up. He had publicly said that he no longer did ambush interviews, and now he's saying they're about to broadcast him doing one. She doesn't let that pass, but challenges him.

WALLACE: Unless the story warranted.
WALTERS: But, Mike, are you for or against ambush interviews? You say that on rare occasions, on some occasions it's okay.

At first she tries to pin him down with "Are you for or against," but then softens it a little by backing off and putting possible words in his mouth. This is effective, because she doesn't want it to be an interrogation. She just wants a straight answer. But then she gives him a little room away from that demand.

WALLACE: Well, I must say that if I . . . I am for and I am against. I know that sounds like a cop-out. But if it's interesting enough, if there is enough that is useful in an ambush interview that you're going to understand the character of the people involved . . . It's the old story, and I've used it so often, of heat for heat's sake or heat for light's sake. Heat for heat's sake, in my estimation—and I confess that years ago probably I used to do it—is useless. It's just . . . it's a pure audience getter. Heat for light's sake, in other words, making things a little bit difficult for the object of your scrutiny, in order to really try to help the audience understand, to me, is acceptable.

WALTERS: Have there been some people who we would be surprised, had we thought, you know, would be great interviews, who you did and then couldn't even use on the air because it just didn't, you know, was so . . .

Even though she doesn't quite get to the question (Wallace is great at anticipating what the question is going to be and starts answering before she's finished), it's a good one. There's no transition from the ambush interview segment, but that's okay. Her approach works well here because Wallace has interviewed hundreds of people. Some of them might be surprising in how dull they were. It's a good placement for this question as well, because she had just pressured him to commit to his journalistic practice, and this question can let him breathe a little.

WALTERS: I want to give you a quote from 1957. Before the women's movement, before many of the changes.

WALLACE: *(clears throat)* Oh, here we go . . .

Again, no transition, but it works. Walters is reaching into history. In the interview, Wallace changes position in his chair, as if to brace himself for something unpleasant. The throat clearing signals the same.

WALTERS: Here we go. And you said of your wife, complimenting her, that you felt that she was like a European woman, not like an American woman. You said, quote, "You have that certain deference to the male, which I confess, I like. I am not suggesting that a wife should walk one step behind her husband, but it helps. It's a 'by your leave, my lord' attitude that I like. European women have it, American women don't have it."

Clearly she's venturing into the topic of how Wallace views women. It's dicey, but fair game, in my view.

WALLACE: That's 1957?
WALTERS: Mm-hmm.
WALLACE: And you know something? Even I grow.
WALTERS: (laughs) Would you like to refute it? Or would you like to say, you know what, deep down I feel just the same way today?

This shows great reflexes on Walters's part. I doubt that she knew how he was going to answer, but she is quick to follow up and probe a little more deeply into how he views women.

WALLACE: No, I don't feel that. I don't feel that way anymore. I really don't feel that way. It depends what you're talking about. Professionally I don't. No. But for a companion? For a relationship? Yeah, they're different. You're different. Or at least I search for that difference.

WALTERS: Getting harder to find.

This is also a great follow-up, even though I don't really know what she means. What she is doing is signaling him to go even deeper. They're into some strange water here, and I love how she pushes him to explain himself further. The viewer has no idea whether she is agreeing with him. She's simply encouraging him to keep talking.

WALLACE: It is! It is getting harder to find. That's true. And I think women to a certain degree are mixed-up because of it.

This is a bombshell sexist statement by Wallace. He has just generalized and stereotyped women, essentially saying that because women are no longer deferential to men, they're mixed-up. Hoo boy. I think it's interesting that Walters chose not to challenge that statement. Now, it's possible that she did in the original interview and it was edited out. But ultimately I think it was the right call to not follow up in this case: Challenging further could have devolved into an argument that would have gone down a trail other than the one Walters wanted. So she chose to let it go. Viewers could see that Wallace's statement was sexist. They didn't need Walters to point it out.

WALTERS: Are you religious?

This is a curious question. I like it, but it seems abrupt—out of the blue. Asking questions like this without any transition can elicit raw and honest answers because they surprise the source. Still, it felt forced.

WALLACE: Certainly no formal religion. I'm Jewish, and was brought up Jewish. I occasionally go to temple. But not often. I like to believe that my religion is "Do unto others as you would have others do unto you." The only manifestation of my religion is that, to this day, when I go to sleep at night I recite a little Hebrew prayer.

WALTERS: What is it?

Great follow-up question. It's the question the audience would want to hear. It showed she was actively listening.

WALLACE: *(recites the* Shema Yisrael *in Hebrew)* Hear O Israel, the Lord our God, the Lord is One. I am just not comfortable going to sleep, for whatever reason, until I say that.

WALTERS: You have been accused of being—

She says this in a gentle, almost apologetic tone, but it is an excellent follow-up to what Wallace just said.

WALLACE: *(interrupts)* A self-hating Jew. Right?

WALTERS: Right.

WALLACE: Yeah. So?

WALTERS: So?

I love this little ping-pong exchange. The back-and-forth hap-pens very quickly. Wallace doesn't want to get into it, so he turns the tables on Walters. She doesn't let him take the reins of the interview, though, and quickly knocks it back to Wallace. Again, great reflexes on her part. Remember what I said about how someone will always control the interview? Wallace briefly tried to take control of it, but Walters wouldn't let him. Very adroit on her part, and a good try on his. It's further evidence of how an interview can be like a great fencing match.

WALLACE: *(scoffs)* Well, I mean, it's quite apparent that I'm not. Why would one hate oneself because one is a Jew? Those who have from time to time accused me, charged me, with that are upset because I have done evenhanded stories on Arab countries. And if you are a partisan of Israel, sometimes you misapprehend what a reporter does when he tells an evenhanded story.

This is a great answer, and it reveals a lot about why certain groups don't like good journalism. If groups want just their version of the truth portrayed, then it upsets them when someone comes along and tells multiple sides to the story. Certain groups want propaganda more than news. Wallace understands this, which is why he doesn't take the charge personally.

WALTERS: Does it bother you?

This is an attempt to reveal his humanity, his complexity. It's a great question.

WALLACE: No, no.
WALTERS: Why not? It would bother me if people thought I was a self-hating Jew, or a self-hating Catholic, or whatever it was.

This is a great attempt at connecting with Wallace at a human level. It's a "help me understand why" kind of question.

WALLACE: I know what I am, and I think that comes with the territory.

Walters then wades into even more personal questions. She asks Wallace about his childhood and his best memories of it. But anyone who has seen a Barbara Walters interview knows that the question is just setting up the next one. You can see it a mile away. Still, it's a fair question and it elicits a side of Mike Wallace that few ever saw.

WALTERS: What was the saddest part of your life?
WALLACE: When I lost my son.
WALTERS: Your son died in 1962. He was nineteen years old.
WALLACE: *(nods)*

WALTERS: And he died in a mountain-climbing accident.

WALLACE: Mm-hmm.

WALTERS: The horror was that you discovered his body.

WALLACE: Mm-hmm.

WALTERS: Do you ever get over that?

This is vintage Barbara Walters. Personally, it strikes me as sappy and invasive in the way she asked it, because it feels as if her objective is to make him cry. That said, it is revealing to talk to a person about loss. There are many ways to ask personal, humanity-revealing questions. Your best approach is to be authentic to your own personality or style. Since I am a parent, I would have asked it more along the lines of, "I think there is one thing in life that I could not overcome, and that would be the loss of one of my kids. How were you able to keep going?" It's a legitimate question (and an important one), but it comes from a shared humanity perspective, and feels less emotionally manipulative to me.

WALLACE: *(inhales, clearly struggling with his emotions)* Yeah. I mean, you never really get over it, sure, sure. There's always the tag, I mean there's always that, the memory of this poet and athlete and I mean, Peter was a just a . . . *(nods, tries to regain his composure)*

His nod to her was his signal that he was done talking for the moment. Paying attention to body language is part of good interviewing. She picks up on it.

WALTERS: It changed your life, didn't it?

She clearly already knew the answer to this question, which is why she asked it this way. It is making an assumption, but in this case it was a safe assumption. If you are in a similar situation but you don't already know the answer, you would ask it more as "Did it change you in some way?" Followed by "How so?"

WALLACE: Yeah, in the sense that up to that time I had moved from one thing to another and always said that I had to support the kids, and that's why I was doing some things. There was nothing shameful in them, but it gave a direction to my life. I was finally able to say to myself, "Hey, you sure don't have Peter to support anymore, so let's go and make a virtue of necessity."
WALTERS: What kind of a father were you?

This is a good follow-up to what Wallace just said. It's open-ended, an invitation for him to explain. Asking a black-and-white question here like, "Were you a good father?" would have limited their subsequent discussion about parenthood, and work-life balance. In the arc of the interview, Walters is portraying him as a human being with feelings, not just a hard-hitting journalist who took on the U.S. military brass.

WALTERS: I want to talk about the Westmoreland case. I don't want to ask you questions about the case itself, I want to ask you about one specific thing about you,

which is interesting, and which perhaps is painful
to you, perhaps not. Don Kowet, who coauthored
the *TVGuide* article that originally caused so many
questions about the whole Westmoreland case, has now
written a book, and in the book he says that George
Crile, the producer of the Westmoreland hour,[2] wrote
virtually all of your questions. True?

*This is a skillfully crafted question. She announces the territory
they're headed into, and makes it clear she's not going to ask him
questions that will be asked at the trial. She knows better than that.
She's entering into Wallace's methods. She tells him she knows it
might be uncomfortable, the way a nurse might say before giving a
shot, "This might sting a little."*

WALLACE: He wrote a lot of questions. And all
producers who work with me on investigative pieces
write a lot of questions. I read those questions, as I
remember it, and threw them back and said, "Too
many, too much, how 'bout this, how 'bout that," and
he gave me another set of questions. But as I'm sure
that you are—I don't know about you—but I'm sure
because I know how magazine broadcasts like this
work, the same thing is true with any producer on
20/20. You get questions from your producers, you

---

[2] *The Uncounted Enemy: A Vietnam Deception.* The CBS News special
report, hosted by Wallace.

get research from your producers, you work on that
research . . .
WALTERS: I'm talking about interviews. Research
is one thing. I'm talking about having questions
written.

*Good clarification on her part. She also cuts him off, keeping him
from rambling. Well done.*

WALLACE: Understood.
WALTERS: In the interview, the one-on-one
interview with General Westmoreland, we have
George Crile's original list of questions—the
first memo that he gave you. He wrote sixty-six
questions in his first memo.
He gave you sixty-six questions. Of those sixty-
six you used fifty-five of them. Forty-four of them
you read verbatim. Now, Don Kowet then says,
"Mike Wallace, America's most feared investigative
reporter, had really been a puppet on George Crile's
knee."

*She is putting him on notice that she is so well prepared that
he'd better not even think about dodging her questions. You can
feel the vise tightening. With the Kowet quote she is inviting him
to respond to a pretty serious charge of Wallace being used by his
producer.*

WALLACE: Do you think so?

WALTERS: What do you think, Mike?

This is a beautiful parry and riposte. Wallace is trying to take the heat off of himself and ask the questions. Walters will have none of it, and won't let him off the hook. How about my mixed metaphors there?

WALLACE: Of course not. Of the fifty-five questions—how many questions did I ask him?

WALTERS: He wrote sixty-six, you used fifty-five of them, forty-four of them verbatim.

She said this in an even-toned manner. Even though she's boring in on him, it doesn't feel aggressive or personal.

WALLACE: And how many questions did I ask in the, what was it, two hours?

WALTERS: Two-thirds of the questions were written by George Crile. You asked approximately eighty-nine, ninety questions, so two-thirds were written by him.

WALLACE: Fine.

WALTERS: Is that the way you usually work, with two-thirds of your questions written by someone else?

Boom. She's in the zone, asking a difficult question, but still not attacking or interrogating him. It's a fine line she's walking, but she's doing it well. It's all in her tone, which brings us back to your mom saying, "It's not what you said, it's the way you said it." A more aggressive approach would have been "Have you always been a puppet and done whatever your producers told you to do?" That would have set up a more adversarial vibe, and he would have gotten defensive, jeopardizing the quality of the rest of the interview.

> **WALLACE:** *(exhales)* Sometimes I work that way and sometimes I don't. In the case of this very complicated business with General Westmoreland— and I have no reason to doubt your figures, obviously—that is the way that I worked, because it was a difficult, complicated—and I was at that same time trying to do a good many pieces on *60 Minutes*, and so forth. And so I did not work the same way on the Westmoreland broadcast that I work on *60 Minutes.*
>
> **WALTERS:** So why did they need you, I mean if somebody else is writing . . .

Great question. She's not letting up. And by the way, whenever someone says "I have no reason to doubt your figures . . ." that is exactly what they're doing. It's an age-old tactic to try to sow some doubt into the accuracy of the accusation. It's like the politicians and celebrities who say they're leaving their posts so they can spend more time with their families. That is generally code for "I'm about to get indicted, or someone is about to charge me with groping them." And, as David Letterman so famously said when he left The Late Show

*to "spend more time with his family," and then returned to television a
few years later, "When people say they are leaving their jobs to spend
more time with their families, they should probably first check with
their families."*

WALLACE: Well, that's a perfectly good question. Not to
have something to do with the so-called star system . . .
WALTERS: Well, you don't want to be thought of as an
actor who comes in and reads questions.

*Again, she's hammering him here. Accusing him of merely being
an actor? That's big! Again, the careful word choice is evident. She
could have said, "So, what you're saying is that you're just an actor
who comes in and reads questions?" That would have gone more on
the interrogation side.*

WALLACE: And I, and I think that you're—
WALTERS: And you're not. And you're not.

*It's as if she realized that she may have crossed a line with him.
She immediately backs off.*

WALLACE: That's right. Okay. So what's the question?
WALTERS: Doesn't it—trouble you? To be called
a puppet? Doesn't it trouble you to have someone
say, "Mike Wallace did this very strong and very
important interview and almost all of it was written
by somebody else"?

This is similar to the question about whether it bothers him when others call him a self-hating Jew. It's a good way to get him to explain how he thinks and feels about the controversy he is involved in.

> **WALLACE:** Well, the way that you characterize it, Barbara—
> **WALTERS:** It's the way it was characterized. I'm quoting Don Kowet—

She's still backing off here, making it clear that she's not attacking him, but simply quoting a magazine article that attacked him. It's a good way to create some separation.

> **WALLACE:** Well, you're quoting Don Kowet. We are in a collaborative medium. And because we're putting on twenty-five pieces a year, each one of us, it should be apparent that we cannot do all of the investigation by ourselves. And particularly if I do a lot of investigative pieces, it becomes apparent that I'm not gonna be able to spend as much time on each piece as ideally I should.

Once Wallace explains himself and gives a mea culpa, that is enough for Walters, and so she moves on to quoting from his book. Just like that, we're back to Mike Wallace the human being, instead of Mike Wallace the journalist who is being sued for libel.

WALTERS: Are you comfortable with yourself now? Are you at peace with yourself?

I like this question because Wallace's journalism career has been one that disrupts and causes havoc in others. She's asking him a big-picture question, a forward-spin question, now that they've talked about a lot of particulars.

WALLACE: By and large, I'm heading into a period that's of a certain tension. The Westmoreland trial, that's going to be difficult. And trying to find myself living really basically alone for the first time in a long time, that doesn't make for serenity.

WALTERS: What's the toughest question I could have asked you that perhaps I didn't?

That's her signal for "The interview is over now. Let's get back to being buddies." It's a nice return to rapport.

WALLACE: I think you've done pretty well. The Westmoreland thing, and not writing your own questions, that's the one that reached me. Because you know, Barbara, that I'm nobody's puppet. But I mean that's a kind of a "gotcha" and that probably will be a difficult question to answer on the stand, too.

WALTERS: That was my "gotcha" question.

WALLACE: *(nods)*

WALTERS: But then you can't interview Mike Wallace without kind of doing a Mike Wallace interview, right? You wouldn't have respected me if I didn't have one "gotcha" question.

She's giving him respect. She's acknowledging that she learned her tactics from him—the best in the business. It's a nice coda to a tough interview.

WALLACE: I couldn't agree more.

Me too.

CHAPTER 8

Before and After the Interview Ends

How to Wrap It Up Well and How to Ensure Accuracy

GOOD ATHLETES ARE ALWAYS AWARE of how much time is left in the game. Especially with just a few minutes left, you'll see a basketball player receive an inbound pass at one end of the court and look up at the clock as he makes his way toward the other end. He or she is calculating what needs to be accomplished in a very specific number of minutes or seconds. Knowing where they are in relation to time has a direct impact on what they do next.

If a hockey team is behind in the game by a goal or two, it is common practice for the coach to pull the goaltender. That means the goalie comes to the bench and another skater gets into the action so that the team can create one last push until the game is over. Coaches do this only in the last couple of minutes of the game, though.

Teams in both of those sports make an extra effort once they realize the game is coming to an end.

And, you guessed it: It's the same with interviews.

Interviews have a time limit (or at least they should!), so it is your job to know where the trajectory of your conversation is in relation to the time that is left.

We have all watched sporting events where it seemed that something great was about to occur, but the players just ran out of time. It's frustrating for everyone.

In other words, you have to think about how you are going to end things.

With each interview you want to give your source a chance for a final thought, and you want to leave a door open for future contact. You want to clarify points where you're confused and you want to make sure you heard the source correctly. You might even want time to do some negotiating about what you can use and what you can't. You have to factor this into the time you have left.

End Every Interview This Way

If the interview's purpose is mostly to just get information, such as for a news story, I give the source a bit of a heads-up and say, "I have just two more questions." Then the source knows that my questioning does, in fact, have an end point. When I'm done I say something along the lines of "Thank you so much for taking the time!" Those interviews have a more defined "The End" quality to them.

But even in situations with an obvious conclusion, there is something you can do to leave the door open for further discussion and better information. When I'm done with one of these straightforward interviews, I will say something like "Just let me be sure of a few things before I go." Then I quickly try to ask the same four questions. If you do the same, you will be surprised at the responses you'll get.

1) "Can you give me the exact spelling of your name?" One source's name was, I thought, Amy. That is what it sounded like when she said it. I was interviewing her in the aftermath of her husband being killed in a car accident. But when I asked her to spell it (regardless of how obvious it sounded), she nearly jumped out of her chair in gratitude. It sounds like Amy, but it is spelled Ami. After I asked for the spelling, she wanted to talk further with me because she trusted me.

It may not seem like that big of a deal to you, but let me elaborate on this whole spelling-of-name thing.

When you see your name misspelled in a story, or anywhere else, it makes you mad. You think, "Does this person not care enough to know how I spell my name?" My wife's name is Marcia. It's pronounced "Mar-sha." Several close friends, and even a couple of relatives, continue to spell it "Marsha." How hard is it to notice how she signs her name? And could you all please stop doing the "Marcia, Marcia, Marcia" gag from *The*

Brady Bunch? It was funny the first ten thousand times. Actually, it wasn't even funny then.

Most people have something written about them maybe once or twice in their lives. Your article may well be that one piece, and, ugh, there it is: Their name is misspelled. Sure, you can post a correction, but if the story is in print, then you're out of luck.

In the journalism classes I teach, I give students a zero for the entire story they've written if they misspell a name—it can be the source's name, or the name of a building or company or city. When I get to a misspelled name I draw a circle around it and write in the margin, "I stopped reading here." It usually only happens once per student. (The exception was one particular student who, upon receiving his third zero in one month, tore up his story into little pieces like it was the losing ticket at the racetrack, and then stormed out of the classroom shouting insults at me about my ridiculous rules. The irony is that he eventually became an excellent sportswriter.)

Students get upset because they put all of this effort into reporting and writing a story, but a misspelled name stops it in its tracks. "Think about it from your source's perspective," I tell the offending (and offended!) students. "That source put all of this time and generosity into letting you talk to them, and you pee all over it by not even going to the trouble of spelling their names right? How do you think they feel about how careful you were about the rest of the story?"

The people in the class who have had their names misspelled by the news media don't complain about my policy.

They get it. Jonathan is sometimes Johnathan. Steven is sometimes Stephen. Carl is sometimes Karl. Smith is sometimes Smythe. Jones is sometimes Jonz. Brittany is sometimes Britney. Tom is sometimes Thom. Beckum is sometimes Bekham. Nelson is sometimes Nelsen. Marsha is sometimes Marcia.

It's the easiest question you'll ask in the interview. And for some people, it may be the most significant. If the person's name is complicated and you spell it correctly, you have a source forever.

2) "Is there anything I should have asked you that I didn't ask?" This one can create an angle that you didn't even know existed. Your source may have been ready to talk about a development, for example, but if it didn't come up in your conversation, this is their chance. Think about being in a doctor's office, and the doctor says at the end of your physical, "Is there anything else going on that we didn't address?" You'll be surprised at how many times a patient will be having an inner dialogue, thinking, "I wonder if I should bring up this other issue that we haven't talked about yet. Should I do it? She seems in a hurry. Maybe I shouldn't." And then the doctor asks that question and you're finally addressing what might be the most pressing issue of all.

You never know whether what a source says in response will be worthwhile. Most people won't say, "I'll bet you're here to talk about . . ." and then give you their juiciest sound bite. Most aren't that bold or outraged. But many will have something else to say, yet they won't say it because you didn't ask them. Give them the chance.

Always ask this question.

3) "Who else should I talk to?" This is crucial, because this potentially will reveal who has the best knowledge on your topic. There is always someone who knows more, someone behind the scenes, someone who isn't quoted or sought out very often. Those people are gold mines. But you'll never hear about them unless you ask.

4) "May I contact you later once I write this in case I need some more information or clarification?" Leaving the door open with your source will pay off in many ways. If the interview has gone well, then your source has some skin in the game and wants the story to turn out well. He or she won't mind if you call or write to get the story more precise. It will also give your source time to think about what else he or she thinks you should know, and is more likely to have even more to say at some point.

Or End with a Forward Spin

If the interview has a broader purpose than trying to get an eyewitness account or to extract some specific information, you can think about the ending differently. You still have to be aware of the time, but you don't have to be headed toward a period at the end of a sentence. Sometimes it's appropriate to just send the conversation into something deep and un-resolved.

Near the end of my interviews with writers, I usually try

to get them thinking outward, toward lessons they've learned about the craft, and advice they have for people getting started. This allows them a chance to think beyond what they have written, address the art of it, summarize their knowledge, and inspire those in the audience. I try to get them thinking about the big picture.

This approach is helpful in other situations as well. Social workers aren't just interested in facts (although those are important); they're also looking at the mental, emotional, and physical environment of the client. Human resources professionals aren't just looking for the candidate to tell them about how they overcame a professional hurdle, they're looking for whether that person will fit in with the organization's culture. When my doctor talks to me about my migraines, he isn't just looking for the best medicine to take the pain away. He also asks questions about the root of the issue. That's a bigger picture.

From a writer's perspective, that bigger picture is also more interesting: It reveals a shared humanity. It was instructive, for instance, to hear the great crime writer Joseph Wambaugh say, toward the end of my interview with him, that his writing gets harder with each book, not easier. For young writers who struggle with their own enthusiasm levels, this was both encouraging ("I'm not alone in my dread and self-doubt!") and discouraging ("You mean it's going to be this difficult forever?"). But it was a great way to look ahead. The satirist Christopher Buckley told me that if he had known how difficult writing was, he might have chosen a different vocation.

Anne Lamott said that she still has trouble with discipline, and she likened her writing self to a dog with a chew toy, chasing it over to one side of the room, throwing it in the air, and chasing it to the other side of the room. But ultimately, she said, it's like each of us has a hundred dollars of creativity to spend each day. How will we spend that hundred dollars? If we have just two hours available to write today, we could spend some of that time on the internet—maybe fifteen dollars' worth. Then we could focus on getting our work done—wisely spending the remaining sixty-five dollars. Then we might take a rudimentary math class to find out why it didn't add up to a hundred. Whatever amount of time you have in a day, know that you can use some of it in a creative endeavor. You can't put it in the bank for tomorrow. You get a hundred dollars today.

It was good advice from someone who has years of experience to draw from.

You get those kinds of responses when you ask broader conceptual questions, and they are usually best addressed toward the end of the interview, after trust and rapport have been established. When I asked Jeannette Walls, author of *The Glass Castle,* whether she had forgiven her parents for the way they raised her, I got a much more profound response than I would have had I asked it at the beginning.

Having sources address these topics at the end of an interview is another example of how conducting an interview is similar to writing a story. In stories, sometimes instead of resolving the conflicts or tying up the loose ends, we just send readers in a direction they can ponder. We give what is called a "forward spin" to the stories so that the stories resonate for a long time after the reading is finished. Readers keep thinking about where the characters are headed, well after the book has concluded. If you have seen the movie *Three Billboards Outside Ebbing, Missouri,* you know what I'm talking about.

With news stories, that's why you often see them end with a quote from one of the key sources. It provides a punctuation mark other than a simple period. When I ended a story about a school shooting with a quote from a girl who had been at the school, and who had just come out of trauma counseling—"I grew up too fast today"—I wanted to leave the reader with a feeling that would linger. An ending like this engages the reader at a deeper level than if I were to just finish a story with a concluding fact like "The teenager accused of the shooting is in custody." One ends with a reverb. The other with a thud.

Or when I concluded my story about Merita Shabiu in Kosovo with a quote from her father as to whether he thought Merita's killer should be executed for his crime—when he said that one weeping mother was enough, I hoped readers would then have to think about their own response to that question. That would lodge the story more deeply in the readers' psyche and, I hoped, would make them think about the complexity of the issue.

Some interviews are similar to stories that end this way. They can end with your subject challenged, energized, and engaged. After an interview with a social worker, therapist, nurse, or human resources person, someone might leave with a big picture—maybe even a solution to a problem.

In my experience, interviews that have more open-ended conclusions leave the door open for further discussion down the road. For my interviews with writers, I like to leave them (and the audience) with an impression more than a resolution.

But When Is the Interview Actually Done?

Defining the end of an interview creates an interesting ethical conundrum. I mentioned this earlier, but it needs more explanation. When you have turned off your recording device, closed your notebook, stood up, and thanked the source for his or her time, and then the source tells you something useful, can you use that information?

There are different schools of thought here. Some people would say that there is a tacit agreement that the interview is over when you stand up and don't have a notebook or recorder in your hand anymore. The source assumes that what he tells you from that point on is "off the record" and is not usable.[1] Is that a fair assumption for your source to make? Some reporters would say yes. The interview is over, they would say. There is an expectation that you're just two people yakking, and the source can let his guard down.

That's not how I see it. Just because you put the tools away doesn't mean you stopped being a reporter. If the source tells

---

[1] I'll get into terms like "off the record," "background," and "not for attribution" in Chapter 10.

you something useful in the doorway of his office or as he walks you to the elevator, it is still part of the interview, in my opinion. That's why I try to never actually put my notebook away. I use those small reporter's notebooks that you can hold in one hand while you write with the other. It's in my hand all the way to my car, exactly for situations like this. Then, as soon as the person is gone, I re-create what he said and note at the top of the page "On way to elevator" or "Walking to car." You must do this, too. Write it down immediately and tell when, how, and where it was said.

I once had a politician tell me things as he walked me out of his office, and then even call my phone before I was out of the parking lot, to tell me more stuff he was upset about. Then he said he was surprised when he saw it in my story. He thought it was just two guys talking. Nope. It was a politician talking to a reporter. The whole time.

Some people think it's unethical to use information revealed after the formal interview was over. I don't. If the source didn't want it in the story, he shouldn't have told you. To paraphrase *Green Eggs and Ham,* not in the room, not in the hall, not in the parking lot, not in the stall. You can use it, Sam-I-am.

Ensuring Accuracy

In Chapter 9 I'll address the issue of note-taking and recording. For now, though, I want to explain what to do with those notes and recordings when you write your stories.

After the interview ends and you have written a draft of your story, report, book chapter, or whatever you're doing with the information you gathered, you have a decision to make about the quotes you used. If you did not record the interview, you can: A) trust your note-taking and assume you have an accurate representation of what your sources said; B) call your sources and read the quotes back to them and simply ask, "Did I quote you accurately?"; or C) send your sources the quotes you plan to use and ask if they are accurate.

Calling the source back to clarify and verify quotes is an honorable practice, in my opinion. I don't do it all of the time, but on deeper, more complicated stories I try to. I consider it part of the interview process. As you can imagine, though, it comes with risk. The upside is that if you got something wrong, your source can tell you before it is posted, published, or broadcast. You don't want to put something out there that is incorrect or out of context. I have called many sources over the years just to say, "I'd like to read the quotes I have from you just to make sure they're accurate. This is not an invitation to change something to sound better." Then I read the quotes and say, "Have I quoted you accurately?" Sometimes it's awkward because your source might not like what he or she said. But most of the time the source will acknowledge that yes, you got it right. The downside is that occasionally the source will say, "No, that's not what I said at all," and try to deny it. At that point you have to decide whether your notes are trustworthy and the person is just trying to save face, or whether you really might have misunderstood something.

In the Tony Campolo story I mentioned, I did a lengthy phone interview with the head of a very prominent and highly regarded religious organization that had decided to pressure Campolo off of the speakers' list for that major convention in Washington. The religious leader was reluctant to pull his support of Campolo, he told me. He and Campolo were friends, and he secretly shared many of Campolo's provocative and political viewpoints. But the entirety of the conference was at stake—it was on the verge of being canceled—and major funding for his own organization was also about to dry up if he didn't side with the "Cancel Campolo" camp. He felt trapped financially and ethically, and his conversation with me reflected that conflicted position.

When I had written a draft of the story and knew which of his quotes I planned to use, I called him and asked if I could read his quotes to him for the sake of accuracy. He sounded grateful for the call, and I began to read. I didn't read the story to him—I didn't want him to infer that he had veto power over the conclusions I was making—I read only his quotes.

The whole time I read to him I heard him moaning. I thought at first that he was getting sick or was trying to pass a kidney stone or something, but eventually I realized that they were moans of regret. When I read the line where he criticized another religious organization, saying, "They believe in a plastic Jesus that jumps off the dashboard and into your heart," it sounded like he had an abscessed tooth.

"I just wanted to check to see if I have quoted you accurately," I said. To his credit, he didn't deny it.

"I said those things, and I meant them," he said, still moaning. I envisioned him talking to me while he pondered jumping off of a skyscraper. "But this is going to cost me. My constituents are going to hate this. So are the people who run these other ministries. My job might be on the line." There was a long pause. He was looking down at the traffic below, no doubt, toes over the edge. Remember what I said about being okay with silence? I chose to remain quiet. Finally, he said, "What would it take for you to not use those quotes?"

I found it gratifying to know that religious leaders were open to cutting deals.

"The only scenario I can think of where I would not use these quotes is if you were to give me something better," I said.

More silence. Vertigo was setting in.

"Can I call you back in a couple of hours? I need to gather my thoughts."

I didn't promise not to use the quotes. I promised that I would listen to what else he could come up with.

When he called back, I was so glad I hadn't played tough guy and said, "Sorry, dude. A quote is a quote. You said it and it's going into the story." He really did give me something far better. He went into the financial and political pressure these ministry groups were under to satisfy their constituents, regardless of how the groups themselves wanted to act. The new quotes were less inflammatory, less juicy, but much deeper and more complex. Instead of the "heat for heat's sake" quotes I had originally, I got "heat for light's sake" quotes. Totally worth it. The story was more profound, and I had a source and friend for life.

Remember, I could have used those original quotes. He verified that he said them. But I got something better by negotiating.

Some people will send sources their quotes through texts or emails. It's a defensible way to verify quotes, but I have seen a lot of sources see this as license to change, modify, even cross out sections of the quotes so that the source sounds "better." You must make it clear that you're asking simply "yes" or "no"—"Is this what you said?" Sources may feel the need to change their quotes, but it's ultimately up to you as to whether you use those changes. It's your story, not theirs. My observation is that when someone returns his or her "cleaned-up" quotes, the source has often taken all of the humanity out of the quote and now it sounds like you talked to a robot. You want the comments to sound like that person. I'll say more about cleaning up quotes later. But because of how dicey this can get, I prefer to verify quotes over the phone. It's too easy for a source to tinker with his or her quote via email. Even when you tell the person that the purpose of your sending those quotes is to ensure accuracy, a source will often take the note as an opportunity to improve how they come across. That makes it awkward for you.

If you call the person, though, and say you want to read the quotes, and the person disputes what you have, you can deal with it, negotiate, even play back the recording, right there. Typically, I will say something like "Hi, this is Dean Nelson from [name the organization I'm writing for]. I spoke with you a week ago for the story I am writing, and I am calling so that I can read you the quotes I plan to use. I just want to verify that I am quoting you accurately. Do you have a moment for me to read them to you? I want to make sure I got it right."

Writers are very sensitive (or they should be!) when a source claims he or she was misquoted. This is why recording the interview is usually a good idea, and so is developing a good note-taking system. I address both of those issues in the next chapter.

Sometimes we really do get the quote wrong. We heard it wrong, wrote it down wrong, remembered wrong. Rarely, in my observation, is it done intentionally. Those who think that journalists are enemies of the people will disagree, of course, and claim that we misquote and fabricate quotes and facts all the time. There have been instances where writers who work for the more sensational tabloids have admitted to fabrication and distortion, and it occasionally happens with the more serious media (thanks, Jayson Blair, Patricia Smith, Stephen Glass, *Rolling Stone,* Janet Cooke, Jack Kelley, and the rest of you), but most of us who have worked in journalism for a long time consider accuracy to be sacred. And especially sacred is the accuracy of quotes.

I'm going to go out on a limb, here, and some people will disagree with me. I'm okay with that. In fairness, I haven't done a scientific study, but based on what I and many of my colleagues have experienced in several decades of journalism, I'm willing to bet that when someone claims he or she has been misquoted, what the person is *really* saying is, "Damn. I wish I hadn't said that in the interview. How can I deflect the damage off of me? Of course! Blame the reporter! Say I was misquoted!"

As I said, this is not always the case. But there is a time-honored tradition of shooting the messenger. It goes back at least to ancient sagas, where, according to legend, if the king didn't like the news about the battle, he would kill the person delivering the news. In our society we rarely kill the messenger (although it does happen with more frequency these days); more likely, we try to discredit and/or sue the messenger (killing their credibility or career). When a source sees a quote in the story, it looks different from how it felt when he or she said it, they regret saying it, and they go on the attack. Shift the blame.

We had an administrator at my university try this tactic when he said something dumb about diversity on our campus, and the student reporter used it in a story. The administrator blew a gasket, went on a tirade about how unethical that student was for "making up quotes," and then banned anyone in his office from speaking to that reporter.

I asked the student how he was sure the quotes were accurate and used in context, and he said that he had recorded the interview. He played the interview for me, and, sure enough, the administrator said it. The comments sounded just as dumb on the tape as they did in the story.[2] I mentioned this the next time I saw the administrator. At first he denied it, but I reiterated that

---

[2] More on the benefits of recording an interview in Chapter 9, but this is certainly an important one!

I had heard the recording. He went silent, but still maintained the ban on that particular reporter. Ain't it funny when you get caught and you can't wriggle out of it? Like a fox in a trap, some people would rather gnaw off their own leg before admitting that they were caught in their own accurate quote.

My favorite examples are when athletes Charles Barkley and David Wells both claimed they were misquoted. When it was pointed out to them that reporters had lifted sentences directly out of the athletes' autobiographies (where, you know, the guys allegedly wrote what they wanted to say. That's kinda what the "auto" part in the word "autobiography" implies), both men used the ingenious approach of claiming they had misquoted themselves. Brilliant! How do you argue with that kind of intellect? And what messenger do you shoot?

I do think there is often a legitimate complaint from sources who say interviewers take quotes out of context. Years ago, *60 Minutes* was caught splicing an answer from a utility executive into a completely different question from what he was asked. That's wrong; it's fraudulent and it's lying. Don't do it.

Compress, but Don't Distort

Sometimes we take things out of context inadvertently, and we should be called out for it when we do. I'll tell you how this can happen.

It is an acceptable practice in journalism to write an entire page of quotes in a notebook during an interview, and then compress the idea from one sentence in one part of your notes into a sentence from another part of your notes, so that it reads as one sentence—even though it's part of one sentence that skipped a bunch of other sentences, and then it's combined with a different sentence on the same thought and now looks like one unified sentence. It's a necessity for space and, in my opinion, an acceptable practice.

For instance, when I interviewed Madame Brigitte, the voodoo priestess in Haiti, I asked her about how one learns to become a priest. She said, "It is something passed down from generation to generation. But there are also apprentices who can learn this whose families were not priests." Then we talked about her community, the aftermath of the 2010 earthquake, her family, and other topics for at least thirty minutes and toured the grounds of her temple. I asked her how difficult it would be for me to become an apprentice of hers. She said, "You could be an apprentice. Come to our ceremony in October and I will teach you."

Remember, those statements were made at least thirty minutes apart, with a lot of talking in between. Even so, I think it's perfectly acceptable for the quote to read like this: "It is something passed down from generation to generation," said Madame Brigitte. "But there are also apprentices who can learn this whose families were not priests. You could be an apprentice. Come to our ceremony in October and I will teach you."

See how I mashed those statements into one unified quote? I didn't change the context or meaning. I compressed the sentences and grouped similar items together.

If you're uncomfortable with compressing quotes this way, an alternative would be to have the original quote like this:

"It is something passed down from generation to genera-tion," said Madame Brigitte. "But there are also apprentices who can learn this whose families were not priests." Then you could add narrative that shows time elapse—such as, "We walked through the temple grounds, looking at symbols, icons, and the pole where the spirit ascends from the earth." Then you could add the rest of the quote: "You could be an apprentice," she said later. "Come to our ceremony in October and I will teach you."

The goal is an accurate representation of both the content of her statement and her intention. These abridgements seem to satisfy both criteria and so, in my opinion, are accurate rep-resentations of what she said.

Confirmation vs. Approval

Steve Weinberg,[3] a legendary investigative reporter, author, and former head of Investigative Reporters and Editors (IRE), sends quotes and facts to his sources, but not for their "ap-proval." He does it to ensure accuracy. If someone wants to change a quote, Weinberg says he makes it clear that he is checking only for accuracy. If a source wants to change an interpretation or tone or conclusion, Weinberg says he will

---

[3] Not to be confused with the physicist Steven Weinberg, whom I mentioned earlier.

listen, but won't guarantee that he will make those changes. Just the changes that improve clarity and accuracy.

If a source says that something is misquoted or taken out of context, Weinberg goes back to his notes or recording and checks. If the source is right, Weinberg changes the quote.

"We regularly miscommunicate with our spouse, our children, our parents," he wrote.

So why should we expect perfect communication with a source we barely know?

If the context needs changing, I change it. If the source is acting in a self-serving way that impedes rather than serves truth, I change nothing. In any case, discussion before publication is preferable to publishing an out-of-context remark. It is also preferable to hearing from an angry source after publication, a source who had no opportunity to review the manuscript and who is now threatening a lawsuit. Never has a source who had an opportunity to review the manuscript threatened to sue me after publication. Furthermore, not once have I made a change against my better judgment.[4]

If the source just wants to sound better, Weinberg doesn't change anything. The point is to have the most accurate story possible.

---

[4] Steve Weinberg, *The Reporter's Handbook*, 3rd edition (New York: St. Martin's Press, 1996), 495.

Another benefit to prepublication review is that sources trust you more, Weinberg said. "Next time I go to those sources, their doors are likely to be open. Furthermore, they will tell future sources about my desire for accuracy, opening additional doors."[5] One uncooperative source was so impressed by Weinberg's commitment to accuracy that the source, who previously demanded that most of his remarks be "off the record," granted a full interview—for attribution.

Yet another benefit of sending sources comments they made is that it will jog the memories of sources as they are reading their comments, and they might give you even more information.

"One such source wrote me an eight-page, single-spaced letter filled with gems while reading a manuscript chapter on Armand Hammer," Weinberg wrote. "I had interviewed him multiple times; he has been a fount of information. But reading the manuscript opened a section of his memory that had been closed until that point."[6]

THE BEST WAY TO ENSURE that you haven't changed the meaning or made a person look bad or good, or let your own bias seep in, is to do what Weinberg suggests. When possible, let the sources see how you have quoted them.

I do an exercise with my journalism students where I have them interview one another for five minutes, then read

---

[5] Weinberg, 496.
[6] Weinberg, 496.

out loud to the class the most significant quotes from the interview. At least once in every class the person who is being quoted will say, "That isn't what I said at all."

Quoting someone accurately is one of the core values of any interviewer. But there's another consideration beyond just your commitment to accuracy. If you misquote someone or take something out of context, you not only have a story that is not true, but also have damaged your reputation. As writers, our only commodity is our credibility. When that is damaged or lost, you will have difficulty getting it back.

And the damage isn't just to you. Sources and the rest of the public have memories like elephants. If they got burned by a writer, they simply won't trust other writers who come to them. Your carelessness has made life for the next generation of writers much more difficult.

Don't poison the well.

CHAPTER 9
Note-Taking and Recording

You Probably Won't Get Sued If You Do This Properly

I MENTIONED PREVIOUSLY THE ADVANTAGES and disadvantages of note-taking and recording, but it bears going into more depth. Depending on the seriousness of the topic you're writing about, you may want to record your interviews. If it is a famous person, a politician, a public figure, or a public official, definitely record it. Lawyers? For sure. You don't want someone (especially someone with easy access to the court system) reading your story and saying, "I never said that," or "You took that out of context." A recording solves that dilemma.

You may think you're the next Truman Capote (who famously claimed he didn't need to take notes because he had a photographic memory), but you're not (and, as it became clear decades later, neither was he!). You may have a good memory, but believe me, it's not that good. If you have some means—

written or recorded, or better yet, both—you will have a more accurate portrayal of what the person said. You will also be able to defend yourself better if someone claims you got the quote wrong, or that you made it up.

Whomever you are interviewing, you simply must have a record of what the person said.

Having some kind of proof would have simplified Janet Malcolm's life when she interviewed Jeffrey Masson and published a lengthy profile of him in the *New Yorker* in 1983 and a book about him called *In the Freud Archives* in 1984. Masson had been a project director of the Freud Archives, and Malcolm's portrayal of him was less than flattering. In the more than forty-five-thousand-word story Malcolm wrote in the *New Yorker,* Masson felt that five quotes attributed to him were libelous, and he sued her. He claimed in court that he never said those particular things, and that they damaged his reputation.

The simplest response for Malcolm would have been "Of course you said those things—here is the recording of your saying them." Trouble is, there was no such recording. And there was no notebook with those quotes, either. That's a red flag so big it could cover Yankee Stadium. She recorded most of her interviews with Masson, *and* took notes, but when it came to proving that those specific quotes existed, she couldn't do it.

What's the word I'm looking for when you interview a public figure, quote him saying provocative things that could damage his reputation, and then can't prove he said them? Oh yeah: risky. The dispute went on for ten years and cost both parties millions of dollars in legal fees. In the end, a federal district court ruled that, while some of the quotes might have been false, they didn't rise to the definition of libel. When it involves public figures (which Masson clearly was) in a libel case, plaintiffs have to prove that the journalist knew the information published was false, or at least showed a reckless disregard for the truth. While Malcolm couldn't prove that Masson actually said what she quoted him as saying, the court said that Masson didn't prove that she published those quotes with the knowledge that they were false. She might have been lazy or sloppy in her note-taking, but she didn't show a reckless disregard for the truth, according to the court.

WHAT IS LIBEL?

"Libel" is a written statement that contains false information that damages a person's reputation. It is often used interchangeably with the word "slander," but slander is the spoken version of a false statement that damages a person's reputation. Both libel and slander fall under the broader term "defamation." It's not illegal to write something about someone that damages that person. It can be illegal, though, to write something false about someone that damages that person.

When a person sues someone for libel, the burden of proof is on the person filing the lawsuit. That person is called the plaintiff. The person she is suing (hopefully not you) is the defendant. In most cases the plaintiff must prove that the statement was published, was false, and did damage, and that the person who wrote it was negligent in the manner in which he sought the truth. Having to prove all of those elements makes it very difficult to win a libel case, which is how the courts designed it. They don't want just anyone who got his feelings hurt to sue people and tie up the courts—to say nothing of taxpayers' time and money—out of revenge.

It's even harder to prove libel if you are a public figure or a public official. You still have to prove that something was published, was false, and did damage, but you also have to prove that the person who wrote it *knew* it was false, or at least showed reckless disregard for the truth. That means you have to be able to prove what the writer was thinking. Check out the significance of the U.S. Supreme Court case *New York Times Co. v. Sullivan*. It's a brilliant ruling, in my opinion.

What does the writer have to prove when someone sues him for libel? Since the burden of proof is on the plaintiff, not the defendant, if the writer can show that he or she had reason to believe that the information published was true and that he pursued the truth in a manner that is generally accepted by nonfiction writers, he should be on solid legal ground. Sounds simple, but it's amazing how dumb a prosecutor can make a writer feel during a trial. Best advice? Verify your information and record your interviews.

One additional consideration about libel: The Iowa Libel Research Project went back through years of libel suits against the news media, and researchers asked plaintiffs for more information about why they sued. Many of them said they weren't going to sue at first, but when they contacted the news organizations and were treated rudely, then they wanted revenge. News organizations could have saved themselves a lot of money and effort had they responded to the initial complaint by listening and being civil. They don't have to back down (when they are correct), but a little shared humanity goes a long way.

Remember, this took ten years out of everyone's lives. *Ten years!*

As the adviser to our university's news media, I have had many conversations with faculty colleagues, administrators, and others about libel. If they don't like how they were treated in a story written by the students, some of them have told me they were suing the paper (and me) for libel. I always go over the story with them to see where it was inaccurate. We occasionally find a factual inaccuracy, but we always find something they didn't like. Sorry, pal. Just because you didn't like it doesn't make it illegal. If the student's notes or recording verify what the person said, and the quotes were put in context, you aren't going to win that suit.

I got a call from the provost of our university, who said, "Should I be concerned that I just gave an interview to one of your reporters about a new academic policy and she never took one note?"[1]

"Did she record it?" I asked.

"Not that I know of. And I think I'm supposed to know it if I'm being recorded, if I understand the law correctly."

You can see where this conversation was going. Basically he was warning me that there had better not be a provocative story that misquoted him on this new policy.

I chatted with the student journalist.

"So I hear you just did an interview with our provost and didn't record it or take any notes?"

"That's right," she said. "I have a really good memory. When I write the story I'll remember what he told me."

---

[1] It's always one of "my" reporters if the student has screwed up. It's one of the university's reporters if she wins a national award.

May I just go on the record and say that this is a terrible idea?

"Type up your notes now as you remember them and send them to him," I said. "Just to make sure."

She did, and the provost had all sorts of corrections for our young Mensa member. Lesson learned.

LET ME REPEAT MYSELF. RECORDING interviews, or at least taking good notes, will save you a lot of trouble. If you have a recording of what the person said, and the person sues you for saying something he felt was damaging and false, then the recording will be a good defense for you. If you didn't record it, but you took good notes, then that's going to help you, too. In the previous sentence, I said "good notes." By that I mean they need to be legible so that a jury would be able to see the same words on there that you used when you wrote your story. Good notes will help you convince a jury (in the event that you need to) that you weren't being negligent or sloppy, or making stuff up.

A federal appointment during the Reagan presidency was delayed in part because of a column written by a reporter, when he quoted Kenneth Adelman characterizing arms control talks as a "sham." But when the reporter, Ken Auletta (remember him from the "tree" question he asked Barbara Walters?), produced his notes, it showed that he drew a line through the word "shame" and wrote "sham" next to it. Auletta insisted that the word Adelman used was "sham."

But you can see that this caused some confusion.

Not only did Adelman deny saying "sham," but he also said he never gave an interview to Auletta. On that second point at least, Auletta was covered: His phone record showed the two had talked. But not having clear notes put him in a lot of hot water that, frankly, he didn't need to be in.

Politicians and public figures aren't the only people who need special record keeping in interviews. Other kinds of sources worth recording are people who struggle with the language, people who use the language in a very colorful way, and children. The reason you want to record them is so that you can accurately capture how they construct their sentences and what kind of expressions they use. You don't have to use all of it, of course, but it gives you a feel for how they said things.

The Etiquette of Recording

Always ask permission to record the interview before turning on the recorder. Yes, *always*. Even if the law in your state doesn't require it, the best policy is always mutual knowledge and consent. It's unethical and possibly illegal to record someone without their permission. I usually pull out the recorder and make sure its presence is acknowledged by the person I'm interviewing. If the source says no to the use of a recording device, I usually give them a chance to reconsider, by saying something along the lines of "Really? This is actually the best way to protect both of us. It's more dependable than my notes. Have you seen my handwriting?" Usually when a source doesn't allow a recording device, she doesn't want you taking notes at all (more on "off the record" interviews in the next chapter).

When I am recording an interview I put the device at an angle where I can see the digital time display. That way, when I am also taking notes (did I mention that you *must* do both?), and someone says something that I know is significant, I can look at the display and write the time in the margin next to my notes. Then I can go right to that quote later and won't have to hunt for it. Here are some other things to consider when recording an interview:

- Always have the device fully charged. If you can keep it plugged in, that's great. If it takes separate batteries, put new batteries in the device before each interview, regardless of how little they have been used in the past. I have a container full of partially used batteries that I can use for less important purposes. I would create less of a carbon footprint if I used rechargeable batteries, but I almost never remember this.

- Set it off to the side so that it's not in the sight line of the source. It can be a little distracting to be reminded that *everything* said is being recorded. But keep it well within your own sight line. You want to make sure it's working.

- Have the person say (and spell) his or her name at the beginning or the end of the interview so that it is part of the recording. This is part of your proof of who you talked to, how the person's name is spelled, and that you had the person's permission to record the interview.

- Download the recording to a flash drive, the cloud, or somewhere other than the original device immediately after the interview. Devices get lost or stolen or crash. Sometimes they are confiscated by police, Border Patrol, or TSA agents. Customs and other law enforcement types sometimes try to assert their authority this way. It's the equivalent of how authorities made photographers open up their cameras and expose their film, ruining their pictures. War correspondents frequently have trouble with this. It's not always legal, but people in uniforms aren't willing to have that debate on-site. And it's a little late to prove them wrong after you have lost your information. I repeat: Have your information in multiple places.

- After listening to yourself interview someone, ask how you could improve your interviewing skills. Do you take too long to get to the point of your question? To turn to my favorite example—

hockey—if you watch a lot of hockey you'll
notice that certain referees (technically called
"linesmen") have the duty to drop the puck for
a face-off between two opposing players. But
invariably there will be a linesman who forgets
his true role and lectures players about face-off
etiquette, and throws one of the players out of
the circle, and then delays dropping the puck,
until both the crowd and the players are furious
with him.[2] Well, interviewers can have similar
tendencies, and the best way to know is to listen
to your recordings: Do you cut the person off
before she is finished? Are you argumentative?
Did you miss a good follow-up question because
you were concentrating too much on your
next question? Do you laugh or cough or do
something else that might seem annoying? I
noticed that I said "Uh-huh" *way* too often. *Shut
up, Dean, and let the person talk!*

Speaking of "Shut up, Dean," I remember interviewing
the business reporter Lou Rukeyser, who hosted a Friday public television program called *Wall Street Week*. I was doing a

---

[2] I suspect that some of these showboats never got their kids to listen to
them, and now they are making up for lost time. I read one account
where a player said to a linesman, "You realize that people didn't buy
tickets to watch you drop the puck, don't you?" I believe that player
was tossed out of the circle.

lengthy piece on the changes in business and economic reporting and wanted his perspective. After a great deal of persistence on my part, Rukeyser finally agreed to talk to me for just a few minutes before he was about to tape his next television program. I thanked him for agreeing to talk to me, complimented him on his successful career and interesting show, and launched into the full background of my article, then asked a question that had *way* too many parts. He finally interrupted me.

"If you'll stop talking, I'll answer your question," he said.

That may strike some as rude. I was actually grateful. Once my train had left the station, I had no idea where it was going to stop. Luckily for me, he didn't let it get very far. Then he gave me some excellent information. And, as usual, he was very quote-worthy. When our few minutes were up, he said he needed to go. Thanks, Lou!

And in case you were still wondering . . .

Did I mention that if you record an interview, you should also take notes? Because you should. You *must* take hard-copy notes. On paper. With a pen or pencil.

Note-taking is a tricky business, regardless of your profession. Journalists, therapists, social workers—you have to do it quickly enough that you can keep the conversation moving, but not so quickly that you can't read what you wrote. You want to be able to show that the person said "sham" and not "shame." You also don't want to be so slow and methodical in your writing that your source is waiting (perhaps patiently, perhaps not) while you finish your sentence. It takes great practice to be able to talk to someone, look her in the eyes, glance down occasionally at your page while you write, and act as if it's a seamless conversation.

When I am interviewed by people, I often want to coach them a little by saying, "Hey, the conversation is up here!"

With students in my classes, I have them interview one another, and we work on eye contact, nonverbal cues, body language, *and* accurate note-taking. I mentioned this in an earlier chapter, but the way you lean in, the way you use facial expressions, the way you use silence, the way you must write in your notebook while looking at your source, the mmm-hmms and uh-huhs, are a lot to consider, but all of those elements are crucial. They get better with practice.

I have a colleague who learned shorthand, just so she could be a better interviewer. For those of you under a certain age threshold, shorthand was a necessary skill for secretaries back in the day (think *Mad Men*) so that if they took minutes from meetings, or dictation from their bosses (who were apparently incapable of writing their own memos), they could write quickly and with 100 percent accuracy. If you look at a page of shorthand notes, it looks like hieroglyphics. I have no idea what my colleague's notes say. But she does, and she has had a very successful journalism career with no one ever accusing her of misquoting, mischaracterizing, or taking quotes out of context.

Most of the rest of us, though, just develop our own cryptic shorthand.

When I take notes I do not write down everything the person says. My mind is constantly toggling between "important" and "not important," so I write down the "important" items for sure, and skip the repetition or background that I already know or don't care about.

But: You can't stop writing and look at your source until he or she says the next interesting thing and then write *that* down. If you're just staring at your source, or smiling and nodding, and a while passes before you write again, your source is thinking to herself, "Am I not saying anything interesting here? Did I get off the topic? Why isn't she writing this down? I'd better say something interesting!"

Or worse, your source is thinking, "I hope she's getting this, because I'm throwing down some awesome pearls here and if she doesn't remember it accurately I could be in big trouble."

The key is to keep writing whether the person is saying something interesting or not. This is an opportunity for you to go back and flesh out earlier notes, or jot down a follow-up question. If I am waiting for the person to finish a (needless) thought, I am still writing, but what I am doing is filling in sentences that the source said before, where I had only written key words. It will take some practice to fill in old sentences while also paying attention to what the source is saying, but you can learn it. I know that the studies say multitasking is a crock, and I generally agree with that conclusion. But for a few seconds at a time, I think it's possible to do two things at once.

When I take notes (in person or on the phone), I write sentence fragments. I write down a lot of nouns and verbs and a portion of something that was said in an interesting way or was really important. If I hear a statement that I think is *really* important, I will stop the source and say—"Hold on. I want to get that exactly the way you said it." Then I will either take a moment of pure silence while I write it down, or I will ask the source to repeat it. Usually when I do that, the source picks up on the signal that the statement bears some explaining and will go on in more depth. You can do that only a few times per interview, though, so choose wisely. Otherwise it will feel like a lurching elevator where someone pushed all of the inside buttons—starting and stopping frequently and never getting any momentum.

If a source has told me something that is *very* important, and maybe a little complicated, I might follow up with what I call a softball question—something I already know about, or something I know will get the source headed down the trail of an anecdote I don't need—just to buy time to fill in the sentences from the previous answer. If that tactic isn't possible, I will write "clarify" in the margin and then come back to it before the interview is over. I'll say something like "A few minutes ago you said something about X. I'm not sure I completely understood what you were saying. Can we go over that again?"

Believe me, the source wants you to get it right. She won't mind.

You're Still Not Done

When the interview is over, your work is not over. You have a crucial responsibility as soon as you can get by yourself. You absolutely must take your notes and fill in all of those sentence fragments with complete sentences. You must take those unique verbs and nouns and put them in a sentence as close to how they were said as you can imagine. And you must do it immediately. Your short-term memory is pretty good. But it will last minutes, not hours, and especially not days. So if your interview took place in a person's office building, duck into the bathroom before you leave the building and re-create those statements into whole sentences.

I have done this and, while standing in the middle of the bathroom (I didn't think to go into a stall), the source walked in and saw me writing furiously. That was a little awkward.

"Just trying to fill in the gaps," I said with a forced smile. He just nodded and walked past me and peed. Again, awkward.

So from then on, when I do this, I go to another floor and duck into *that* bathroom.

It's also acceptable to wait until you get back to your car and fill in before you leave the parking lot. Or stop in at a coffee shop nearby. The longer you wait, the greater the chance you'll miss some well-crafted metaphor or sentence or illustration.

If you wait until you get back to your house or office, you have already lost a lot. If you wait until you have conducted several other interviews and you're ready to write a few days later, I hope you have libel insurance.

After making your handwritten notes complete sentences, there is one more step that I recommend: Type them up. That's right, take the notes you wrote out and type them. Now they're legible and clean and easy to move around when you organize how you'll use them.

Best Ways to Transcribe Quotes

When you record an interview, there are some things to keep in mind. Transcribing the recording is dull, monotonous, and annoying. You could hire someone to do it for you (thanks, interns!), but I think it's best to transcribe it yourself. You know what you were asking, you know how the person said it, you know what the ancillary noise is. And no, you don't include all of the "uhhhhs" and "ummmms" and repetition in the transcript. An intern will include everything because the intern isn't yet thinking independently. His still potentially reptilian brain is fixated on following your directions ("Transcribe this") rather than using good judgment. You know what's important and what's not. So you (and only you) will know what you can skip.

This raises a very important ethical dilemma for every writer. Should you clean up the person's grammar and sentence structure when you use the quote? What if something is said in bad taste or is potentially offensive? I'll answer that question the same way virtually every journalism ethics question is answered.

It depends.

It depends on several variables. Is the source very media savvy? Is this the first time the source has been interviewed and quoted? Is English the source's first language? Is it a child? Does the person speak in a manner that would perpetuate harmful stereotypes? For purists, none of these questions should matter. We should quote the person exactly as he or she said it. But that kind of fundamentalism can look like we're making fun of the person, mocking the way he or she speaks. It can appear condescending if we don't clean it up, but it can look dishonest if we do.

One of the considerations is whether the interview was recorded by others. If there is a recording that will potentially go online or be broadcast, then there is no decision to make: You must quote the person exactly as he or she said it.

The practice of cleaning up quotes from public figures was evident during the time Dwight Eisenhower was president. He simply mangled the language. He was not an orator by any stretch. But if you read his quotes in a newspaper, everything seemed normal and pithy. If you heard what he said on the radio, it was a completely different experience.

This also created a challenge for the White House reporters who covered presidents George H. W. Bush and his son George W. Bush. Every English teacher wept when those two spoke off the cuff to answer a reporter's questions. But with the prevalence of broadcast and online media, print reporters could no longer make subjects and verbs agree as an act of presidential courtesy.

Let's talk about courtesy for a moment. It can look like you're trying to embarrass someone if you quote the person verbatim when he or she uses the language incorrectly. The student newspaper and website at the university where I teach used to love to take letters to the editor from faculty and administrators and, if there were errors in grammar, spelling, syntax, whatever, the editors would gleefully point out the errors by putting the bracketed word "*sic*" after each mistake. The "*sic*" usage is Latin for "exactly as written." So when students placed that after mistakes, they were pointing out to their readers, "We know that this is wrong, but this bozo obviously doesn't. Can you believe we're being taught by these morons?" Or something to that effect. Students love to embarrass faculty and administrators. I get it—there is a level of accountability that is useful. But sometimes it just seems mean.

When we quote others, we have to consider our intent. It's a judgment call. I lean more on the side of courtesy, but sometimes the public should see exactly how this person communicates. For example, I try to use quotes from children exactly as they spoke, because they often say things in creative ways, and it adds a lot of personality to the story I'm writing. It makes the story feel authentic.

Quoting people when English is not their first language is trickier. I would have loved to have used a quote from a political leader from another country whose English was good, but not perfect, when he described a spiritual awakening he had. "It was like the Apostle Paul when he fell out of the horse," the leader said. He was comparing his experience to that of Paul in the book of Acts in the New Testament of the Bible, when Paul (then called Saul) was persecuting Christians, but had an experience where he heard God's voice, and it knocked him off of his horse and temporarily blinded him. "Off" of his horse is different from "out" of his horse. The latter makes it sound like the guy was reenacting the battle of Troy. The solution to this kind of dilemma is often to paraphrase and say something like "he compared his spiritual awakening to the experience of the Apostle Paul, who was knocked from his horse and blinded when he heard the voice of God, according to the biblical account."

What if a person used bad grammar? Do you clean it up?

It depends.

What would be the point of quoting someone who said this: "I seen the robbers run out the store," as I saw in a *Los Angeles Times* crime story? It doesn't add color or character to the story. If you're writing fiction, the rules are different. Huck Finn and Jim can talk any way you want them to talk. But if you're writing nonfiction, a quote like that can look tone-deaf. It will read immediately like you're making fun of the person. Again, the solution is to paraphrase. Instead, write, "Witnesses said they saw the robbers run from the store."

If you do clean it up, even if it's just a little, is it still acceptable to put quote marks around it?

In my opinion, yes. I think it is acceptable to fix subject/verb disagreement, pronouns, tense shifts, if the quote is important to the story. For some news organizations, though, quotes are sacrosanct. You simply don't alter them for any reason.

But if it is a story that goes into more depth about the character, and there is a need for lengthier quotes, then it might be more authentic to leave the quotes as they are. It depends on the purpose of your story.

The thing about quoting from notes is that very few writers can get everything the source has said with complete accuracy. When we put quotes around a statement from a source, what we're saying to the reader is that it's really close to what the person said. The public sees those quote marks and thinks they signal a word-for-word account of what was said. But unless we recorded it, what we're really saying is that it's as close as we could get.

You see the problem, here, right? When we take notes, we're probably already editing what the person said. We're probably unconsciously cleaning up the person's grammar, substituting the correct word if the wrong word is used. Then, when we put the quotes into our stories, we tend to clean them up a little more. There are all sorts of opportunities to alter the statements, make the person seem smarter or dumber, and shoehorn the quote into the point we're trying to make.

Mostly we do this unconsciously so the story will read better.

If you don't believe me about how easy it is to change what a person said when taking notes, find a person you can interview for about ten minutes and do your best note-taking.

But also record it. When the interview is over, transcribe your notes into the actual quotes, using whole sentences. Then compare them with what you recorded.

Whether you choose to record your interviews or not, learn from Janet Malcolm and be ready to defend your decisions. Keep good records, decide why you're quoting what you're quoting, and don't trust your memory alone, Truman.

CHAPTER 10
Terms You Should Know

We Use These Phrases, but What Do They Mean?

WHEN I GOT THE CALL from the national desk of the *New York Times* asking me to check out a house where it appeared there had been a mass murder, I left a note for my wife and kids and drove up to an area north of San Diego called Rancho Santa Fe. It's the wealthiest part of San Diego County, with mansions on several acres—not jammed together the way some of them are in La Jolla. Rancho Santa Fe houses have horse stables, nearby golf courses, and a lot of unmarked streets. If you don't know where youre going, then you probably don't belong there.

The editor didn't have an address, so I headed up to the area hoping I could figure it out. I stopped at a fire station in Rancho Santa Fe and asked the people there. No HARO (Help A Reporter Out) from them. But as I walked from the fire station to my car, I noticed a helicopter in the air, hovering, with a spotlight shining down. It wasn't even circling. It was fixed in that one spot.

I drove the unmarked streets, keeping an eye on the chopper, hoping I could find my way out again, and I finally got close. The number of police cars and flashing lights was a dead giveaway. I parked my car and walked toward the scene under the spotlight. Police officers stopped me a few times, but my news ID allowed me access past the yellow tape. On my way toward the house I asked several people what had happened, and all I got were these cryptic half sentences about "mass murder," "invisible spaceship," and "Hale-Bopp Comet."

When I got to the house, I approached a sheriff's deputy who was clearly standing guard at the front door. I introduced myself and asked the young man if he could tell me what happened.

"No, sir, I cannot," he said.

"Did a bunch of people die in this house?" I asked.

"I cannot comment, sir."

He looked straight ahead, not establishing eye contact. Like one of those guards at Buckingham Palace.

"I heard it might have been a mass murder—is that right?"

"I cannot comment, sir."

"Are the bodies still in there?"

"I cannot comment, sir."

"May I go in there and look around?"

"If you attempt that, sir, I will arrest you."

"So it's a crime scene, but you can't tell me what happened?"

"I cannot, sir."

Props to him for staying in character!

Then it dawned on me. I knew a sheriff's deputy who worked in this part of town.

"Where do you think I would find . . ." I said, and then I named the deputy.

The guard at the door visibly twitched and looked at me for just one second. Then he regained his previous posture, looking straight ahead.

"You might try him at home, sir."

I went back to my car and called the deputy's house. He answered the phone.

"I'm at this house in Rancho Santa Fe, for the *Times,*" I said. "Have you been up here?"

"Yes."

"What happened?"

"I can't really tell you."

"Why aren't you still here?"

"I had to go to the hospital."

"Whoa! Why?"

Long pause.

"We thought there might be something still in the air in the house, so I had to get checked out."

"Wait—you were in the house?"

"I'm the one who discovered the bodies."

Now it was my turn for a long pause.

"Are you okay?"

"Yeah—I'm fine."

Another long pause.

"How many bodies are we talking about?"

"Dozens."

"How did they die?"

"That's what we're trying to figure out. Look. I really can't be talking to you about this."

"Sure. Sure. Is there a time when you *can* talk about this? I'd love to hear about what you saw. I can come to your house if that's better."

"No. I can't be a source for you on this."

"Sure. I understand. Who else can I talk to who will know as much as you, though?"

Long pause.

"Meet me at the sheriff's station first thing in the morning. Don't come in, though. Park at the far end of the parking lot."

I hung up and went back to the house where the deaths had occurred. More police were there, and now more reporters. The sheriff arrived and gathered the news media around so he could make an announcement. He said that the house was the site of a mass suicide. Thirty-nine men took their own lives in order to join an invisible spaceship that was traveling behind the Hale-Bopp Comet the night before. The group called themselves Heaven's Gate.

I spent the rest of the night reporting, talking with neighbors, local merchants, police, religious leaders, and medical examiners, and working with the rest of the *New York Times* team that had driven down from the Los Angeles bureau—

they rented rooms in a nearby hotel and used it as their news headquarters.

The next morning I drove to the sheriff's station and parked where my friend had instructed. I got out of my car and my friend walked out of the station, dressed in civilian clothes. He motioned for me to walk in the opposite direction of the station.

"Let's take a walk," he said, when he caught up to me.

I asked how he was, and why he wasn't in uniform. He said he was fine, but they didn't want him coming back yet because they weren't completely sure how the Heaven's Gate members had died. Was it through the air vents? Whatever they had done, it wasn't violent or bloody. So far it was mysterious and invisible.

When we got a ways from the station, my friend said, "Here's what you got right in your coverage, and here's what you got wrong. And no, you can't quote me or even acknowledge that you have a source in the sheriff's department. But I want this as accurately reported as you do. When everyone is speculating and they get it wrong, it makes our job a lot harder."

For the next thirty minutes or so, we walked and he told me what the investigation was and was not revealing, and where certain news reports were way off base.

We did this for the next few mornings as coverage of the event escalated and transfixed the entire world.

He didn't know this journalism term, but what he was doing was talking to me "on background." He was educating me, guiding me, even criticizing me when we got something wrong. And at no point could I let on that he even existed.

On a smaller scale, he was my Deep Throat, the secret source Bob Woodward had in the U.S. government when the *Washington Post* was exposing the Watergate scandal. His source, decades later, was revealed as Mark Felt of the FBI. As the story goes, only Woodward, Carl Bernstein, and their editor, Ben Bradlee, knew the identity of Deep Throat. About ten years after Watergate, I met Bradlee through a mutual friend. The friend introduced me as a journalist and a journalism professor, and Bradlee flashed that big smile and, with his gravel-filled voice, said, "I'm happy to meet you, and happy to answer any questions you might have—except one!" He kept the secret of Felt's identity until 2005, more than thirty years later, when Felt himself revealed his identity as Woodward's source.

If my source follows Mark Felt's pattern, it will still be a few years before he identifies himself.

Anyone dealing with a complicated topic needs someone who can give him information "on background." That's especially true for journalists, but it's also true for anyone trying to get a head start on how to talk to experts about a topic. Social workers, lawyers, human resources professionals, customer service representatives, and anyone else who talks to people for a living knows that they need people who can educate, react, and guide them—from offstage.

In journalism we use some specific terms when it comes to these "interviews before the interviews." The terms are "on background," "not for attribution," "off the record," and "on the record." We all think we know intuitively what these terms mean, but the reality is that very few people actually agree on their definitions. I read one writer's attempt to put the confusion to rest. He asked five *Washington Post* reporters what each term meant, and none of them could agree on any of these terms.

So I will explain them according to the definitions I was taught and according to the definitions I practice as a writer. Here's the thing, though: Whether or not you agree with my definitions doesn't really matter. What matters is that *you and your source agree* on the definitions. So before you agree to talk with someone "on background," make sure you both know what you think that term means.

"On Background"

When I talk with someone on background, I am asking that person to educate me on a topic. I am not asking for the source to provide me with statements that I can quote in my story. I am just talking with someone who knows more about a topic than I do and is willing to tell me what some of the big issues are. Maybe that person can tell me who would be good sources for actual "on the record" conversations.

Background interviews are crucial. Even though they are for your educational purposes only, you still have to be prepared before you go into that interview. It can be less formal, but it's not as if you can ask the person to educate you on the difference between stocks and bonds. You can read about that on your own. But you can ask the person why, in certain economic times, one is a better investment than the other.

I did a lengthy story about Native Americans who lived on the U.S.-Canada border and produced an influential newspaper. In addition to reading as many of the back issues as I could find, I talked with several people who are Native American and who are involved in the social issues that paper wrote about, just to gauge the paper's popularity, effectiveness, and veracity. If I felt that I wanted to quote any of them, I would circle back to them later and ask their permission. But since I was just trying to figure out my angle for the story, I asked general questions on what they knew about the paper, and what they thought I should ask the editors when I went to the border to spend a few days with them.

Talking to others before your big interview is a way to get ideas you hadn't thought of. I often ask people, "If you were talking to [fill in the blank], what would *you* ask them?" That doesn't mean you're going to use those preliminary conversations in your story. It just means you're letting those conversations inform and even shape your story. Background interviews are crucial.

To repeat, though, in my definition of background interviews, you cannot use what they told you in your story. You can use that information to guide you, or try to confirm it elsewhere with additional interviews or reporting, but you cannot use it publicly.

For example, I once reported a story about a rock and roll band, and, while doing background interviews, I heard about one of the main band members' health problems. My source had told it to me on background, so I couldn't use it in my story. But here's what I did instead. When I interviewed the band member, I said, "It's amazing you guys are all still healthy and still rocking. How have you been able to keep your stamina?" It's a pointed question—of course, I already knew that this musician's stamina was at issue. Once the musician himself said, "Actually, I've been having some health problems," and he discussed them at some length, I was able to include it in my piece. I'm not sure I would have thought to ask that question had I not been given a heads-up by someone else.

This may sound complicated, but we let background information inform our questions even when we aren't working on a story. If you know that a friend of yours is dating someone, but the person who told you made you swear you wouldn't tell, you will probably say to your friend something like, "So, are you seeing anyone?" You already know the answer because you got it "on background," but now you can ask follow-up questions.

In a sense, I am always doing background interviews. I'm always working on some kind of a story, so I'm always thinking about what I'm writing. That means if I'm at dinner with some friends, they might ask what I'm working on, and I'll usually tell them. Then I'll ask what they would want to know about a topic, and what they would ask if they were interviewing the person I'm about to interview.

The answers I get aren't always useful, but crowdsourcing (or informal polling, asking around, or whatever you want to call it) it can bring up something you haven't thought of. Most often, the useful part of this comes when I mention a topic to friends, and they run across something on that topic that catches their attention. I have gotten several articles, speeches, interviews, links, etcetera, sent to me later, with a note along the lines of "You mentioned such and such topic at dinner. I just saw this and thought of you." Those are often *very* useful. It's like having a small group of researchers in your back pocket.

You have to be careful, though, if you're crowdsourcing. Not everything everyone tells you is necessarily fair game, even "on background." For example, my wife and I had been married two years when I was just getting started in journalism. She was working with patient accounts at a big hospital. One night we were having dinner at a restaurant, catching up on each other's day, and she started telling me about a patient who came to see her with a conflict regarding his insurance coverage. The hospital had been doing gender confirmation surgeries for a while, apparently, and trying to keep it a secret. This particular patient's quandary was that he had started the process to transition, and his insurance coverage stopped. He was in somewhat of an in-between place and couldn't continue to pay for it. The hospital wanted to be paid, the patient couldn't do so without insurance, the insurance company said no, so the hospital essentially said to the patient, "Let us know when you can pay for the rest of the procedure and then we'll finish the job."

When my wife finished telling me this gut-wrenching story, I saw her look at me kind of funny. Then she looked down at the table in front of me and her eyes narrowed. I hated when she did that. As she had been telling me this story, apparently I had moved my dinner plate to the side and had filled the paper placemat with notes. I swear I didn't realize I had been doing this—it was pure instinct. This story had all of the elements I had been taught in journalism school—conflict, impact, proximity, timeliness, novelty, and human interest. It was perfect.

My wife, unfortunately, didn't see it that way.

"What are you doing?" she asked.

"This is an amazing story! Do you think I could talk to the patient?"

Horror. And even narrower eyes.

"No, you can't talk to the patient! It was a private conversation between a client and his account representative! That would violate all sorts of privacy and ethics rules. He would know where you got the idea and I would get fired and the hospital would be liable for invading his privacy. Are you nuts?"

Nuts? No. Dumb? Maybe. Clueless about husbands and wives? Definitely.

"Besides," my wife continued, her eyes narrowing even further. "This was just us talking at dinner. You can't take notes on dinner conversation. This was private. I'm not one of your sources. I'm your wife."

She took the placemat from in front of me and tore it into tiny pieces.

It was a good lesson for our marriage and a good lesson

for journalism. I just wish I could have first taken a photo of the placemat before she shredded it.

But I have to confess that I did figure out a way to leverage the "on background" nature of that conversation and get a story out of it.

The next day I read up on the topic and saw that for a person to go through this process, a psychiatrist had to be involved and sign off on the surgery. We were living in a medium-sized city, so I started calling all of the psychiatrists in town. My approach was something like this:

"I'm working on a story about all of the work that goes into gender-confirmation surgery, and I understand that there is a psychiatric component to it," I said. "Could I talk with you about what that component looks like, and what you're looking for as a doctor before approving that the procedure may continue?"

The first few I talked to said they hadn't come across the situation, and didn't want to speculate.

After a few more calls, a psychiatrist said, "Well, you know we do that surgery here in this city, right?"

"Really?" I said. "Are you involved in some way?"

"Yes."

"May I come over and talk to you about it?"

When we met I never brought up that I knew about the patient with the insurance conflict, but I did ask if insurance covered all of the medical care involved.

"Sort of," he said. "There is one situation where it's still being sorted out."

We talked about "the situation" in general terms. I asked if he would allow me to talk to that patient, and, predictably he said, "Of course not." I had to try.

So the story I wrote wasn't about that patient with the terrible predicament, but more about what qualifies a person for this kind of operation at this local hospital, and how it is covered, or not, by insurance. The story had only an oblique reference to the person my wife encountered.

That conversation in the restaurant was sort of a "background" interview. I didn't connect anything to my wife, but she educated me on the issue and I was able to find out more as a result.

She also educated me on the difference between a background interview and a "how was your day" conversation between a husband and wife. More than forty years later, she will often still start a sentence with, "Now, you can't use this *anywhere*," and make me look at her directly in the eyes and tell her I am not working at the moment, but just listening to something interesting.

Occasionally, if it's really juicy, and if I know she'll know I'm joking, I will find a scrap of paper and start writing down things she's saying. But I don't use it. At least not so it can be traced back to her.

"Not for Attribution"

"Not for attribution" means that I can use the information, and even quote the person, but I can't say specifically where it came from or even write it in such a way that a reader could figure out who said it.

Interviews that can't be attributed to a specific person are useful, but in a limited way. They can show readers that you have sources who have knowledge about the subject, and that you have a reason to believe them. But just because you believe them doesn't mean the public believes them.

There are reasons why people tell you things but don't want their identities revealed. They might not be authorized by their employers to speak publicly about an issue. They might be bothered by something and want the public to know about it but fear for their job or safety. They might want to just help you out but are afraid of being associated with a reporter or a story. They might have an ax to grind.

When we talk about "not for attribution" interviews we are essentially talking about anonymous sources. This is an important and time-honored practice in political journalism, and really, in any kind of journalism that is in the public interest. When a president doesn't want the public to know something, such as, let's just use a hypothetical, maybe, a secret bombing campaign in a Southeast Asian country, and people associated with the White House think that Americans might be interested in the fact that we might be—again, this is a hypothetical—carrying out a secret, unauthorized, unwinnable war that is costing thousands of American soldiers' lives and billions of American taxpayers' dollars, those concerned people might contact a reporter with a heads-up. They might tell the reporter some information, with the agreement that the informant's identity will be protected. They might even drop off nine thousand pages of photocopied documents.

These are called leaks. Presidents hate them (unless they are the leakers themselves, and they sometimes are), and they all claim that they are going to plug them. Richard Nixon even called a group of henchmen "plumbers" so that he could end the leaks of secret information coming out of his administration.

Leaks are crucial for democracy to work. They are sometimes the only way the public can be informed. They often create transparency of actions where secrecy was desired. They are a way to maintain accountability of powerful people and entities. Whether it is about sexual harassment, poisoning the air and water, secretly bombing a country, or products that cause cancer, there is a lot of information that some people want to remain hidden. Profits and reputations are at stake. But so are people's lives if the information remains hidden.

Is it possible to abuse the practice of leaking information and using anonymous sources? Absolutely. Competitors use leaks to sabotage policies, programs, and products. Reporters must have their eyes wide open when they enter into the realm of anonymous sources. One of the problems with anonymous sources and not-for-attribution statements is that the public often doesn't trust them. A reader or viewer might ask, "How do I know that the reporter didn't just make this up and attribute it to an anonymous source?" It's a fair question.

I talked to the editor of a news organization in Mexico that is known for its aggressive coverage of drug cartels and government corruption. They use anonymous sources all the time. In fact, that is the only way they get a good amount of their information for their hard-hitting stories.

"How do you know that that the anonymous sources are telling you the truth?" I asked.

"We verify the information with at least three other sources who are not associated with that person," she said. "It's the only way we will publish information from someone we don't name."

That paper also has a great quote in large letters on the wall of their conference room: "It is better to lose a story than to lose your credibility." Tattoo-worthy.

The Associated Press has more specific rules for using anonymous sources:

1. The material is information, and not opinion or speculation, and it is vital to the story.

2. The information is not available except under the condition of anonymity imposed by the source.

3. The source is reliable and is in a position to have accurate information.

I will use anonymous sources on occasion. But that is only after I have worked very, very hard to try to convince that individual to let me use his or her name. Sometimes a source will talk to me only on the condition that his or her identity is protected. After some discussion about the merits of being on the record, if the source still refuses, I will agree to it. Even then, though, when I go to write the story, I will ask the person to reconsider. Sometimes sources change their minds. I never stop trying to negotiate this point. Ultimately, though, you must honor your agreement.

Many news organizations have a stated policy that they simply don't use anonymous sources. Then they wait a beat and say, "Unless the story warrants it and there is no other way to report this important story in a responsible way." Even the student media at the university where I teach have this policy. But to avoid the charge that a source was a fiction, we employ the Ben Bradlee rule: If a student journalist wants to use an anonymous source, the reporter has to tell the source that one other person will know their identity. That other person will be either the editor in chief or me, since I am the faculty adviser.

There have been times when the student media reported something and not named a particular source, and school administrators read the story and demanded to know who was being quoted. Or they accused the reporter of fabricating a source. I have had great confidence in telling the suits that this person really does exist, and I know who it is. But I won't reveal the person's identity.

Thanks, tenure!

But again, readers and viewers typically hate the use of anonymous sources. The practice should be used sparingly and only if no other way is possible to tell an important story.

Don't forget that anonymous sources always have their own agendas. Sometimes it's to protect themselves and their privacy, such as when a story is being done about gang activity, abortion, self-mutilation, criminal activity, or something that could affect how that person is seen in his or her community. But often the agenda is more self-serving. The information given to you can expose something a person believes is unjust and hypocritical, but it usually involves something that the source disagrees with or wants to expose in order to inflict damage.

I mentioned earlier that I wrote a magazine story about a district attorney's race. Part of the story described an alleged atmosphere of rampant sexual harassment. A female deputy district attorney told me that "the only way for women to shatter the glass ceiling in the office was horizontally." She said I could use the quote if I protected her identity. In this instance, it was a price I was willing to pay. It was a great quote, of course, and it illustrated the view that women in the office had about the locker-room atmosphere they worked in. Did my readers believe that a real person said it? I hope so, because I know who it is. But you—and your source—lose credibility when you let them drop a bomb of a quote and hide behind anonymity.

Good reporters do everything they can to get a person to agree to be identified. The story's and reporter's credibility are at stake. And let's face it—credibility is the *only* thing a reporter really has to offer an audience. Any moron who knows how to type or speak can provide information (accurate or otherwise—thanks, Alex Jones!). You have to be able to provide credible information that the public can trust. *That's* your commodity. And anonymous sources put that credibility at risk.

Using anonymous sources can create legal problems, too. There have been several cases where courts have demanded that reporters name their sources, despite the reporters assuring the sources that their identities would remain anonymous. Judith Miller of the *New York Times* went to jail for twelve weeks in 2005 because she would not reveal her source on a story and the court found her in contempt. Not until her source gave her permission to reveal his identity was she released. It's rare that reporters are jailed for protecting the identities of sources, but it has happened. It's another reason to go to all lengths possible to identify your sources.

Sometimes you just can't. The movie *Nothing but the Truth* is based loosely on the Judith Miller case. Don't worry, I won't spoil it, but if you watch the movie you realize why the Kate Beckinsale character simply could not reveal the identity of her source.

Most states have passed shield laws, which protect reporters from having to reveal sources, but there isn't yet a federal shield law, so if the case is in federal court, you can't invoke it.[1] But even if you are in a state with a shield law, it's still no guarantee that you can keep the information to yourself. Sometimes the First Amendment protection for the news media comes in direct conflict with the Sixth Amendment,

---

[1] At the time I wrote this, the following states did not have shield laws: Idaho, Iowa, Massachusetts, Mississippi, Missouri, New Hampshire,

which states that people have a right to a fair trial. What if a judge is convinced that the only way a person can get a fair trial is to find out where you got your information for your story?

This is a sore point with me. It's such a sore point that I sort of relished it when I got booed and hissed at a journalism and law conference where I was on a panel talking about this very topic. We were debating whether journalists really had the right to refuse a subpoena order to reveal their sources. For years I have advised journalists to say something along these lines when a judge demands information that they said they would keep confidential: "Your Honor, under the First Amendment to the Constitution, and under the shield law of this state, I respectfully decline to reveal this information." Lawyers, of course, think that if you have information that can help their case, they should have access to it.

"Let me see if I have this straight," I said to the lawyers at this conference. "To be a lawyer in this country, a person typically must go to college, then take a rigorous admissions test, then apply to law school, get admitted to law school, graduate from law school, and pass an even more rigorous test called a bar exam, right? And a lot of you spend a lot of money to do this and go into great debt just so you can get some kind of governing board to say you can now practice law in this state. If you mess up, then you get kicked out of the club because you didn't measure up to these very high standards."

South Dakota, Vermont, Virginia, and Wyoming.

The lawyers in the audience knew they were being set up, so they gave me that pseudo-bored look, as if to say, "Go on, say what you're going to say."

"But in this country," I continued, "pretty much anyone who wants to cover something, or post or publish something, can say they're journalists. They don't need to obtain a license, pass a test, satisfy a board of regents, go to college. And they are always underpaid, especially compared to lawyers.

"And oftentimes, lawyers work in firms that have investigators—groups of people who can dig into records, find surveillance, dig and dig and dig, and bill for lots of hours. Yet you're telling me that your team, with all of their training and professionalism and degrees and resources and clerks, have to depend on a *journalist* to do their work for them? You should be ashamed of yourselves. You should be able to find this out on your own."

Controversial, I know. You can likely see why the response was hissing and booing. Even my fellow journalists on the panel raised their eyebrows at me, as if to say, "Be careful driving home tonight. Check your brake fluid."

The point is that the shield law is not an absolute. It may come up against other rights, and a judge will ultimately decide whose rights need the most protection at the time. Obviously, I think the rights of journalists should be up there and shouldn't be abused by investigators and lawyers who should do their jobs better.

When we promise someone that we will protect his or her

identity, we want to have the confidence that we will stand behind our promise. Remember, your credibility is all you have.

"Off the Record"

Of all the terms that get used by reporters and sources, the most confusing and problematic term is "off the record." I have said it when I have been interviewed. Others have said it to me when I was interviewing them. "Can I tell you something off the record?"

But does anyone *really* know what it means?

I'll tell you what I was taught and what I practice, and what I teach my students. It means someone is telling you something that you simply can't use in your story. Period. It's not information you can refer to the way you would with a "not for attribution" arrangement. No saying, "Sources have confirmed . . ." Nope. Can't use it.

Part of the debate about the term is whether you can use the knowledge you gleaned from the "off the record" comment and find someone else to say it. That would be closer to the "background" agreement. The person who told you something off the record has trusted you, and if you agree to not use the information, you are in the ethical position of not violating your word. Violating your word could potentially put you in legal trouble, too, which I will explain later.

Again, I say, you can't use it.

Why, you might ask, would anyone tell a reporter something off the record? That's a *great* question. Secondly, why would any reporter agree to hearing something that he or she couldn't use?

I know some reporters who, when sources say they want to go off the record, will say, "Nope. You're talking to a reporter. If you say it, I have the right to use it. If you don't want me to use something, then don't tell me."

When I was writing about the demise of newspapers in San Diego for the *New York Times* (the city went from having three competitive newspapers to one in a matter of months), I sat across the desk from one of the editors in chief, who was explaining how San Diego just wasn't a big enough city for all of that competition.

That didn't make sense to me, so I pressed him and asked why he thought San Diego was still viewed as such a backwater. He told me some pointless trivia about how the city was organized, and I cautiously interrupted him. "That was decades ago. Why is it *still* seen as a city that no one takes seriously?"

He looked at me for a few moments and finally said, "Put your pen down."

Then he told me things about city leadership that only an insider would know. It explained a lot. Then he said, "You can pick up your pen now."

When the interview was over, I circled back to that very damning information.

"What of that can I use?" I said.

"None of it. I just told it to you so that you'd understand why this city will never achieve greatness."

Had I broken my word and used the information—even without revealing where it came from—my source would have known where it came from and that would have been the end of our relationship. This guy was a sort of mentor to me and I valued my friendship with him, so I wasn't willing to risk it.

But what if I hadn't liked this person and didn't care if we would be friends? Then is it okay to break your word? Of course not. Remember that tattoo-worthy slogan? *It is better to lose a story than to lose your credibility.* As a journalist, all you have is your credibility—not just with your readers, but also with your sources. You don't make and keep friends by being trustworthy only some of the time. It's the same with your relationship with your sources. Either you're trustworthy or you're not. I'm a utilitarian to a point, but even more fundamental is that I want my word to count for something. If I say I won't use it, I won't.

Breaking your word can also put you in serious legal trouble. That's what happened in the 1980s in Minnesota. Dan Cohen, a campaign operative for a Republican candidate for lieutenant governor, wanted to dish some damaging information about the Democratic candidate to local reporters. But before he gave them the information he made them promise they would not reveal where they got it. Unfortunately (in my opinion) they agreed. They should have walked out of the room. The "damaging" information was pretty tame. The Democratic candidate had been arrested years before at a street protest, he said, and another time for shoplifting six dollars' worth of sewing supplies. Some reporters decided there was no story there. Two others continued with their stories, but their editors felt that the source of this lame information should be named. Over the objections of the reporters, the editors named Dan Cohen as the person spreading this "dirt." Cohen was fired, and he sued the papers essentially for breach of verbal contract. It went to the State Supreme Court and Cohen won.

But now we get to the sticky part: If a source wants to go off the record, it matters when the source actually says this. If she gives you a magnificent interview, full of concrete information, pathos, and quotes that would make a reader cry, and then says, "This was all off the record, by the way," you have a dilemma. Option one is to respond the way the character Ben Shepard does when he talks to Billy Cusimano in *The Company You Keep*. After Cusimano tells Shepard a few important things for Shepard's story, Cusimano says:

"I'm not saying anything else. Everything here is off the record."

"Ah, see, it doesn't work that way," Shepard says. "You gotta say 'off the record' before we have the conversation."

"Who says?"

"Those are the rules."

"There's rules for what you people do, huh?"[2]

Well, actually, yes! Those *are* the rules. People who have

---

[2]   LaBeouf, Shia, and Stephen Root. *The Company You Keep.* Theatrical release. Directed by Robert Redford. New York City: Sony Pictures

not been interviewed before might not know that you must say something is off the record before you say it. So you have to gently educate them on this point and perhaps negotiate what you can use. If people with no media experience request that an interview be off the record after the interview is completed, I try to be a little flexible. I will go over the items that I think are crucial and that need attribution, and then discuss why those are so important. If there are some items that the source really doesn't want in there, then I'll negotiate within reason. But I will make it clear that, in the future, when someone agrees to be interviewed, the assumption is that it will be on the record and that everything said is fair game.

If I feel that I'm being played, and that the source is having second thoughts about saying certain things and tries to play dumb with statements like "I didn't know you wanted to use any of this," I will remind the source that she saw my recorder, saw me write things down, and waited until I finished writing until speaking again, and that I have the right to use the information.

Politicians, celebrities, and many others know this rule, but that doesn't mean they won't try to abuse it. A congressman once tried to play this card when I interviewed him for a story about the U.S.-Mexico border. I had identified myself as a reporter and told him what I was working on, and we had a very

Classics, 2012. Paraphrased from https://www.springfieldspringfield. co.uk/movie_script.php?movie=company-you-keep-the.

spirited conversation. When it was all done, though, and I was thanking him for taking the time to talk to me, he said this:

"All of this was off the record, of course."

"No, sir, that wasn't my understanding," I said. "I told you I was a reporter and working on a story and needed your perspective. This was all on the record."

"Listen, son," he said. (Did I sound that young?) "I never give on-the-record interviews. You should know that."

"Then you shouldn't have agreed to the interview, sir."

Now he was agitated.

"Look—if you use *any* of this conversation, it will be the end of our relationship," he said.

What—he thought we were dating?

"That's a price I'm willing to pay, Congressman," I said.

Then he hung up.

He thought he could pull a fast one, but I knew that he knew better. Naturally, I used the information. I never heard a peep from the politician again.

Clarifying the Rules

Of course, it's all well and good for you to know what these terms mean, but what ultimately matters most is that you and your source agree on those definitions. Even more critically, the terms must be agreed to *before* the interview, not after. Trying to negotiate after the fact gets complicated. Settle the issue before you begin. And, again, unless the source set some ground rules ahead of time, you may assume that everything said in the interview is "on the record." That means you can use it all. It doesn't have to be stated as such. If the source sees you taking notes and/or recording the conversation, that is tacit agreement enough. Everything is on the record until someone says it's not.

Sometimes it's not necessary to negotiate verbally. If I am being interviewed by a television reporter, for example, and the reporter and a videographer come to my office, set up the equipment, do a sound and lighting check, and then begin the interview, we can all assume that this interview is on the record. I don't have to say it. The camera is recording. It would be silly for me to exclaim, partway through the conversation, "Wait—I never agreed to this being on the record!" When I sat there and watched them set up and clip a microphone to my shirt, I tacitly agreed—but agreed nevertheless—to an on-record interview.

If a source wants something off the record, he or she must say, "This is off the record." When someone says that to me, I discuss with them why they want it off the record and what their concerns are. I try to address those concerns as well as I can, without being manipulative or pretending to be more knowledgeable about the fallout than I really am. This is still a human being. You are still a human being. It matters how we treat one another. Your credibility is at stake with this person as well as with your readers. I also address why the information is so important, why the story—and therefore the public—would be better served with that information, and why the information will not be harmful (but only if I think that's true).

WHEN SOURCES TELL ME THEY want to go "off the record," there are a couple of things I typically do: If it's a phone interview, I keep taking notes, but bracket the notes with a big bold OTR in the margin. When the interview is over, I say to the source something along the lines of "Let's talk about the things you wanted off the record." Then the source can explain why she thinks it should stay off the record, and I can explain why I think it's important for the story (if I do). It becomes a negotiation.

But if I am interviewing someone in person, and she says, "I'm going to tell you something off the record," then I have an obligation to put my pen down and turn my recorder off so that she can see I am honoring the agreement. When she is done with a particular point, then I will say, "We're back on the record now, right?" When we are all done I will try to circle back to the area she didn't want me to record and try to get at least something usable out of it.

Some reporters won't do that. They don't want to have information that they can't use. That's certainly a cleaner way to go, but I prefer to negotiate.

The only thing that matters is that both you and your source know what you mean when you invoke "on background," "not for attribution," and "off the record." Make sure you both are working from the same definitions, and that everyone sees the nuance between them. And it matters *when* in the interview the terms are used.

Those are the rules, Billy Cusimano. There really are rules for what we do.

CHAPTER 11
Check Your Ego at the Door

Interviewing Those You Love and Those You Loathe

THERE IS ONE LAST THING to consider when conducting an interview of any kind: your ego.

We spend so much time preparing—researching, honing questions, even obsessing over the person and the material we are exploring—that we sometimes forget there is one other person who will play a role in how well this interview goes: you. To be properly, completely prepared for an interview you must give some thought to the role you will play, not just the questions you will ask.

An interview is more than getting this person to talk to you. It is the manner in which the two of you interact that will determine whether this interview will have value. That means you must consider your motives, blind spots, assumptions, prejudices, and, most of all, your ego.

THE EMOTIONS OF LOVING AND loathing (or at least liking and disliking) the people we interact with occur in any circumstance where you have to talk to others on a regular basis. Doctors like talking to certain patients and hate talking to others. Same with cops, same with social workers, same with lawyers, same with human resources people—same with anyone and everyone that you have to talk to in your daily life. There are some people who give you straight, intelligent answers and agree with your assessment of things, and it makes your day easier.

And then there is everyone else.

When I was in high school, I worked as an orderly in an emergency room. This was back when I thought I wanted to be a doctor. There was one ER doctor in particular who intrigued me, and not for the right reasons. It seemed as if he saw every patient as a kind of personal insult, but there was one guy in particular toward whom he was particularly cruel. This guy had been in the ER several times before, each because of an unsuccessful attempt to kill himself. I was in the examination room with the patient, who, this time, had slashed his wrists but was still alive and conscious. When the doctor walked in and saw the patient, he shook his head and said, "You again?"

The doctor took the bandages off of the man's wrists and helped get the wounds cleaned and sewed back up, all the while berating the man for wasting his time.

"Next time you do this, you slice *up* the wrist, not across," the doctor shouted, showing the man exactly where to do the most damage. "I never want to see you in here again!" I don't think I need to say that this is a completely unacceptable way to interact with anyone, let alone a patient in crisis.

Don't be this guy. Whatever your problem is, you need to check it at the door.

At some point in your career you'll be called upon to interact with people in moments where it is simply not appropriate to let them know how you really feel about them. You have a job to do. Regardless of how you feel about any of these individuals, you must exercise some control over how you act and speak in their presence. You're a professional. You have to appear impartial. You simply must let the person speak without your correction or judgment or criticism.

It is in situations like this where you have to remember who you are, and what the purpose is for the interview. An interview is not a way to score points or prove yourself. It's not to show the person how witty or snarky or superior or intelligent you are. Your ego is always demanding to be center stage, ready to defend itself and its self-righteousness, ready to be offended or ready to be stroked. You have to recognize it when your ego begins to inflate, and let the air out immediately. Because here's the hard truth: No matter how much effort you've put into it, the interview is not about you. Repeat that last sentence over and over and over. *The interview is not about you.* Send that sentence to whatever interviewer you are thinking of right now. He or she needs this reminder.

But you have to consider your ego when it could be leading you the other direction, too. Sometimes when you interview someone you get distracted by trying to impress the person. That can be equally damaging, because you can lose track of the purpose of the interview.

When I interview writers for our Symposium, I usually get to choose which writers to invite. They are typically people I admire, whose work is a model for aspiring writers. So I'm already a fan.

I don't have to try to like them—I already do. There will undoubtedly be moments in the interview where I will wade into some tricky situations, but not out of spite or some hidden need to embarrass the person. As I mentioned before, the audience expects thorny questions, and the person you're interviewing expects them. It's part of the deal.

You Can Be a Fan—Just Don't Swoon

On the one hand, it is easy to interview people you admire. You get them talking about things you agree with or want to highlight. It can be a borderline lovefest. On the other hand, it runs the risk of being too chummy, not being illuminating or challenging or complicated. Being a fan of a person can keep you from being a professional. Confronting your fandom and being hyperaware of how it can blind you will keep you on the side of good, solid interviewing. You have to be aware of your ego's attachment before you can set it aside (thanks, Siddhartha!).

The easiest way to do this is to remember the purpose of your interview with that person.

When you are interviewing someone you admire, you have to be even more on your guard that you aren't overlooking something. It's human nature to want the person to like you. But that's not the point, and it's not your purpose. If you want them to like you, buy them a puppy. If you want them to dig into human nature or shine new light on important topics, then you have to take the risk of making them think.

Jeannette Walls, whose writing I admire a great deal, was not surprised at all when I brought up the fact that some people read her memoir *The Glass Castle* and simply didn't believe it. Some even publicly proclaimed it a fraud. After all, books like *A Million Little Pieces* and *Three Cups of Tea* also seemed too good to be true and it turned that that they were, in fact, too good to be true.[1] So it was understandable that readers were suspicious about her bizarre childhood and her lack of bitterness. She was more than ready with her answer. And since I admired her already, I asked it in a tone that wasn't accusing or incredulous. But no matter how fervently *I* believed her, I still had to ask the question.

If I think I am on the verge of being a fangirl, I try to picture someone else watching the interview. I will get the image of a student, or a community member who is struggling with his writing, and craft my interview through the prism of "What does Dave need to know here? What would be useful

---

[1] *A Million Little Pieces* by James Frey, and *Three Cups of Tea* by Greg Mortenson and David Oliver Relin.

to him as he struggles to write his memoir and struggles to find the time and the inspiration?" Focusing on someone in the audience helps me get out of my blind spot. It's one way of getting your ego out of the way and putting the emphasis back on the person you're talking to.

If you're worried about your feelings getting in the way of your interview, you can do something similar. What does your mom, or your friend, or the guy who lives down the block need to know about this person? Thinking about others will keep the interview from becoming an inside-baseball love-in, and ensure that you have a conversation that is worthwhile and evenhanded.

I really had to work at being evenhanded when I prepared to interview my journalism idol, Bill Moyers. I had felt a kinship to him ever since I first started in the field: He was raised in a conservative Christian home (so was I), eventually grew past the narrow-mindedness of that upbringing (so did I), and practiced journalism at a level that explained complex issues and exposed hypocritical leaders of business, culture, religion, and government (something I wished I did). He has a prophetic voice of clarity and honesty in the tradition of the Old Testament prophets. He is the Edward R. Murrow of my generation.[2]

I had spoken to him once as a graduate student, but I got a second chance to really sit down and talk in 2005, when

---

[2] If you don't know who Edward R. Murrow is, read up on him. At least watch the movie *Good Night and Good Luck*.

he came to the Writer's Symposium. In preparing for my interview with him, I didn't want to be like the Chris Farley character when he interviewed Paul McCartney on *Saturday Night Live* and kept mouthing to the audience, "This guy is awesome!" But I was in awe of Moyers.

Moyers was a pro in all ways. He knows the interview process so well that he even sort of hijacked my interview with him just before it began. As we stood offstage, he said, "I'd like to make a few comments to the audience before we begin." He said it in that southern gentleman way of his. I was still so enamored with him that I just said, "Uh, okay." (This guy is awesome!)

So when we got on the stage he talked to the audience about celebrity culture, about the power of images and television, and warmed everyone up with hilarious anecdotes about being recognized in public. Then it was time for our interview. Whatever he thought was going to happen, he had everyone right where he wanted them. Including me.

We talked about his background, about his love for journalism, and his role as a voice crying in the wilderness. Still, I felt that I needed to ask him about a particular season when he was the public spokesman for President Lyndon Johnson when the United States ramped up its involvement in the Vietnam War.

This was the point in the interview where I needed to set my ego aside, where I was going to take the risk of him not liking me. Because the interview wasn't about me. Because, remember, the interview is *never about you*.

George W. Bush was president when this interview occurred, and the United States had invaded Iraq on the false premise that Iraq was one of the countries behind the 9/11 attacks and was about to use weapons of mass destruction on the United States. It took very little sleuthing to discover that the Bush administration's claims were fabricated.

I brought all of this up to Moyers, and he went on a beautiful and forceful rant about governments that lie to their people.

Then I pivoted to when Lyndon Johnson was president, and the excuse his administration used to enter the United States more fully into the Vietnam War based on what was called the Gulf of Tonkin incident. That "incident" was an account that a U.S. Navy ship had come under attack by the North Vietnamese. It gave our military the excuse to send in troops and begin overt bombing raids. Historians have since declared that, in fact, there probably was no "incident" in the Gulf of Tonkin. That narrative was also a fabrication.

"Do you see a parallel between how we entered the Vietnam War and how we entered the Iraq War?" I asked him.

He gave a very thoughtful, nondefensive answer. He was ready for it and wasn't offended.

Just because he was my hero didn't mean I could give him a free pass on something so important. He got a standing ovation when the interview was over. I may have been the first one to stand.

NO MATTER HOW BIG A fan you are, keep coming back to those key questions: What does your audience need to know about this person? What does the world need to know about this person? Focus your energy there. You're probably not going to go out for drinks or sushi after the interview. They have friends and family in town that they're going to hang out with as soon as you're done. Be realistic. Do your job.

I loved the honesty of the writer Ann Patchett after she spoke at a book event I attended. She told the crowd that she would be happy to sign their books, but that she was not going to spend a lot of time doing so.

"Please don't tell me where you first read one of my books or give me one of your ideas for my next book," she said. "We're not going to bond, so keep the line moving."

Some people in the audience were horrified by her comments. They felt that it was insensitive and arrogant and even rude. But I thought it was spot-on. She spoke the truth. And we should take the same approach in our interviews, even with people we admire. If we accept up front that we're not going to become this person's new best friend, then we can be a little more impartial when we ask questions.

The Opposite of "Swoon"

Unfortunately, though, my interviews are not limited to those I love. Yours won't be, either. And it is an awful feeling to realize that, sometimes, I despise the person I am interviewing.

Let me give you an example. A number of years ago, I had invited this writer to come to the Writer's Symposium on the recommendation of someone else (note to self: Never listen to that colleague again), and a few weeks before he arrived, I started reading everything I could that he had written. The more I read, the more disturbed I became. It's not just that I disagreed with what he was saying—which is irrelevant and often leads to great interviews—I actually developed a dislike for the kind of person he was and what he stood for. The more backgrounding I did, the more I concluded that this person was, frankly, despicable.

Let me repeat: When I say that, I do not mean I simply disagreed with the person's ideas. I disagree with lots of people and that's completely okay with me. It's in the exchange and tension of conflicting ideas that real enlightenment occurs. But I found myself in a tricky position: I became judgmental rather than curious, and I didn't want to be associated with him.

The interview went fine, I think. His True Believers thought it was wonderful. His detractors felt that I was too easy on him. My personal goal was that neither he nor the audience would pick up on how I actually felt about him, and I think I succeeded. No, I'm not going to tell you who it is.

While I'm being honest, at times, feelings of revulsion cropped up while I was in the middle of the actual interview, usually sounding a lot like "You're such a jerk" and "I can't wait until I'm done with this interview so I can get away from you" and "I so want to punch you in the face right now."

I hope I do not live long enough for someone to develop the technology that puts thought bubbles over our heads.

This doesn't happen very often. And thank goodness! But it does happen. And it will happen to you. And you *still* have to conduct the interview as a somewhat dispassionate questioner.

Interviewing someone who disgusts you puts pressure on you to remain professional and civil. That doesn't mean you excuse them when they are offensive, but you do not get to be offensive in how you respond to or interact with the person. I used to work in a newsroom that was just a big, open space. We all had desks, but no walls between us—not even partial cubicle walls. We could all see and hear one another. I once heard a particularly volatile colleague conduct a phone interview, and when I heard her shout, "Oh, grow up!" into the phone, I knew she had passed the point of getting any useful information out of her source.

This colleague had moved to San Diego from New York, where she had been a reporter for several years. A few days after hearing her berate this person over the phone, I asked her about it.

"Does that technique usually work for you?" I asked.

"It worked all the time in New York," she said. "It doesn't seem to work in San Diego, though."

Chalk one up for beach culture, dude.

SO WHAT DO YOU DO when you have to talk to people you loathe? Ironically, a lot of the same things you do to focus when you're talking to your heroes. You remember it's not about you. You think about what your neighbor would want to know. You ask the questions you need to as impartially as you can. And then maybe you take a hot shower afterward to wash off the ick factor.

When you're in the midst of the interview, it can be important to remember that you don't have to respond positively or negatively. Your obligation is to remain neutral. You can challenge unsavory statements if it feels relevant. You don't have to laugh at a joke just because the person you're interviewing thought it was funny.[3] What is the obligation of the interviewer in situations like these? Just to reveal the truth.

Of course, "the truth" is hard to pin down. So if I can draw out what the person believes, respectfully challenge him when he makes no sense or is actually harmful in what he is saying, and remind myself that this is not an argument, I'll consider that a success. It covers the minimum criteria of a good interview. It's not about me. It's about the person I am interviewing. Readers, listeners, and viewers can decide for themselves what conclusions to draw.

Hard as it may be, interviews should not devolve into shouting matches.[4] What is accomplished when you start shouting, anyway? How many people do you think have changed their behavior because they lost an argument to you? It is always better to ask, listen, respond, guide, ask differently, and probe—even when you want to scream.

---

[3] Remember Billy Bush laughing at Donald Trump's claim about having so much celebrity that he could grab women's crotches with impunity? You laughed, Billy. You're an accomplice. Shame on you.

[4] Watch Anderson Cooper and Kellyanne Conway, or Jon Stewart and John McCain.

When Megyn Kelly interviewed Alex Jones of InfoWars in 2017, and challenged his claim that the children of Sandy Hook Elementary School were not really murdered in 2012 but were part of a government conspiracy, she let him talk, but occasionally cut him off, saying, "That's a dodge," and "That doesn't excuse what you said." I thought that was acceptable. She didn't then go on a tirade about what she thought about the Sandy Hook killings or what she thought about Alex Jones. She made sure that the interview wasn't about her. She let him continue. But she didn't let a contentious and preposterous statement just lie there. Viewers were left to decide what they thought about it all.

I have no idea what Megyn Kelly personally thinks of Alex Jones, nor should I. I can imagine it wouldn't be positive, since Jones repeatedly criticizes the mainstream news media and Kelly is part of that establishment, but her opinion wasn't the point of that interview. Kelly didn't make it an argument. She didn't try to get Jones to change his mind. She conducted a spirited conversation and respectfully called BS when she thought she saw it.

This is the approach Barbara Walters took when she interviewed Mike Wallace, too. While it was clear that the two of them knew and liked each other, occasionally Wallace said some things that could be interpreted as sexist. He was being vulnerable in the interview, and when he revealed those views, Walters could have challenged him on it and called him a caveman. She didn't, even though I presume she vehemently disagreed with his comments. He was making a statement about his personal views, not accusing anyone of a conspiracy, as Alex Jones was doing. Walters let Wallace's statements linger, as if to let the audience realize what he was actually saying. She trusted that the audience would hear what she just heard. It was an egoless moment, in my opinion. Also, she knew the purpose of her interview, which was to discuss his legal issues.

Occasionally I wonder what our obligation is when we have the opportunity to interview someone who promotes a point of view that you believe is harmful to society or who represents something that that you vehemently oppose. Would I interview a Holocaust denier? A pedophile? A pornographer? A mass murderer? A dictator? A businessperson responsible for looting millions of people's pensions? Someone who got us into a war under false pretense? Someone who claims that those kids in that school shooting weren't really killed?

What line will you not cross? You might not know yet, but it's worth considering.

For me, I try not to make my decisions based on whether I agree with these people or approve of their actions. The point is whether they have a point of view that the world should hear, and whether I can do it in a manner that will not excuse, but will scrutinize. If you make sure it's not about you, and it's about enlightening others with what the interview reveals, then it's probably worth doing.

Where you draw that line goes back to the original questions in this book. Whom do you want to interview? And why? That second question is as important as the first. I have seen interviews where I thought the interviewer was being flirtatious, too gushy, too adversarial, and full of his or her own outrage. Those interviews are annoying and often pointless. They are heat for heat's sake and not heat for light's sake.

Interviews that involve emotion—whether good or bad—are tricky. They take a lot of self-reflection, preparation, and self-control in the moment. Sometimes you don't want them to end; sometimes you can't get out of there fast enough. No matter what circumstances you find yourself in, remember that this interview is not about you. I've said it a million times, but it still bears repeating: The interview is not about you. Period. Remember that you aren't there to prove someone wrong or prove someone right or show off. Keep in mind that you're interviewing the person to reveal what the person is about and to get information about a particular subject. You want their perspective, their insight, their unique point of view, their anecdotes, their expertise, their wisdom, their personality, their ability to point you to a greater understanding. So get out of the way, and let the person talk to you.

An Interview That Started Out Badly and Pretty Much Stayed That Way

Terry Gross of *Fresh Air* Talks to Gene Simmons of KISS

Originally broadcast on February 4, 2002[1]

IN MY CHAPTER ON INTERVIEWING people you love or loathe, I refer to my own experience of interviewing someone whom I realized that I despised. I don't have a recording of that interview, thankfully.

But here is an example of a seasoned interviewer talking to someone who clearly got under her skin. Again, what follows is an abbreviated and annotated transcript, so I encourage

---

[1] 'Transcript of Gene Simmons and Terry Gross, host of NPR's *Fresh Air*, Originally broadcast on February 4th, 2002, transcript by maniahill.com, http://www.ucdenver.edu/academics/colleges /CLAS/Programs/HumanitiesSocialSciences/Students/Documents /Gene%20Simmons%20and%20Terry%20Gross_Fresh%20Air.pdf.

you to find it or listen to it, and you'll see what I'm talking about.

It's easy for me to give commentary on what Terry Gross should or shouldn't have done, since I wasn't the one doing the interview. She's such a pro, and she's the gold standard of interviewing. This is one of her few exceptions. I also know how easy it is to lose focus on why you're doing the interview and on what the audience needs, because it all happens so quickly, and sometimes things catch you by surprise. That's what happened in this interview.

You can prepare for an interview and assume it will go a certain way. If it takes a sharp turn, though, the interviewer must adapt and keep it under control. Gene Simmons said sexist, ridiculous, and hostile things, and it took Terry Gross a while to recover. This interview reminds me of what I heard a hockey coach say when a game got out of control. "You can't always play the game you prepare for," he said. "Sometimes you have to play the game that is there." Who knew that hockey coaches could sound like Zen masters? Must be all those hours of staring at the Zamboni going in circles, laying down a new sheet of ice . . .

What the coach is getting at is that despite what you think the other team is going to do, it might not. There might be an injury. There might be a freak play. The referee might have had a fight with a spouse the night before. You can't engineer it all. But you do have to adjust.

So when Gene Simmons caught Terry Gross by surprise, she had to adjust, and it took her a long time to do so.

She started the interview with an odd question, in my view. The title of his new book was *Kiss and Make-up*. She asked him whether he liked to wear the wild Kiss makeup during a performance because it made him feel less vulnerable, less like his Jewish birth name. I realize that the word Make-up is in the title of the book, and that one of the iconic things about Kiss is the makeup and costumes, but this got weird right away. First of all, asking the person about makeup being used to hide vulnerability as the first question is a bad idea. Regardless of how professional they both are, interviews still need a little rapport-building time. Going right to a question about vulnerability didn't give Simmons time to warm up or even know if Gross is a trustworthy interviewer. And it's clear that he doesn't want to be vulnerable that soon when he immediately insults Terry Gross for her pronunciation of his Hebrew name.

Gross has to immediately put the attention on herself, and that allows Simmons to take the interview even further off track. And they hadn't even gotten *on* track! But instead of pivoting and going to something less personal, she returns to the vulnerability question. Asking a celebrity about whether he is hiding his true self is a legitimate question. But it's a bad *first* question. In my opinion, the interview never recovers. She asks two more questions about makeup, and he rambles aimlessly in his answer. I'm not sure listeners are *that* interested in the details about makeup. This is Gene Simmons of Kiss. He has written a memoir. The first section of this interview feels wasteful.

Remember what I said earlier about someone will control the interview? Up to this point it's been all Simmons. At one point, when Simmons starts off on a trail of how much money he's worth, Gross cuts him off to try to get a handle on things.

GROSS: Are you trying to say to me that all that matters to you is money?

This is a good follow-up question. She could have said it less confrontationally, such as, "Is making money the driving force behind the band?"

SIMMONS: I will contend, and you try to disprove it, that the most important thing as we know it on this planet, in this plane, is, in fact, money. Want me to prove it?
GROSS: Go ahead.

Gross should not have taken the bait here. She could have said, "It's clear that it's important to you. But let's talk more about your book." I realize that an interview moves even faster than a hockey game, but she could have been less reactive here.

Simmons then says something dumb and misogynistic about women selling their bodies. When someone makes a sexist comment the way he did, it's time to cut him off and go back to why you are doing the interview. You want to talk about Simmons' contribution to pop culture, and the new book is the hook into that discussion. Instead, she again loses control of the interview. You can hear the desper-

ation in her follow-up questions. To be fair, I have resorted to desperate tactics, too, just not this publicly. My point is that she should have tried to get this back to his book, his life, or something where he isn't just spouting dumb sentences. When he starts down yet another insulting rabbit trail, she finally cuts him off again.

> **GROSS:** Wait, wait, could we just get something straight?
> *I admire what she did here. She's finally getting control of the interview and the direction it's going.*
> **SIMMONS:** Of course.
> **GROSS:** I'm not here to prove that I'm smart—
> **SIMMONS:** Not you—
> **GROSS:** I'm not here to prove that you're not smart or that you don't read books or can't make a lot of money—

I don't think that's where he was heading, so this actually makes things worse. She could have said something like "You're obviously a smart guy. You have proven that by all of the different entities created by the band."

> **SIMMONS:** This is not about you. You're being very defensive—why are you doing that?
> **GROSS:** *(laughs)* It's contagious.

Now it's an argument. She said he was defensive, he said she was defensive, she replied with the equivalent of "Well, you started it!" If I would have heard this on the radio while driving, I would have changed the channel at this point. Remember in the last chapter where I said, "It's not about you?" Even Gene Simmons agrees with me!

It's one thing to be frustrated with the person you are interviewing. It's another thing to take something personally. Granted, he has accused her of being a Gentile and he demeaned her because she is female, so she is justified in her anger. But she can't let the interview devolve into an argument. No real information or insight comes out of an argument. This is an interview. And, remember, an interview is not about winning. It is about exposing, scrutinizing, uncovering, understanding, deepening. This is becoming a train wreck because Gross has departed from that purpose. She doesn't have to rise to his baiting. She can change the subject and get it back on track.

But she doesn't. She asks yet another question about makeup. This was her chance to hit a re-set button. But now we're back to what got this all going badly in the first place. You don't regain control of an interview by going back into the territory that made you lose control in the first place.

Then, after asking him a few questions about the rest of his costume, she asks him about the bizarre studded codpiece that he wears. He replies with something even more offensive.

GROSS: That's a really obnoxious thing to say.

Terry is right to call him out on his being a pig here. Even though I don't advocate getting into an argument with your source, when he is that insulting, you can't let it go.

SIMMONS: No, it's not. Why should I say something behind your back that I can't tell you to your face?

GROSS: Wait—has it come to this? Is this the only way that you can talk to a woman? To do that shtick?

But now she should have let it go. She's not going to make him a more thoughtful, sensitive person. Now it's personal, and all we're getting is heat for heat's sake, not heat for light's sake. Gross could have said, "But let's get back to your book." Instead, I believe she lost all perspective. He's such a loathsome person in this conversation. But she's letting him have way too much fun at her expense. Eventually she asks him about his relationships with women, and he reveals himself to be even more of a cave man than he had already revealed. This time, though, she showed great skill to not challenge him or comment further. She trusted her audience to form their own opinions. As sports commentators say, when a referee doesn't blow a whistle, this is a good "no call." And even though this is a radio interview, I can almost see Terry Gross shaking her head as she listens to Simmons in this segment. Maybe even puking.

GROSS: Are you interested in music, or is the goal of being in a rock band to have sex a lot?

Gross has decided not to hide her disgust with Simmons, and asks a pretty barbed question here. A better question would have been "How much of Kiss is actually about music?" He replies with more sexism and nonsense.

GROSS: Are you interested in music at all?

I love this question. She's not taking the bait.

SIMMONS: Don't you love this interview? Tell me the truth.

She doesn't really owe him an answer. She could have said, "Let's decide when it's all over," or something like that. But she engages . . .

GROSS: Well, I think it's kind of a drag, because you're making speeches.

SIMMONS: That's right.

GROSS: And you're being intentionally obnoxious.

(laughs)

Unfortunately, she is trying to argue with a caricature. This is pointless. We're back to the argument. She's trying to convince him of something, and she is going to be unsuccessful. Finally she moves on and asks him about the movie Spinal Tap. *This is a good question because it's a movie that spoofs rock bands, and she's asking about it to a guy who apparently also spoofs rock bands. But, as you might have predicted by now, he says something insulting about NPR, and she gets defensive again.*

SIMMONS: . . . Have you ever heard the *Saturday Night Live* version [of NPR]? It's pretty spot-on.

GROSS: Have you listened to it enough to know if it's spot-on?

Now she's even more defensive. I listen to NPR and I saw the
Saturday Night Live *spoof, and I thought it was spot-on.*

When Gross asks Simmons about some of his antics on stage like
fire eating and vomiting blood, the interview changed. After Simmons
answered those questions, he said something very revealing, in my view.

SIMMONS: . . . But what does it all mean? Nothing! It
means for two hours we're going to make you forget
about the traffic jam, and the fact that your girlfriend
is whining, or whatever else is going on in your life,
and for two hours we give you escapism, that's what it
means.

In my opinion, this is the most interesting thing he has said in
the entire interview. He's talking about the bigger role of entertainment
in the world. This could have gone into a much deeper discussion,
because he has obviously thought about it. Gross then asks him about
his childhood in Israel and his mother who had survived a Nazi con-
centration camp. Now we're getting somewhere. The makeup, costumes,
the fire, the blood, are all getable facts from a variety of places. Now
we're getting underneath it all. Simmons then describes the difference
between life in Israel and life in New York, where he and his mother
relocated when he was a child.

This is a fascinating exchange, and the interview should have
started there. It would have set a completely different tone, and he
would have been presented as a more complex character. Instead, Gross
opened in a manner that put him on the defensive. This exchange
about his childhood reveals a deeper, more vulnerable, more interest-

ing Gene Simmons. Who knows how much better things would have gone if she had started here? She then asked him about his religious training, and he contrasted it with what he was seeing in television cartoons. That contrast lets the audience come up with this conflict of images that must have been crashing in his head. His attraction to wild characters started here. That's a lot more interesting than the topic of hiding behind his makeup.

But eventually her disdain for him bubbled up again toward the end of the interview. They discuss his view of humanity, and she said:

> **GROSS:** But my impression is you don't have much sympathy for anyone. You're so into yourself! You're just so deep into yourself.

I think this is too aggressive and attacking. She could have said, "Do you have sympathy for anyone? How about yourself?" But she's accusing him of being a narcissist, which he probably is, but the audience has already come to that conclusion. They don't need Gross to say it and put him on the defensive again, especially since they were on a pretty good give and take of deep discussion. He gives another provocative response, and she follows up with this:

> **GROSS:** I would like to think that the personality you've presented on our show today is a persona that you've affected as a member of Kiss, something you do on stage, before the microphone, but that you're not nearly as obnoxious in the privacy of your own home or when you're having dinner with friends.

This feels like she's taking a final whack at calling him a jerk. I think he's made it obvious that he's a jerk. Whether he was yanking her chain or just role-playing is up to the audience to decide. Asking him point-blank whether he has putting her on strikes me as an invitation for him to yank her chain one last time. Which he does.

SIMMONS: Fair enough. And I'd like to think that the boring lady who's talking to me now is a lot sexier and more interesting than the one who's doing NPR. You know, studious and reserved, and—I bet you're a lot of fun at a party.

That was painful, but it didn't have to be.

Conclusion

The Search for Transcendence

ALL INTERVIEWS TEACH US SOMETHING. There is the content of the interview, of course, where you hope you learn something new. But there is the dynamic of the interview, the exciting part where you engage deeply with another human being, and each time you do it you learn how to do it better.

Occasionally there is the transcendence of the interview, where you simply are in awe of what is happening. That's how I felt when I listened to Terry Gross interview the children's author Maurice Sendak in 2011. Sendak had just released his book *Bumble-Ardy* at age eighty-three, and he was too frail to do the interview in a studio. Gross talked to him on the phone. They talked about aging, death, atheism, love, children, sexuality, and publishing, among other topics. It was deep, heartfelt, and emotional. Just as Gross was wrapping up the interview,[1] Sendak interjected:

SENDAK: You know, I have to tell you something.
GROSS: Go ahead.
SENDAK: You are the only person I have ever dealt with in terms of being interviewed or talking to who brings this out in me. There's something very unique and special in you, which I so trust. When I heard that you were going to interview me or that you wanted to, I was really, really pleased.
GROSS: Well, I'm really glad we got the chance to speak because when I heard you had a book coming out, I thought, "What a good excuse *(laughs)* to call up Maurice Sendak and have a chat."
SENDAK: Yes, that's what we always do, isn't it?
GROSS: Yeah. It is.
SENDAK: That's what we've always done.
GROSS: It is.
SENDAK: Thank God we're still around to do it.

Sendak died eight months after this interview.

---

[1] Maurice Sendak, "Maurice Sendak: On Life, Death, and Children's Lit," interview by Terry Gross, *Fresh Air*, NPR, https://www.npr .org/2011/12/29/144077273/maurice-sendak-on-life-death-and -childrens-lit.

WHEN INTERVIEWS ARE DONE WELL, they have the potential for a human connection that goes past the level of merely gathering information. They become an experience where you are fully present with that other person, and she is fully present with you, and you have a sense of everything aligning just so that this interchange can take place. Just like being in a jazz club where the music goes outside what the players practiced and they enter into what feels like a new orbit, a successful interview can feel the same way. You and your source hit a topic or an expression that surprised you both. Something new was created in that moment. Was it joy? Grief? Mystery? It seems that we all live for moments of shared humanity. Interviews can provide those moments. An experience of shared humanity doesn't happen with every interview, but when it does? It feels like eternity broke into the now.

Jacqui Banaszynski, a Pulitzer Prize–winning journalist, seems to specialize in these kinds of interviews. She has an uncanny ability to go deep and transcendent with her sources. She gives this advice:

"Immerse yourself in your interviews. You must focus so intently that your mind is fully with the person you are interviewing. You need to listen so hard that you can move with the person, take another step forward or pull back. Don't worry about your list of questions, your editor, or your story lede. Worry only about the person in front of you . . . If you do it right, you will feel exhausted when you leave the interview."[2]

---

[2] Mark Kramer and Wendy Call, eds., *Telling True Stories* (New York: Plume, 2007), 67.

Banaszynski embodies her own advice, but one example in particular stands out in my mind. I heard that she did something extraordinary in an interview, so I called her and asked about it. The story she was covering was about a family whose house caught fire in the middle of the night because of a pipeline explosion just outside their house. The man's wife ran to one bedroom, grabbed one young daughter and ran out the front door. The man ran to another bedroom, grabbed their other young daughter and ran out the back door. The wife and the daughter ran right into a wall of flames and died. The man and the other daughter were safe.

Jacqui covered the story of the fire for her newspaper, but what she really wanted was to talk to the father. His decision to turn this way instead of that way changed everything. It was a story everyone could relate to, where sometimes we have to make split-second decisions. If we survive those decisions, we have to live with them the rest of our lives. Talking to someone who just went through it would provide insight into those deep human questions of randomness, instinct, guilt, grief, and where do we go from here?

As you can imagine, the father had no interest in talking with Banaszynski or anyone else. It complicated matters that he was raised not to trust the news media. Through a mutual contact, she was able at least to get enough of a reasonable request to him that he called her. As Jacqui recalls it, he called to say "What business is this of yours?"

Fair question.

Jacqui remembers asking him if she could come to his house and explain her reasoning in person. He said yes. At his house she told him about these deeper questions this tragedy raised. "What happened to you could happen to anyone," she remembers telling him. "And if you talk to me, we can put the story out over the wires so that all news media would have access to it, and you won't have to talk to anyone else. The information will be out there. It's a bigger story about making decisions and living with them."

She told him that if he agreed to the interview, they could stop it at any time. If he didn't like a question, she would stop. She told him that she would try to figure out why he wanted to stop and try to go forward, but he could end it whenever he wanted.

Then she did something she said she had never done before, and has never done since.

She told him that once their interview was done, if he still didn't like how it went, she would leave her notebook with him and walk away.

That's bold.

She said he looked surprised when she offered this.

"You would do that?" he asked.

"You don't owe it to anyone to talk," she replied. "It's your story."

"What will you tell your editor?"

"I'll say I couldn't get the story. I won't be happy about it, but if that's what you want, that's what I'll do."

Banaszynski said she saw him relax in that moment.

What she did was give him control over his story. There is a power dynamic in every interview, as I have said before, and normally you as the interviewer want to be the one in control. But occasionally you experience something where it is worth giving up that power. This father had already lost so much. He could at least retain the power over his story. If he didn't want to tell it, she wasn't going to force him.

"I wasn't going to rob him of one of the few things he had left," she said.

But we have to keep in mind that many times—I would even say most times—people want to tell their stories. They want someone to listen to them. They want to be heard. You are honoring them. And they are honoring you by letting you into their homes and lives.

"When I show up to do an interview, and I am truly paying attention and listening, I am giving them a gift," she told me. "Instead thinking that we're just taking their time, we're also giving them a gift of time and attention."

It's a tradeoff. You have a story to tell. I will listen to you and tell it. We bear witness.

A few days after Banaszynski's story ran, she saw that a television station announce it was doing an interview with the father. She called him and said "I thought you didn't want to talk to anyone else?" He told her that since his interview with her had gone so well, and it surprised him, he was agreeing to another one with the TV station.

It has an even happier ending. In the flood of mail he got after those two stories, one was from a woman who had lost her husband and one of her children in an accident. They met for coffee and, about four years later, married.

I KNOW THIS IS GOING to sound counterintuitive, but just as often as not, your source is going to thank you for the interview you did. Did you get that? You're an intrusion in their lives, you're the one poking your nose in their business, you're the one asking the hard questions, you're the one staring at them in silence while they try to contain, explain, or compose themselves, and they're thanking you. Why? Because you listened to them. You asked good questions. You came prepared. You showed interest in their perspective. You respected them enough to hear their point of view. You might not agree with them, but that's not the point. The point is that you asked, you listened, and you acknowledged that their voices mattered.

They didn't know it until you showed up, but many of them wanted to talk to you.

Very few times in a person's life does one get asked what she or he really thinks. I know it sounds sappy to say that interviewing someone is a way of honoring them and their stories, but I think it's true.

For that they are grateful. Your readers and viewers will be grateful, too. And the story you're telling will be better.

SO. ARE YOU READY FOR that interview? Of course you aren't. You can't plan for everything. There will be variables you didn't anticipate.

But by now I hope you have a sense that conducting great interviews can be part of your practice regardless of your profession. Now you know that it's not always as easy as it looks (and, thankfully, sometimes it is!). Great interviews are the result of some thinking about purpose, of preparation, of establishing a structure, of asking deeper questions, of not backing down, of improvising, of taking risks, of committing to accuracy, of self-awareness, of being committed to improving, of shared humanity, and of being authentically you.

I'm hopeful that now you won't worry quite as much when you say to someone, "Talk to me."

Acknowledgments

As I RECALL THE EVENTS, it was after a phone conversation with Hannah Robinson, an editor at HarperCollins, that the idea for this book began to form. She was being kind in her rejection of a different book I was pitching her, and maybe just throwing me a bone so I'd stop whining. But after I thought about what she said, I realized she was onto something. A few days later I got back to her with a clearer idea. She has been a writer's dream to work with every step of the way.

But even that conversation would not have happened without Elise Capron of the Sandra Dijkstra Literary Agency. Elise has been an advocate from the beginning, and arranged that conversation with Hannah.

Thank you, Hannah and Elise.

Thanks also to the hundreds (thousands?) whom I have interviewed in Tibetan Buddhist monasteries, in huts, homes, offices, playing fields, and death beds all over the world. Thanks to those who have wanted to end the interviews with songs, hugs, and threats. Thanks to the dozens who have let me interview them in front of audiences at the Writer's Symposium by the Sea. Thanks especially to the very first Symposium interviewee, Joseph Wambaugh. I had asked him to come speak at a writers' event I was trying to organize and he said no, that he didn't do speeches. But, he added, if someone wanted to ask him questions, he'd be happy to come. The Writer's Symposium format was born. Thanks, Joe!

Thanks also to Amy Williams, Madison Collins, and Charlie Merritt for their expert transcriptions.

And thanks to Point Loma Nazarene University, where I teach, for believing in the Writer's Symposium by the Sea.

About the Author

DEAN NELSON IS THE FOUNDER and director of the journalism program at Point Loma Nazarene University in San Diego. He has written for the *New York Times*, the *Boston Globe*, *USA Today*, *Christianity Today*, *Sojourners*, *Christian Century*, *Westways*, *San Diego* magazine, and other national publications. He has won several awards from the Society of Professional Journalists for his reporting, and has written or cowritten fifteen books. Nelson is a frequent speaker at writing workshops and retreats.

He has traveled throughout the world covering stories of human interest—India, where he wrote about the slums of Mumbai; Kosovo, where he wrote about victims of terrorism; Tanzania, where he wrote about members of the Black Panther Party who live in exile; Tibet, where he wrote about religious persecution; Central America, where he wrote about poverty and contaminated water; New Orleans, where he wrote about the immediate aftermath of Hurricane Katrina; Haiti, where he wrote about the aftermath of the 2010 earthquake; Iceland, where he wrote about the country's literary scene; Croatia, where he wrote about a part of Europe that is trying to reinvent itself after the breakup of the Soviet Union; Rome, where he wrote about the Canonization of Mother Teresa, and elsewhere.

He has covered the stunning, the moving, the mysterious, the tragic, the amusing, and the absurd.

In addition to directing his university's journalism program, Nelson hosts the annual Writer's Symposium by the Sea, where prominent writers come to discuss the craft of writing. Nelson has interviewed Amy Tan, Anne Lamott, Gay Talese, Anchee Min, Ray Bradbury, George Plimpton, Joyce Carol Oates, Garrison Keillor, Billy Collins, Nikki Giovanni, Dick Enberg, Otis Chandler, Kathleen Norris, Donald Miller, Bill Moyers, Jim Wallis, Chitra Banerjee Divakaruni, Joseph Wambaugh, James Fallows, Barbara Brown Taylor, Eugene Peterson, Philip Yancey, Michael Eric Dyson, Bill McKibben, Chris Hedges, Rachel Held Evans, Luis Urrea, Krista Tippett, Kareem Abdul-Jabbar, Jane Smiley, and dozens of others. Many of those interviews are available for viewing at deannelson.net and on UCSD-TV's website, ucsd.tv. The interviews are broadcast worldwide.

Nelson grew up in Minneapolis.

He has a PhD in journalism from Ohio University in Athens, Ohio, and a master's degree in journalism from the University of Missouri at Columbia.